Charles Soule
Writer-In-Chief

Alberto J. Alburquerque
Executive Artist

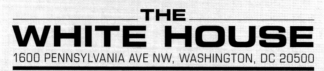

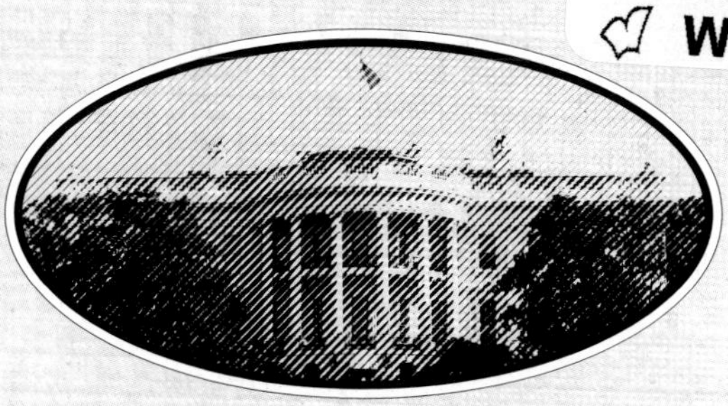

Dan Jackson
Executive Colorist

Crank!
Chief of Letters

THE WHITE HOUSE

1600 PENNSYLVANIA AVE NW, WASHINGTON, DC 20500

FROM THE DESK OF THE 44TH PRESIDENT, STEPHEN HENRY BLADES

TO THE MEN AND WOMEN OF THE CLARKE:

I have never met you[redacted]r will. Even now, as my administration has only just begun, I am certain that this fact will remain, to me, one of the great tragedies of my Presidency. The service you have offered this nation–[redacted] is, quite simply and with no hyperbole intended, unparalleled in human history.

SER-471337.C /// DOS. 102-AC- /// AUTH. JMB*J5

[CLASSIFIED]

All of you chose to leave everything familiar behind, to voyage out [redacted]e. Your rewards are uncertain at best–knowledge, certainly, but there will most likely be no [redacted]. But I will use every power of my office to make certain that your sacrifice is not forgotten. In time, your names will be included amongst the other great explorers of human history.

We do not know the intentions [redacted] at the end of your journey. You will be tasked with making [redacted] I envy you the opportunity. For thousands of years, humankind has looked up and wondered about the possibility [redacted]. You will be the very first to know the truth.

It may seem that you are alone–cut off from the rest of the human race, [redacted] from home, your mission secret. Nothing could be further from the truth. You are not alone. You are never far from my mind. This offer may seem hollow, but if there is anything I can do for you, for your families and friends [redacted], you have but to ask.

Be safe, and discover wonders.

Stephen Henry Blades
44th President of the United States of America

LETTER 44 VOLUME II: REDSHIFT

WRITTEN BY
CHARLES SOULE

ILLUSTRATED BY
ALBERTO JIMÉNEZ ALBURQUERQUE

COLORED BY
DAN JACKSON

LETTERED BY
CRANK!

DESIGNED BY
JASON STOREY

EDITED BY
ROBIN HERRERA

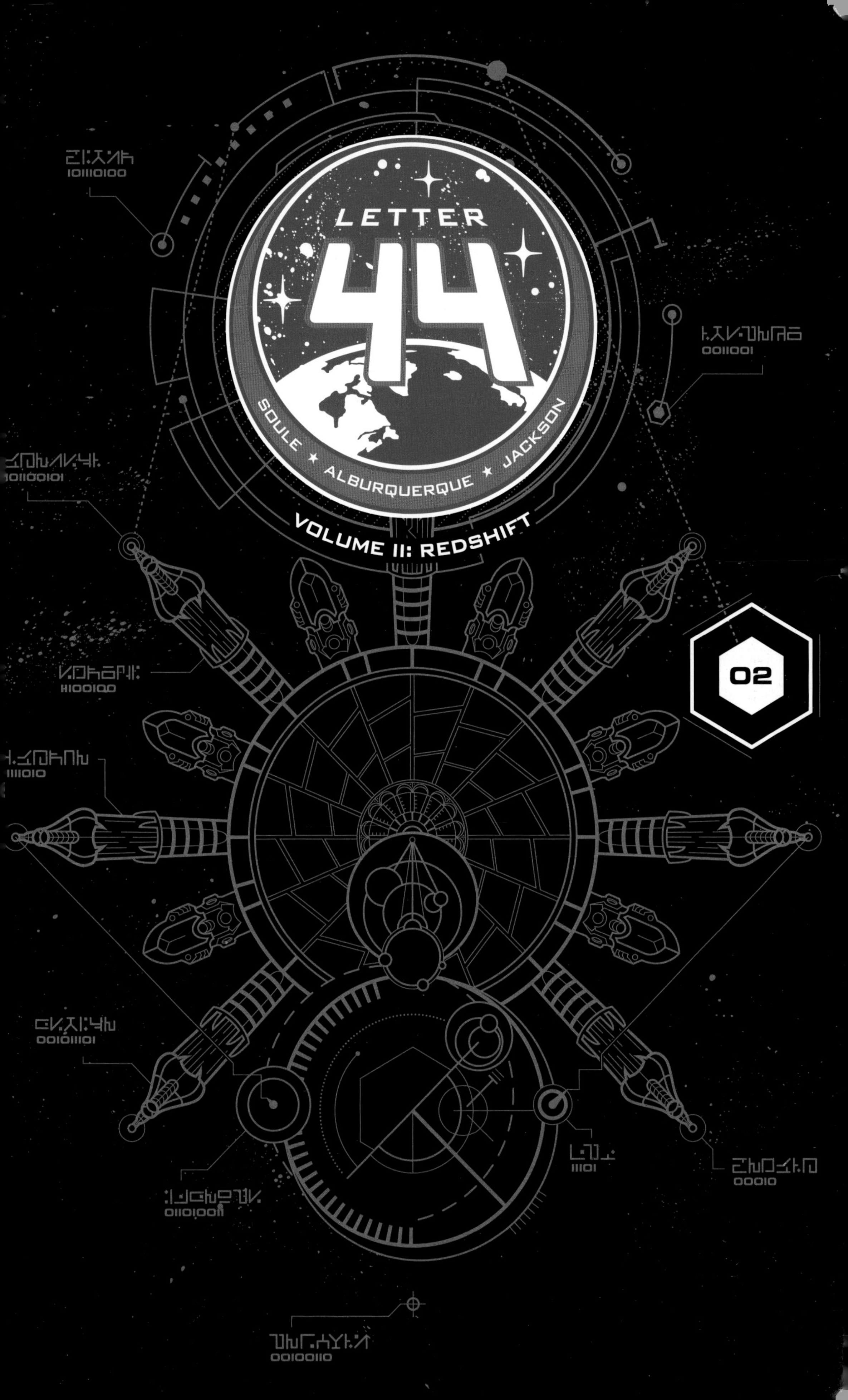
LETTER
44
SOULE ★ ALBURQUERQUE ★ JACKSON
VOLUME II: REDSHIFT
02

LETTER 44

THIS VOLUME COLLECTS ISSUES 8-13 OF THE ONI PRESS SERIES *LETTER 44*

Oni Press, Inc.

Publisher /// **Joe Nozemack**

Editor In Chief /// **James Lucas Jones**

V.P. of Business Development /// **Tim Wiesch**

Director of Sales /// **Cheyenne Allott**

Director of Publicity /// **John Schork**

Production Manager /// **Troy Look**

Editor /// **Charlie Chu**

Associate Editor /// **Robin Herrera**

Administrative Assistant /// **Ari Yarwood**

Graphic Designer /// **Hilary Thompson**

Production Assistant /// **Jared Jones**

Inventory Coordinator /// **Brad Rooks**

Office Assistant /// **Jung Lee**

ONI PRESS

1305 SE Martin Luther King Jr. Blvd.
Suite A
Portland, OR 97214

onipress.com
facebook.com/onipress | twitter.com/onipress | onipress.tumblr.com

charlessoule.com | @charlessoule
ajaalbertojimenezalburquerque.blogspot.com

FIRST EDITION: MARCH 2015

Letter 44 Volume 2. March 2015. Published by Oni Press, Inc. 1305 SE Martin Luther King Jr. Blvd., Suite A, Portland, OR 97214. Letter 44 is ™ & © 2015 Charles Soule. All rights reserved. Oni Press logo and icon ™ & © 2015 Oni Press, Inc. Oni Press logo and icon artwork created by Keith A. Wood. The events, institutions, and characters presented in this book are fictional. Any resemblance to actual persons, living or dead, is purely coincidental. No portion of this publication may be reproduced, by any means, without the express written permission of the copyright holders.

ISBN: 978-1-62010-206-0 | eISBN: 978-1-62010-207-7

Library of Congress Control Number: 2014949045

10 8 6 4 2 1 3 5 7 9

Printed in China

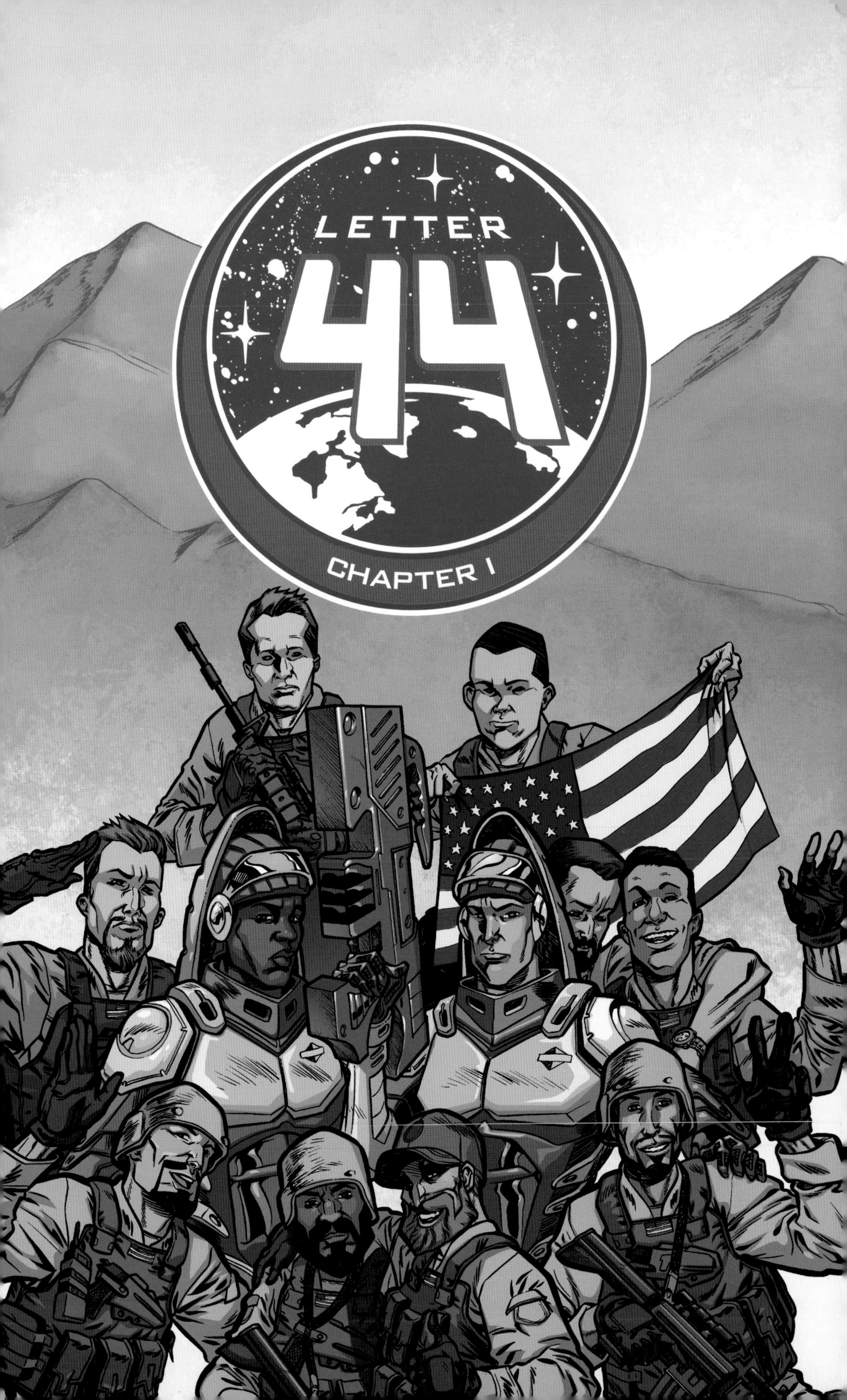
LETTER
44
CHAPTER I

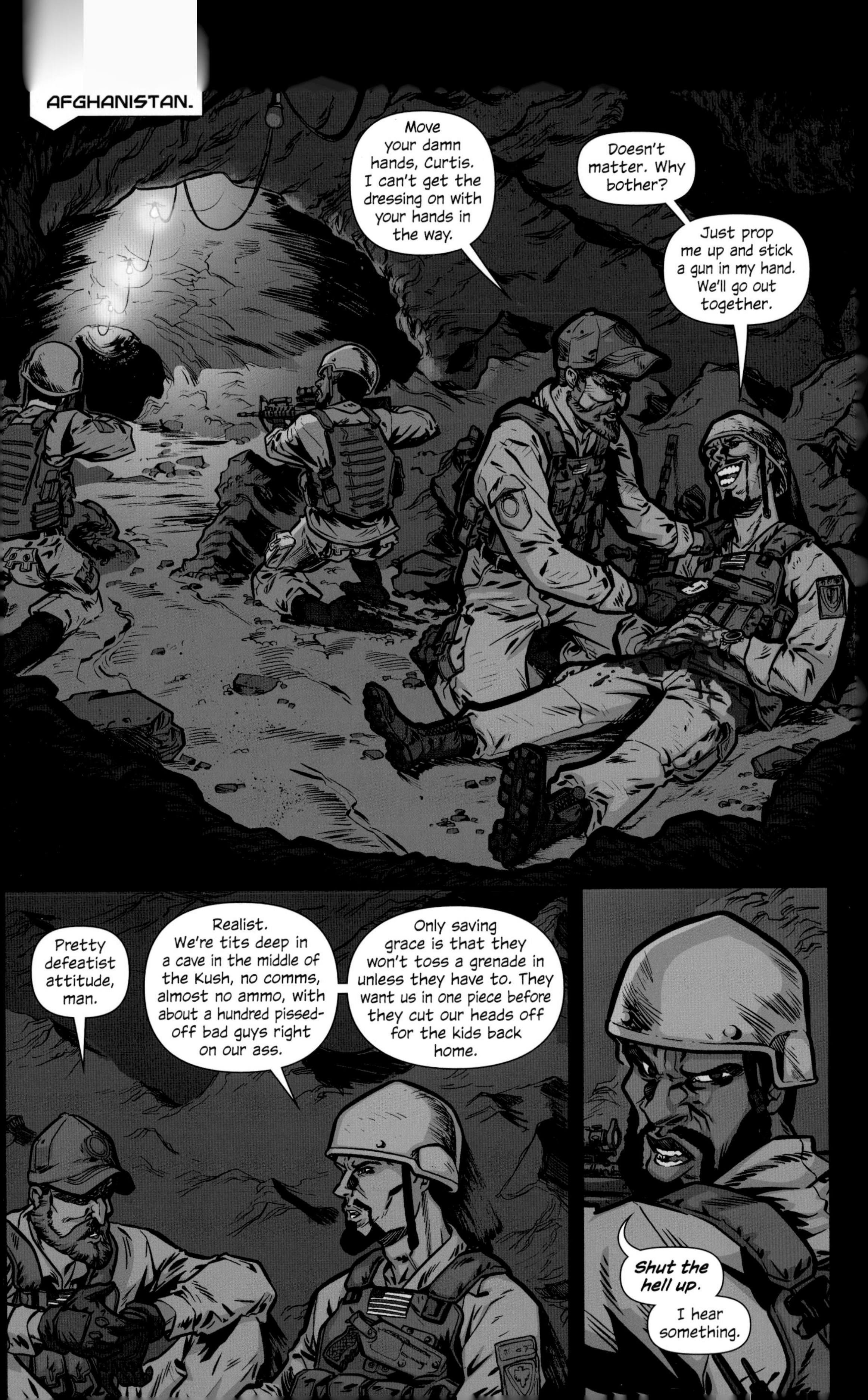
AFGHANISTAN.
Move your damn hands, Curtis. I can't get the dressing on with your hands in the way.
Doesn't matter. Why bother?
Just prop me up and stick a gun in my hand. We'll go out together.
Pretty defeatist attitude, man.
Realist. We're tits deep in a cave in the middle of the Kush, no comms, almost no ammo, with about a hundred pissed-off bad guys right on our ass.
Only saving grace is that they won't toss a grenade in unless they have to. They want us in one piece before they cut our heads off for the kids back home.
Shut the hell up.
I hear something.

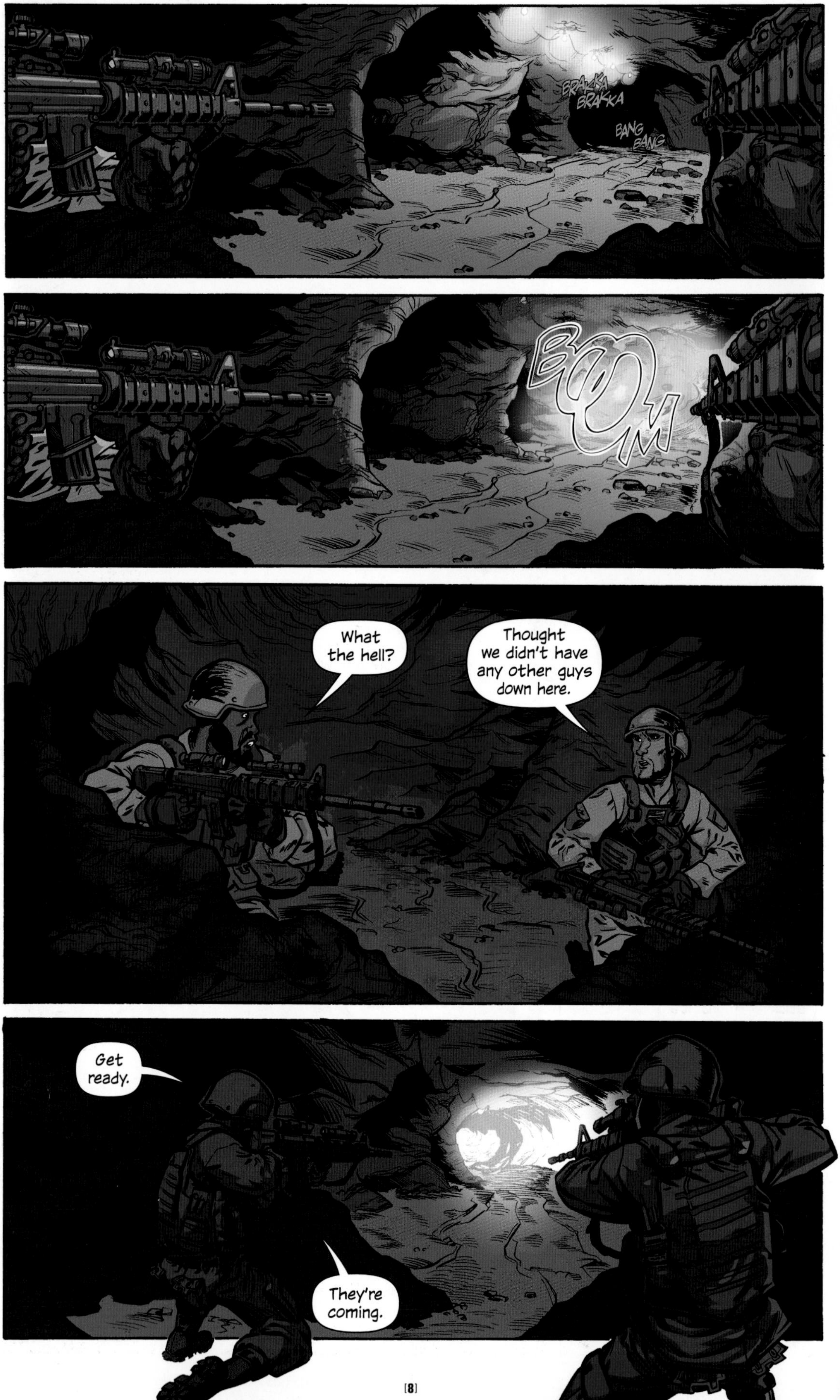
BRAKKA BRAKKA
BANG BANG
BOOM
What the hell?
Thought we didn't have any other guys down here.
Get ready.
They're coming.

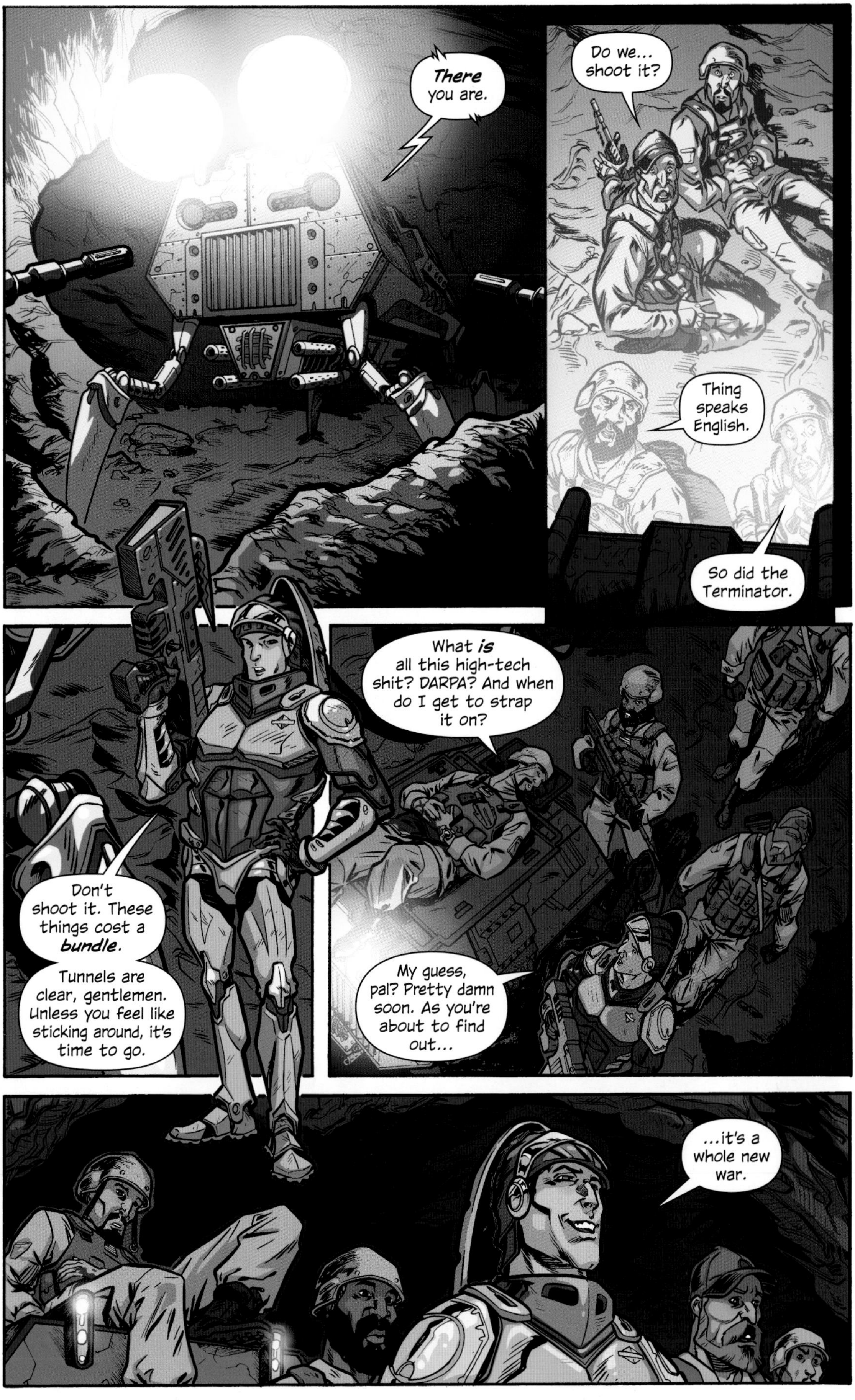
There you are.
Do we... shoot it?
Thing speaks English.
So did the Terminator.
Don't shoot it. These things cost a bundle.
Tunnels are clear, gentlemen. Unless you feel like sticking around, it's time to go.
What is all this high-tech shit? DARPA? And when do I get to strap it on?
My guess, pal? Pretty damn soon. As you're about to find out...
...it's a whole new war.

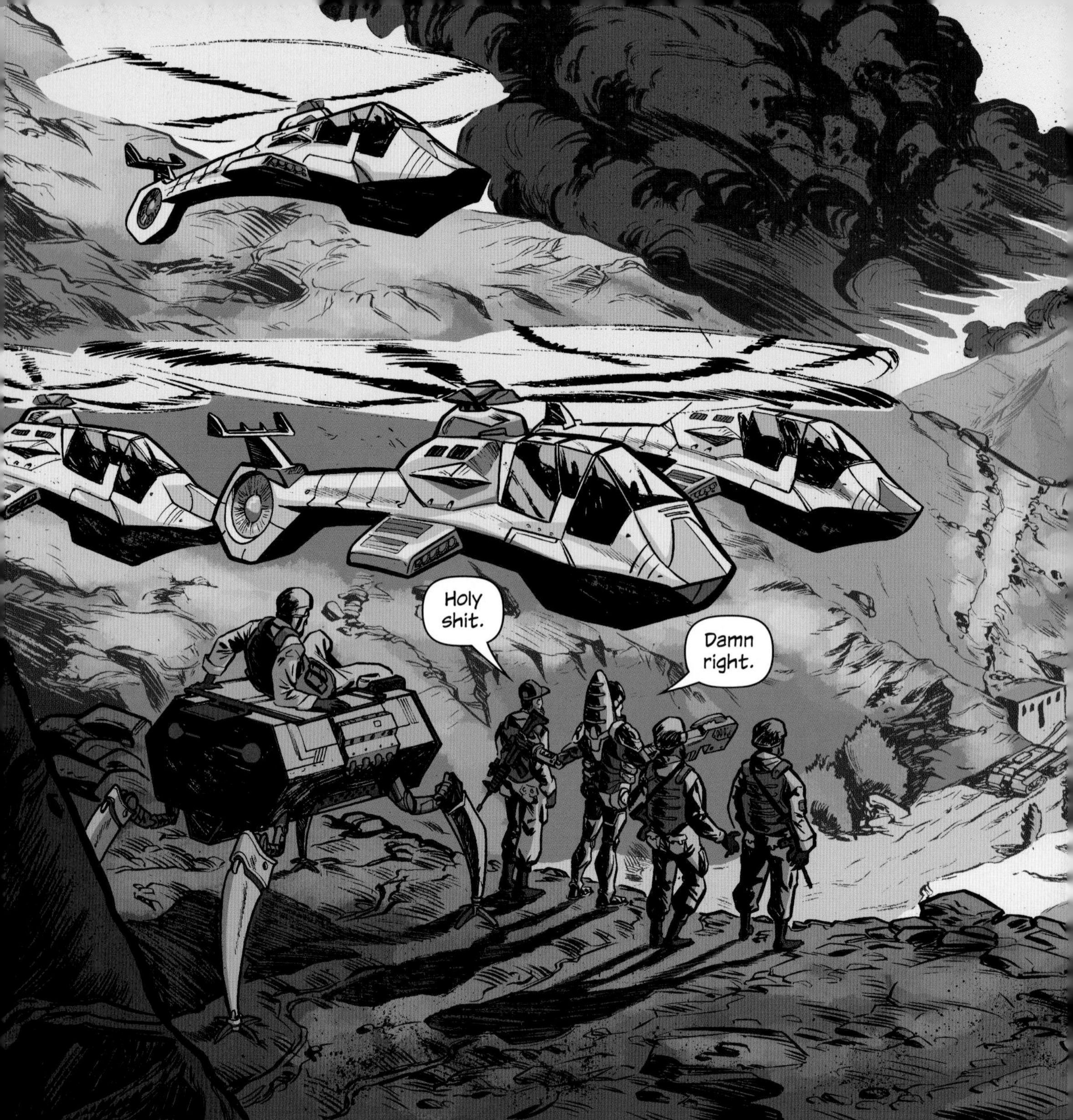
Holy shit.
Damn right.

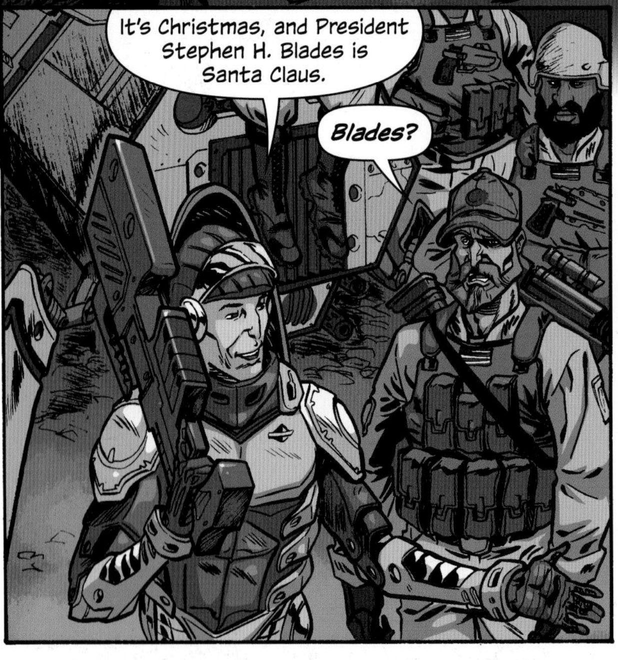
It's Christmas, and President Stephen H. Blades is Santa Claus.
Blades?

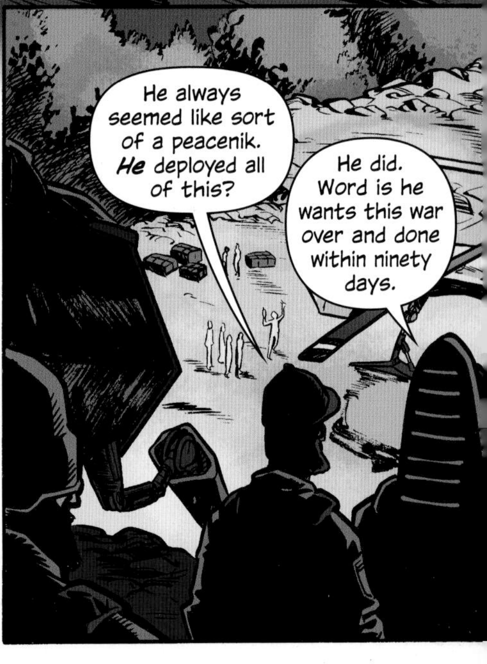
He always seemed like sort of a peacenik. *He* deployed all of this?
He did. Word is he wants this war over and done within ninety days.

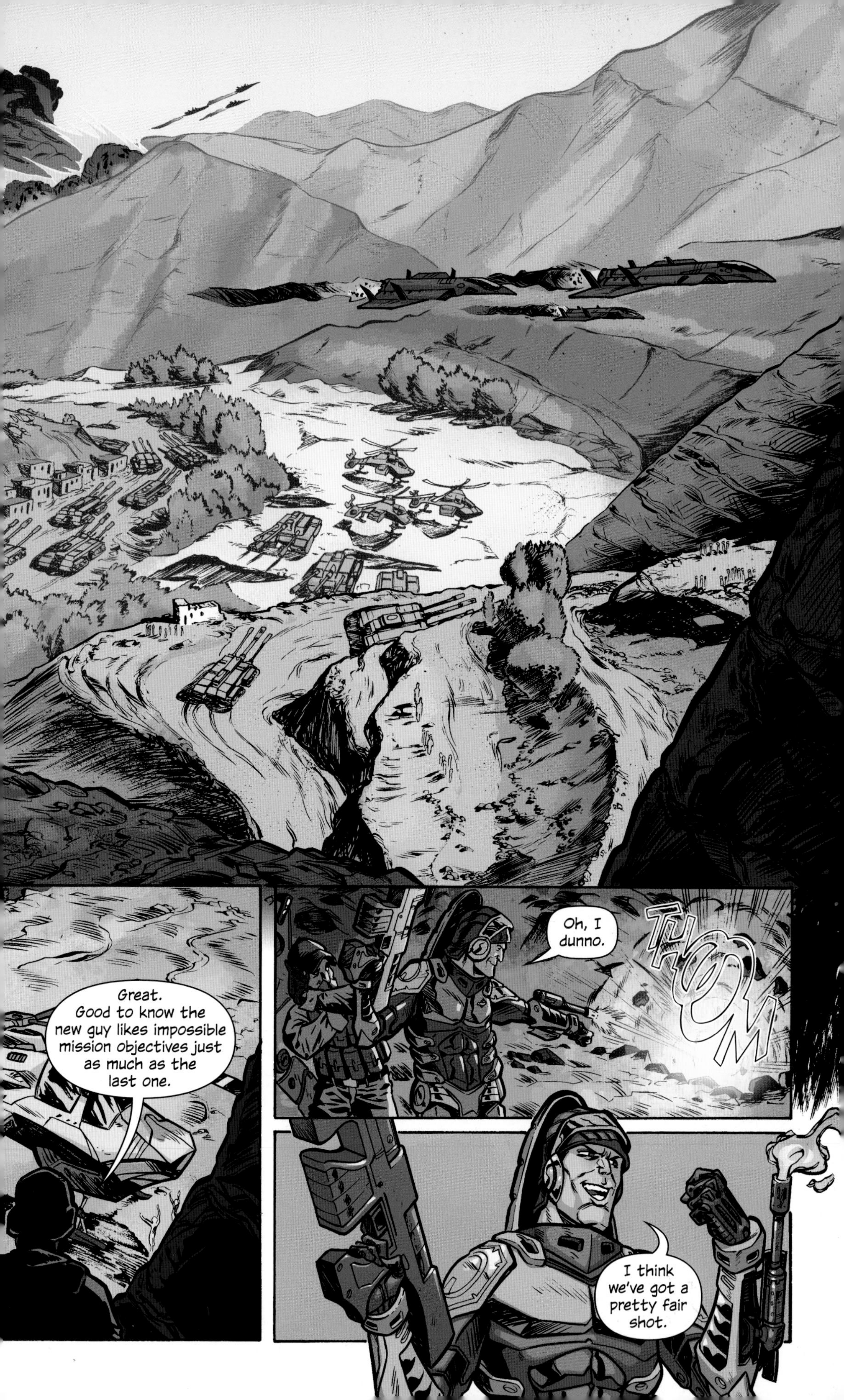
Great. Good to know the new guy likes impossible mission objectives just as much as the last one.
Oh, I dunno.
THOOM
I think we've got a pretty fair shot.

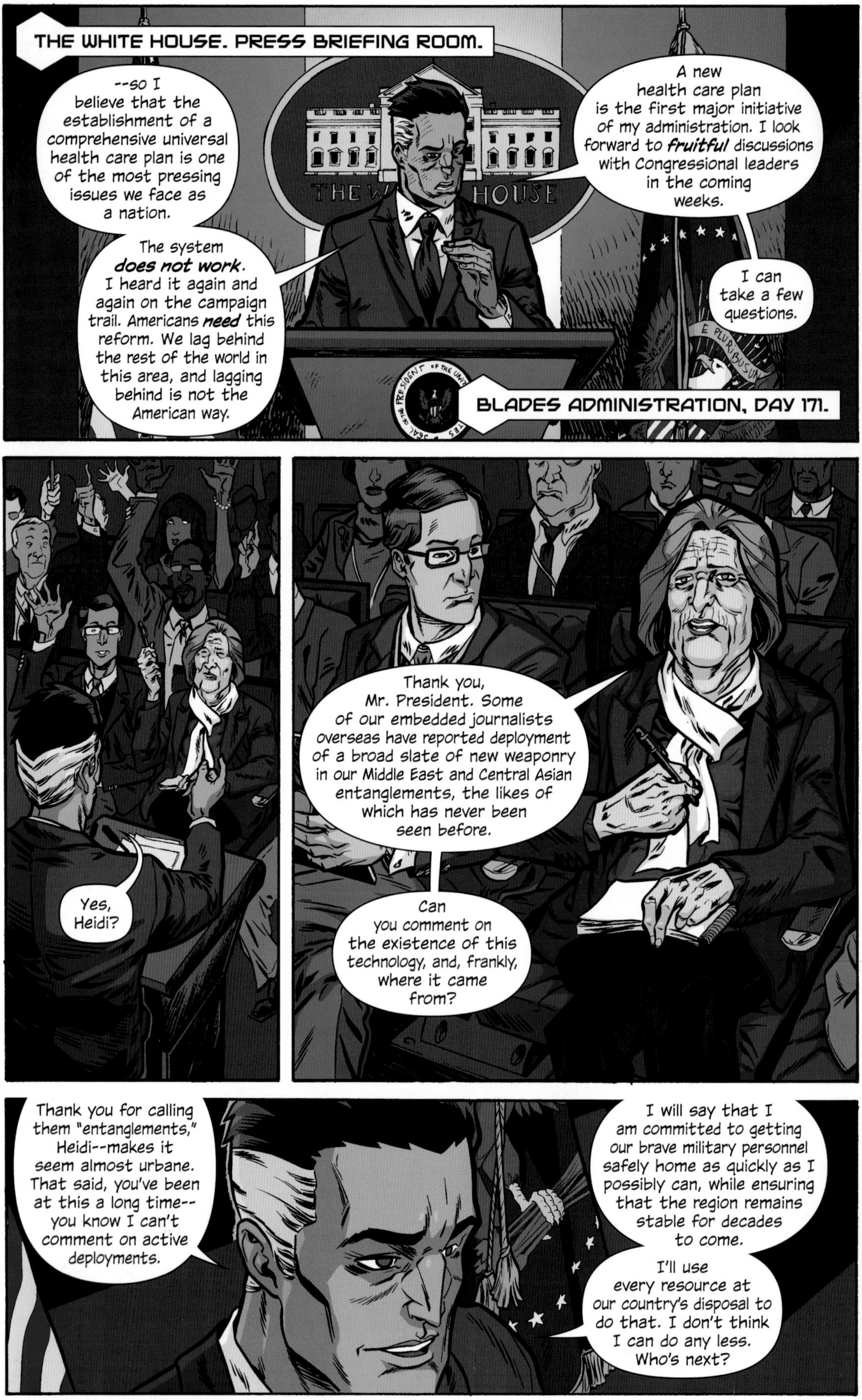
THE WHITE HOUSE. PRESS BRIEFING ROOM.
--so I believe that the establishment of a comprehensive universal health care plan is one of the most pressing issues we face as a nation.
The system **does not work**. I heard it again and again on the campaign trail. Americans **need** this reform. We lag behind the rest of the world in this area, and lagging behind is not the American way.
A new health care plan is the first major initiative of my administration. I look forward to **fruitful** discussions with Congressional leaders in the coming weeks.
I can take a few questions.
BLADES ADMINISTRATION, DAY 171.
Yes, Heidi?
Thank you, Mr. President. Some of our embedded journalists overseas have reported deployment of a broad slate of new weaponry in our Middle East and Central Asian entanglements, the likes of which has never been seen before.
Can you comment on the existence of this technology, and, frankly, where it came from?
Thank you for calling them "entanglements," Heidi--makes it seem almost urbane. That said, you've been at this a long time--you know I can't comment on active deployments.
I will say that I am committed to getting our brave military personnel safely home as quickly as I possibly can, while ensuring that the region remains stable for decades to come.
I'll use every resource at our country's disposal to do that. I don't think I can do any less. Who's next?

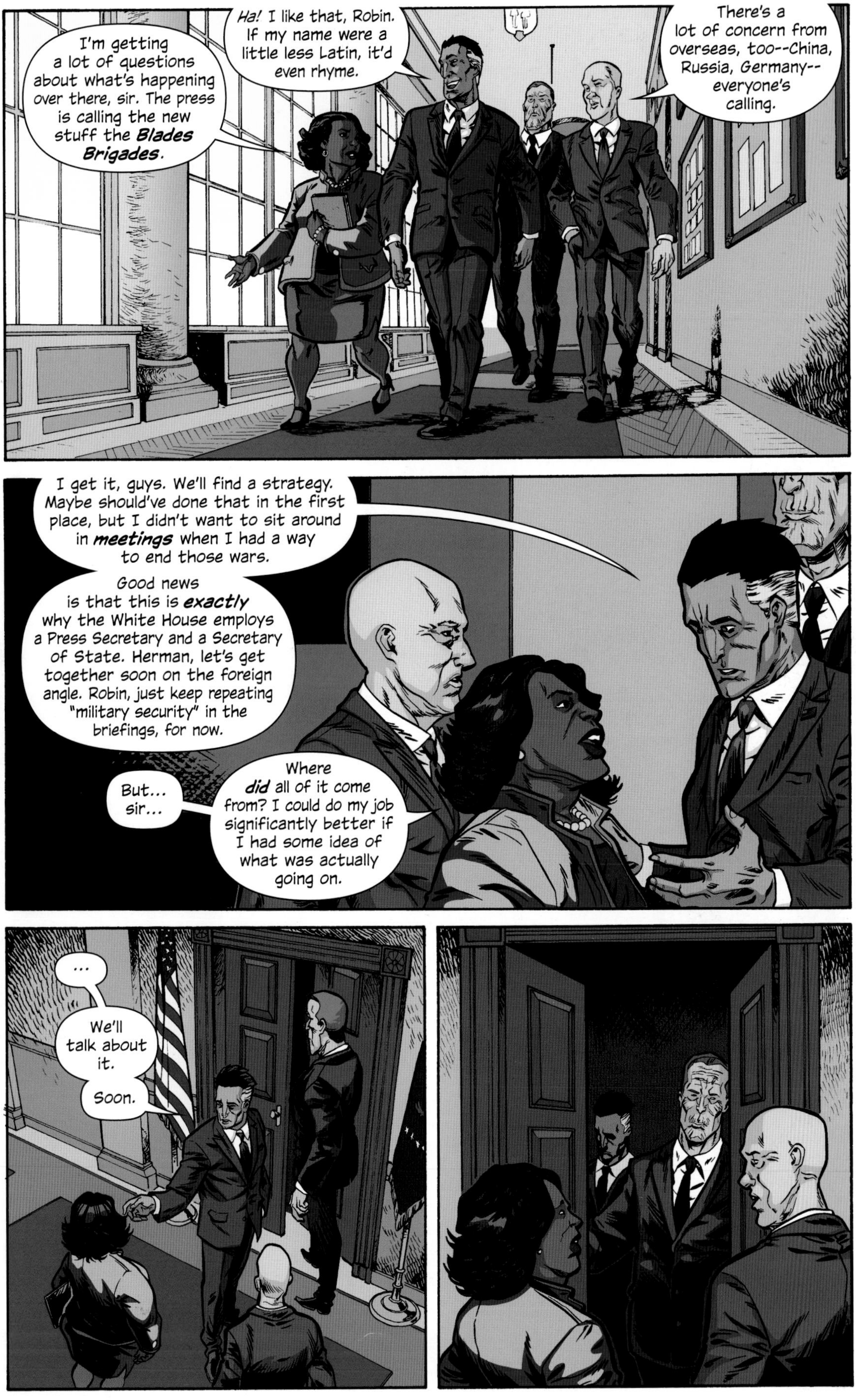
I'm getting a lot of questions about what's happening over there, sir. The press is calling the new stuff the **Blades Brigades**.
Ha! I like that, Robin. If my name were a little less Latin, it'd even rhyme.
There's a lot of concern from overseas, too--China, Russia, Germany--everyone's calling.
I get it, guys. We'll find a strategy. Maybe should've done that in the first place, but I didn't want to sit around in **meetings** when I had a way to end those wars.
Good news is that this is **exactly** why the White House employs a Press Secretary and a Secretary of State. Herman, let's get together soon on the foreign angle. Robin, just keep repeating "military security" in the briefings, for now.
But... sir...
Where **did** all of it come from? I could do my job significantly better if I had some idea of what was actually going on.
...
We'll talk about it.
Soon.

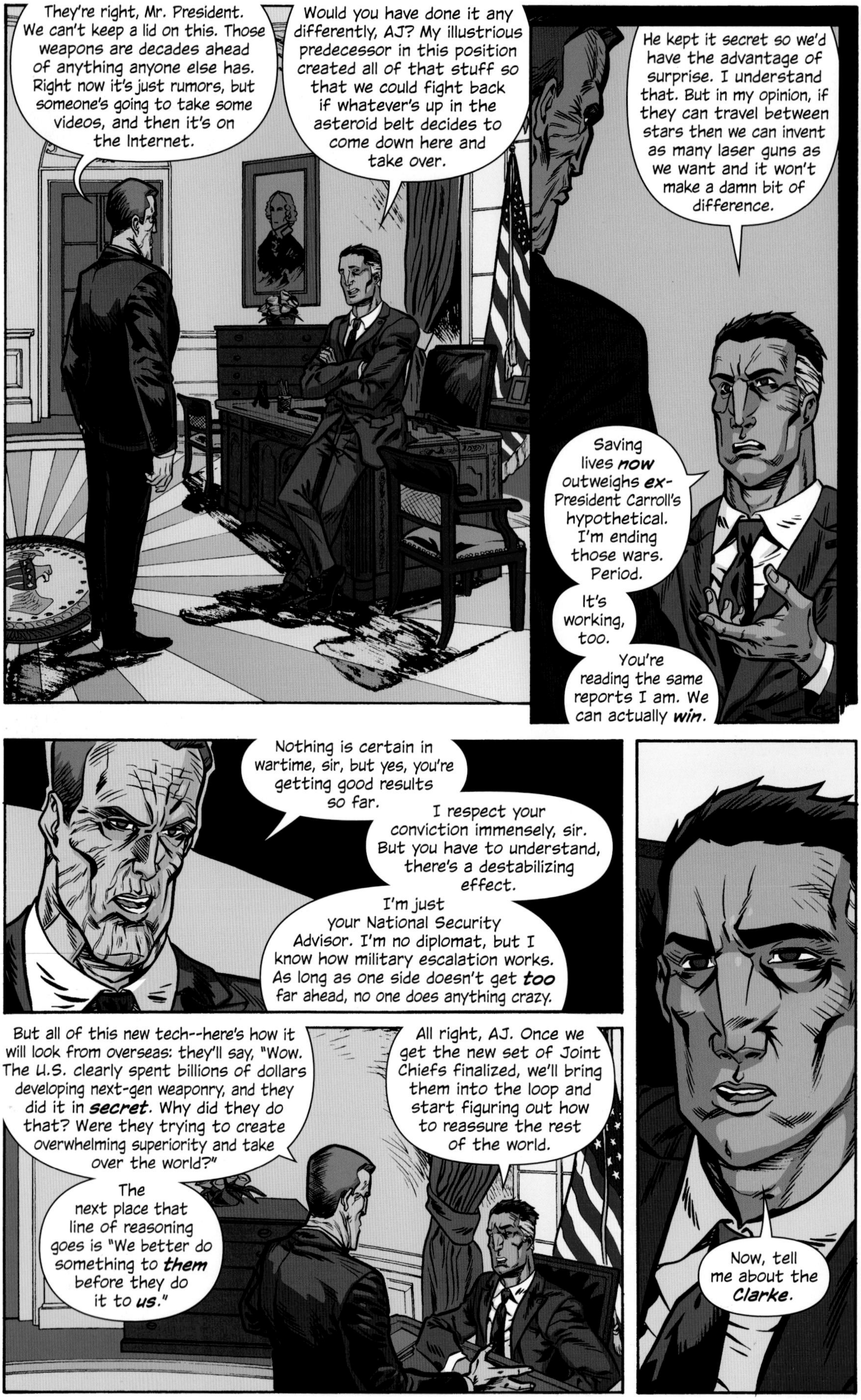

They're right, Mr. President. We can't keep a lid on this. Those weapons are decades ahead of anything anyone else has. Right now it's just rumors, but someone's going to take some videos, and then it's on the Internet.
Would you have done it any differently, AJ? My illustrious predecessor in this position created all of that stuff so that we could fight back if whatever's up in the asteroid belt decides to come down here and take over.
He kept it secret so we'd have the advantage of surprise. I understand that. But in my opinion, if they can travel between stars then we can invent as many laser guns as we want and it won't make a damn bit of difference.
Saving lives **now** outweighs **ex**-President Carroll's hypothetical. I'm ending those wars. Period.
It's working, too.
You're reading the same reports I am. We can actually **win**.
Nothing is certain in wartime, sir, but yes, you're getting good results so far.
I respect your conviction immensely, sir. But you have to understand, there's a destabilizing effect.
I'm just your National Security Advisor. I'm no diplomat, but I know how military escalation works. As long as one side doesn't get **too** far ahead, no one does anything crazy.
But all of this new tech--here's how it will look from overseas: they'll say, "Wow. The U.S. clearly spent billions of dollars developing next-gen weaponry, and they did it in **secret**. Why did they do that? Were they trying to create overwhelming superiority and take over the world?"
The next place that line of reasoning goes is "We better do something to **them** before they do it to **us**."
All right, AJ. Once we get the new set of Joint Chiefs finalized, we'll bring them into the loop and start figuring out how to reassure the rest of the world.
Now, tell me about the **Clarke**.

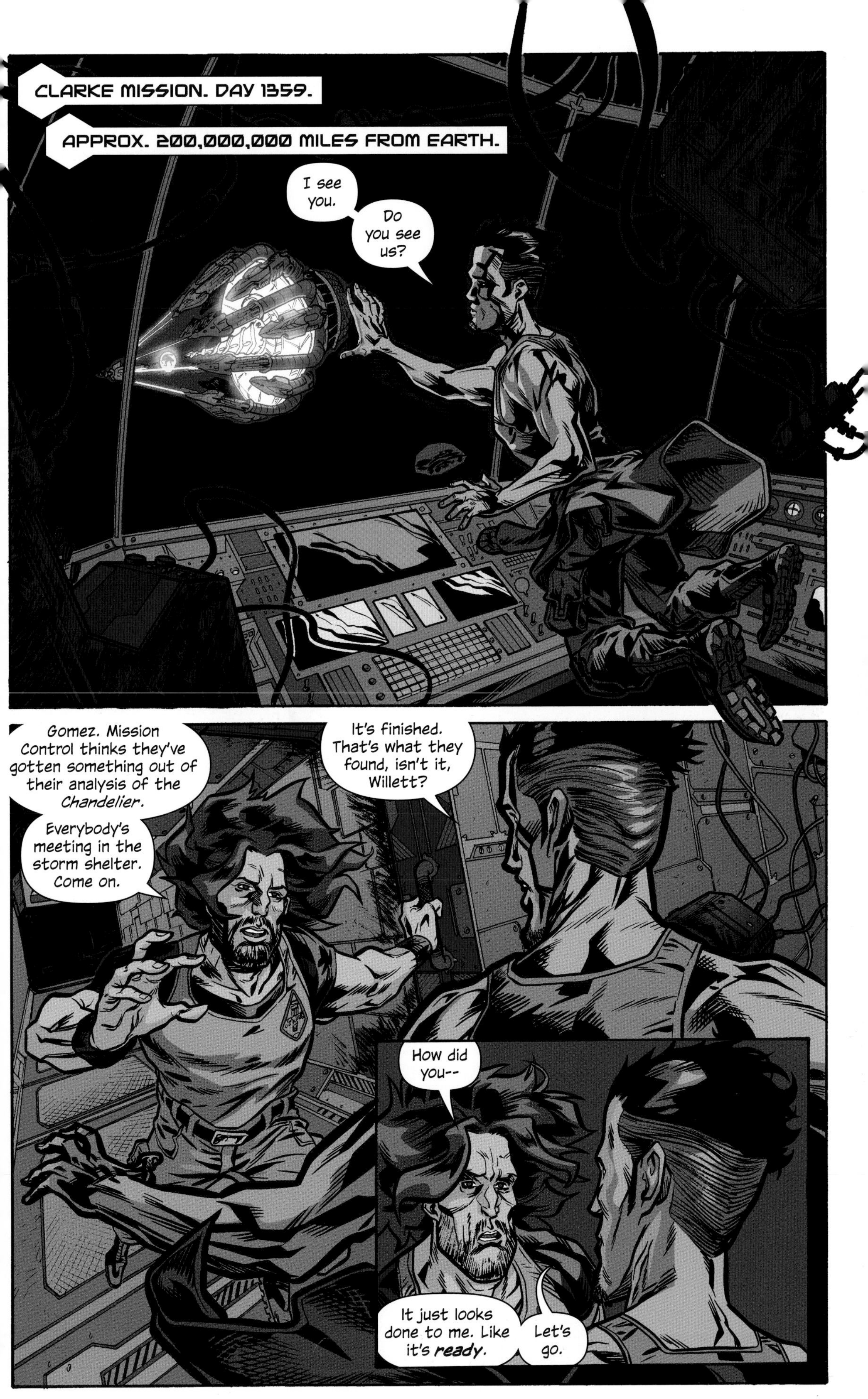
CLARKE MISSION. DAY 1359.
APPROX. 200,000,000 MILES FROM EARTH.
I see you.
Do you see us?
Gomez. Mission Control thinks they've gotten something out of their analysis of the *Chandelier*.
Everybody's meeting in the storm shelter. Come on.
It's finished. That's what they found, isn't it, Willett?
How did you--
It just looks done to me. Like it's ***ready***.
Let's go.

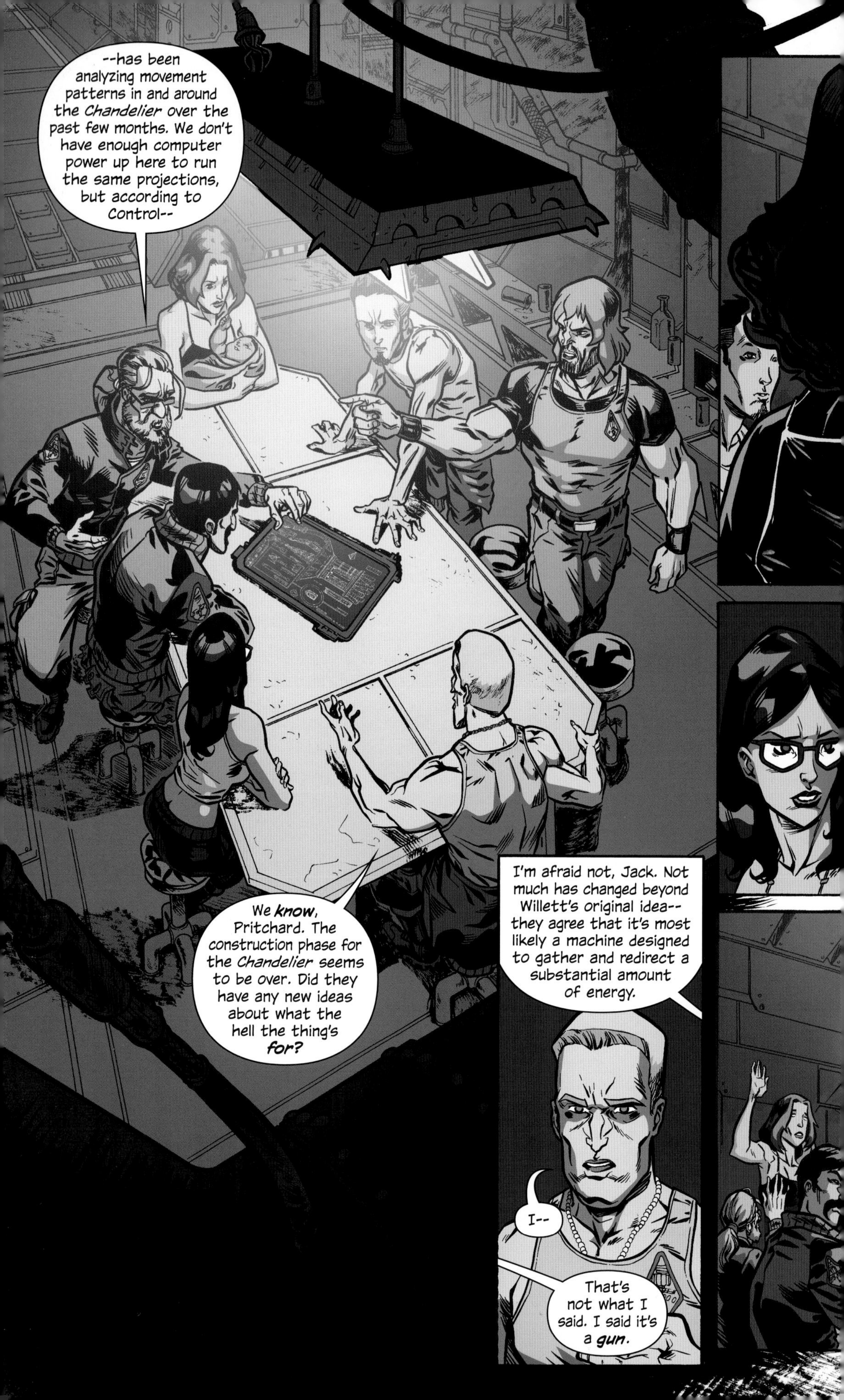
--has been analyzing movement patterns in and around the *Chandelier* over the past few months. We don't have enough computer power up here to run the same projections, but according to Control--
We **know**, Pritchard. The construction phase for the *Chandelier* seems to be over. Did they have any new ideas about what the hell the thing's **for?**
I'm afraid not, Jack. Not much has changed beyond Willett's original idea--they agree that it's most likely a machine designed to gather and redirect a substantial amount of energy.
I--
That's not what I said. I said it's a **gun**.

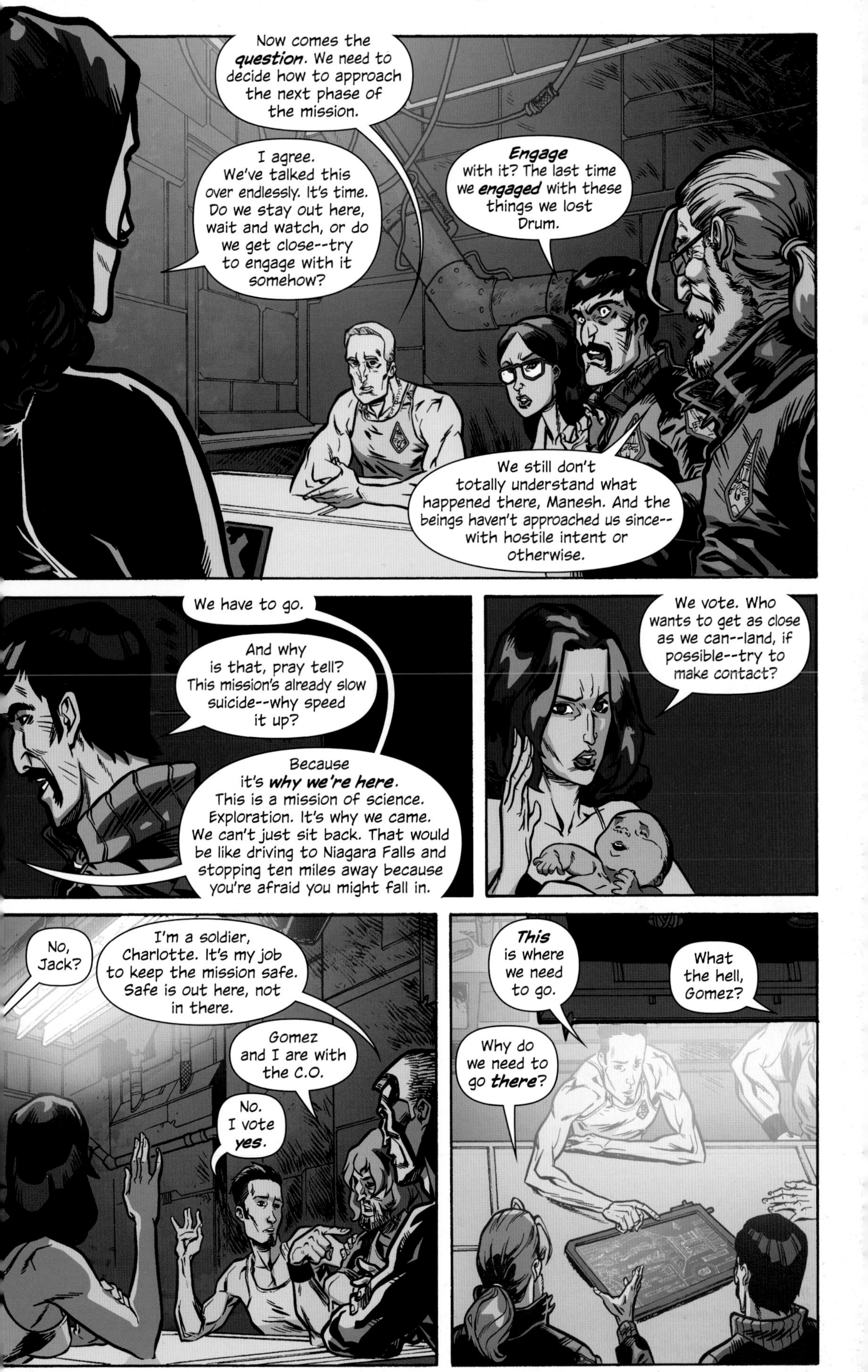

Now comes the *question*. We need to decide how to approach the next phase of the mission.
I agree. We've talked this over endlessly. It's time. Do we stay out here, wait and watch, or do we get close--try to engage with it somehow?
Engage with it? The last time we *engaged* with these things we lost Drum.
We still don't totally understand what happened there, Manesh. And the beings haven't approached us since--with hostile intent or otherwise.
We have to go.
And why is that, pray tell? This mission's already slow suicide--why speed it up?
Because it's *why we're here*. This is a mission of science. Exploration. It's why we came. We can't just sit back. That would be like driving to Niagara Falls and stopping ten miles away because you're afraid you might fall in.
We vote. Who wants to get as close as we can--land, if possible--try to make contact?
No, Jack?
I'm a soldier, Charlotte. It's my job to keep the mission safe. Safe is out here, not in there.
Gomez and I are with the C.O.
No. I vote *yes*.
This is where we need to go.
What the hell, Gomez?
Why do we need to go *there*?

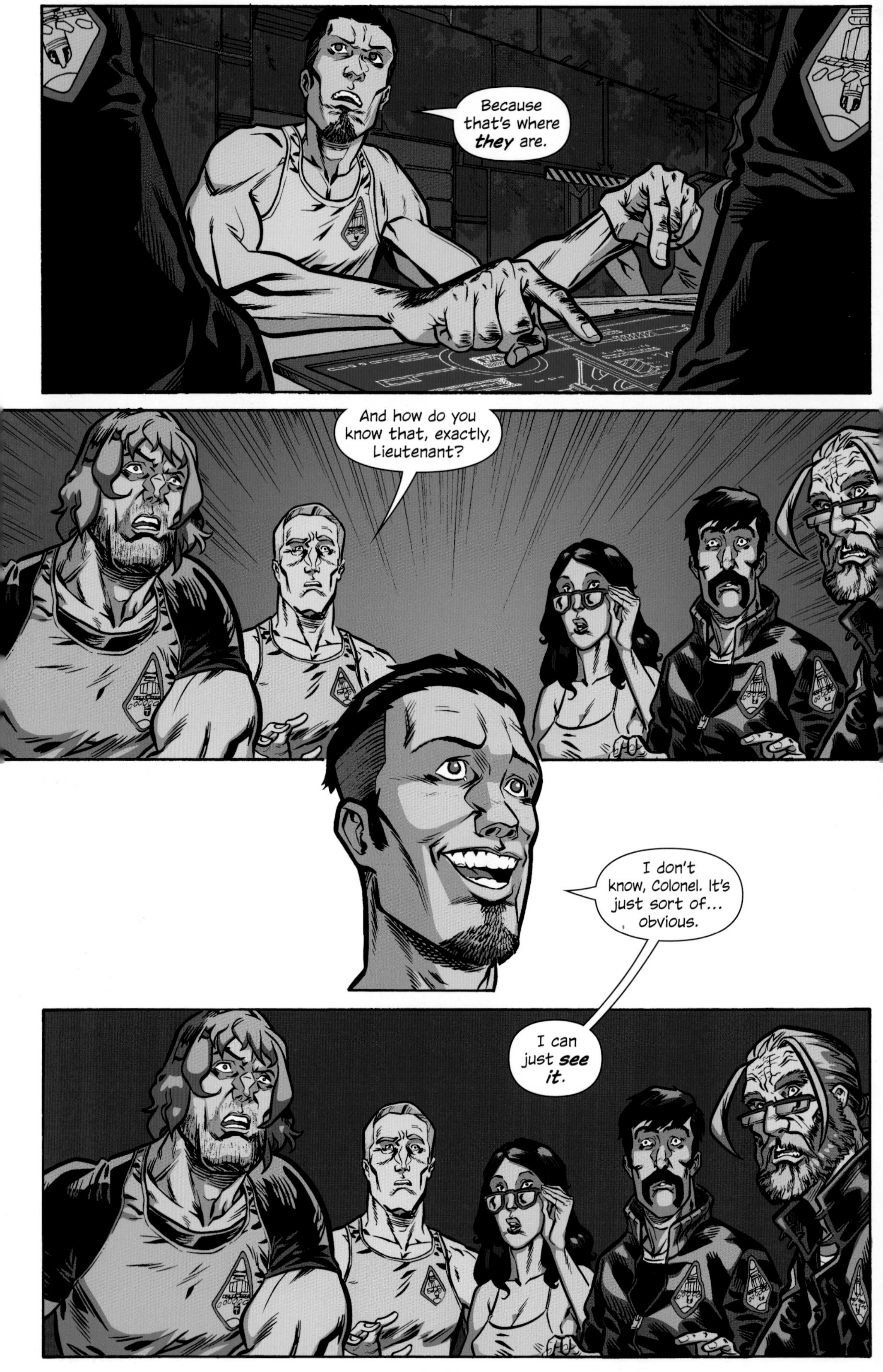
Because that's where *they* are.
And how do you know that, exactly, Lieutenant?
I don't know, Colonel. It's just sort of... obvious.
I can just *see* *it*.

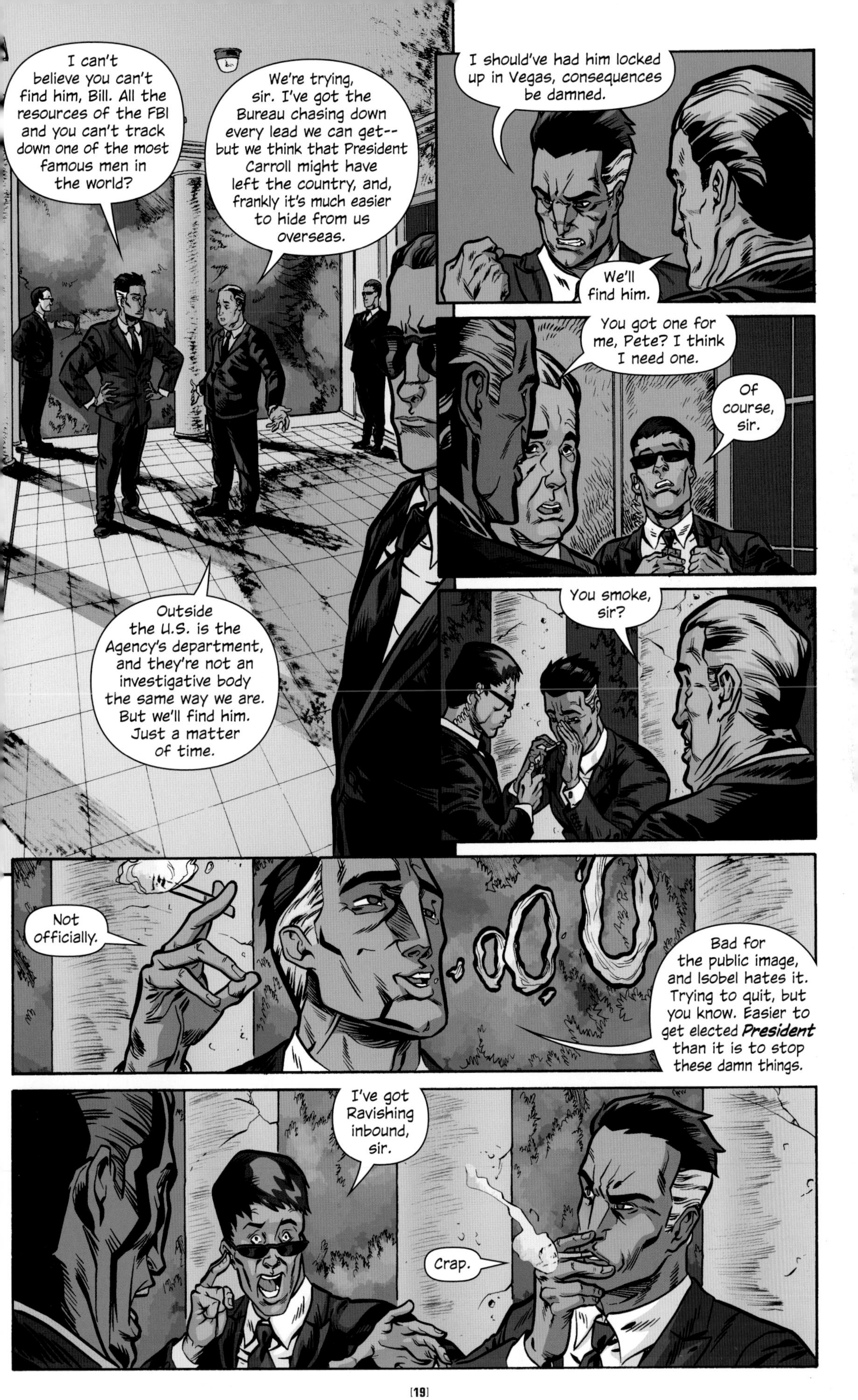

I can't believe you can't find him, Bill. All the resources of the FBI and you can't track down one of the most famous men in the world?
We're trying, sir. I've got the Bureau chasing down every lead we can get--but we think that President Carroll might have left the country, and, frankly it's much easier to hide from us overseas.
Outside the U.S. is the Agency's department, and they're not an investigative body the same way we are. But we'll find him. Just a matter of time.
I should've had him locked up in Vegas, consequences be damned.
We'll find him.
You got one for me, Pete? I think I need one.
Of course, sir.
You smoke, sir?
Not officially.
Bad for the public image, and Isobel hates it. Trying to quit, but you know. Easier to get elected *President* than it is to stop these damn things.
I've got Ravishing inbound, sir.
Crap.

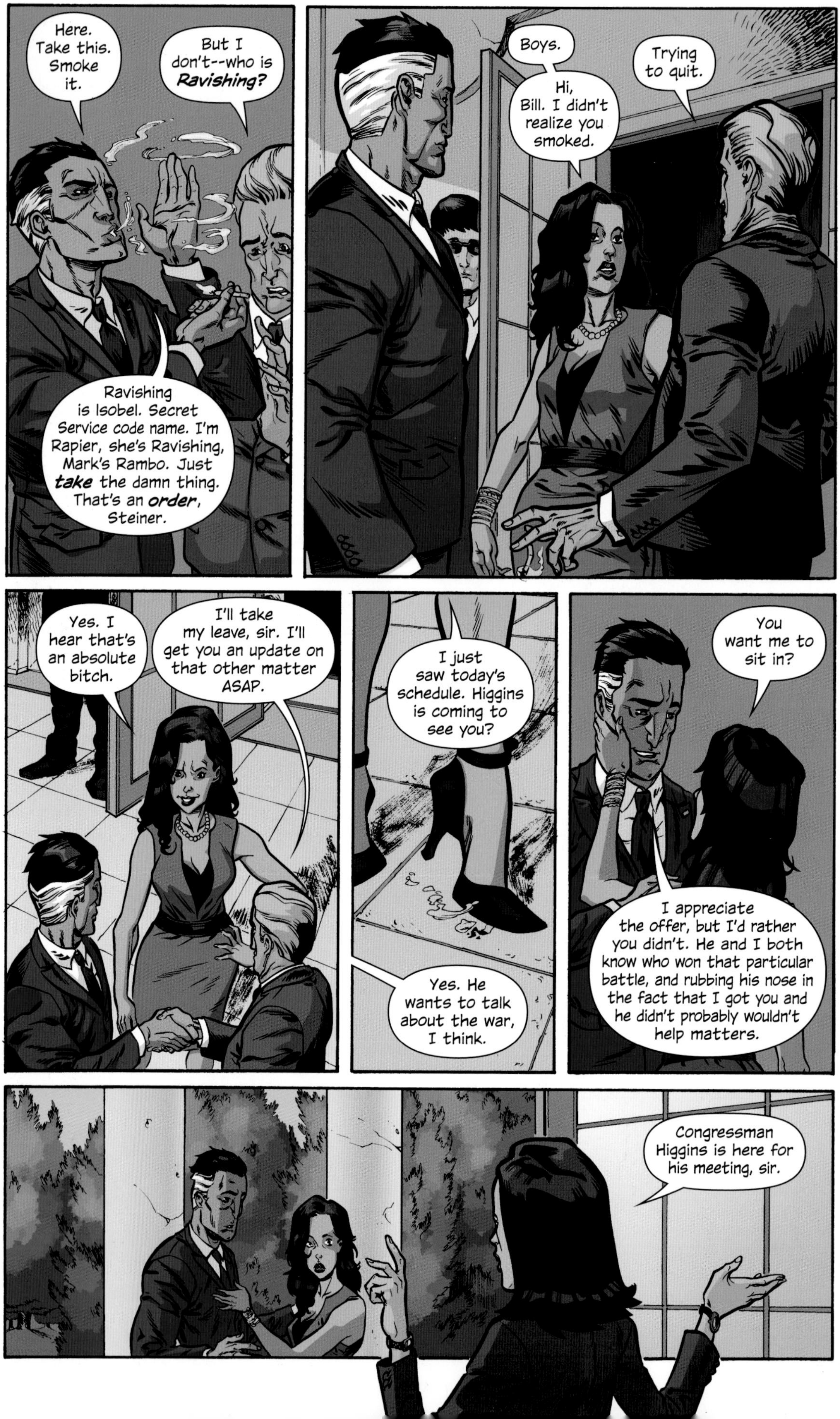
Here. Take this. Smoke it.
But I don't--who is *Ravishing?*
Ravishing is Isobel. Secret Service code name. I'm Rapier, she's Ravishing, Mark's Rambo. Just *take* the damn thing. That's an *order*, Steiner.
Boys.
Hi, Bill. I didn't realize you smoked.
Trying to quit.
Yes. I hear that's an absolute bitch.
I'll take my leave, sir. I'll get you an update on that other matter ASAP.
I just saw today's schedule. Higgins is coming to see you?
Yes. He wants to talk about the war, I think.
You want me to sit in?
I appreciate the offer, but I'd rather you didn't. He and I both know who won that particular battle, and rubbing his nose in the fact that I got you and he didn't probably wouldn't help matters.
Congressman Higgins is here for his meeting, sir.

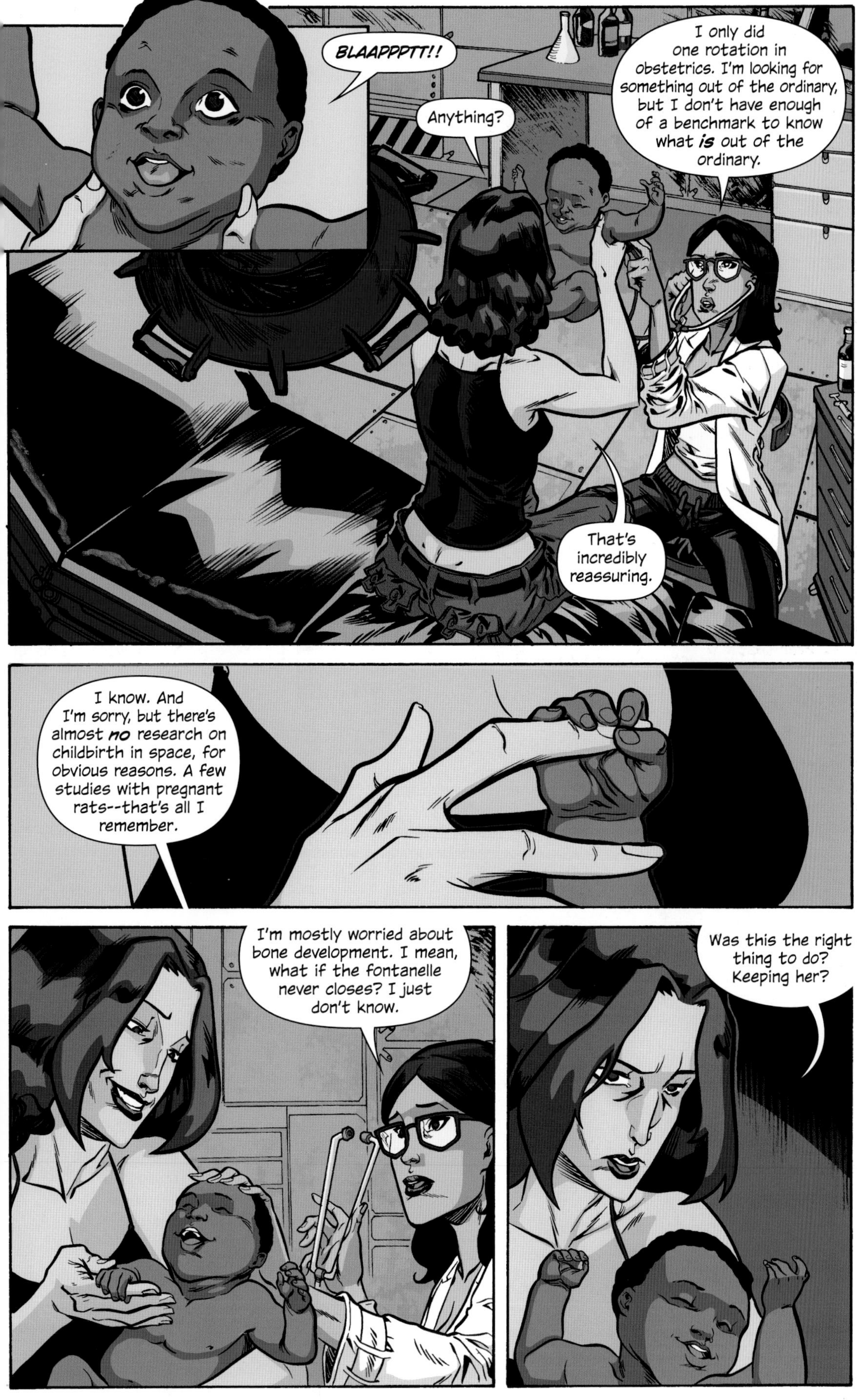
BLAAPPPTT!!
Anything?
I only did one rotation in obstetrics. I'm looking for something out of the ordinary, but I don't have enough of a benchmark to know what *is* out of the ordinary.
That's incredibly reassuring.
I know. And I'm sorry, but there's almost *no* research on childbirth in space, for obvious reasons. A few studies with pregnant rats--that's all I remember.
I'm mostly worried about bone development. I mean, what if the fontanelle never closes? I just don't know.
Was this the right thing to do? Keeping her?

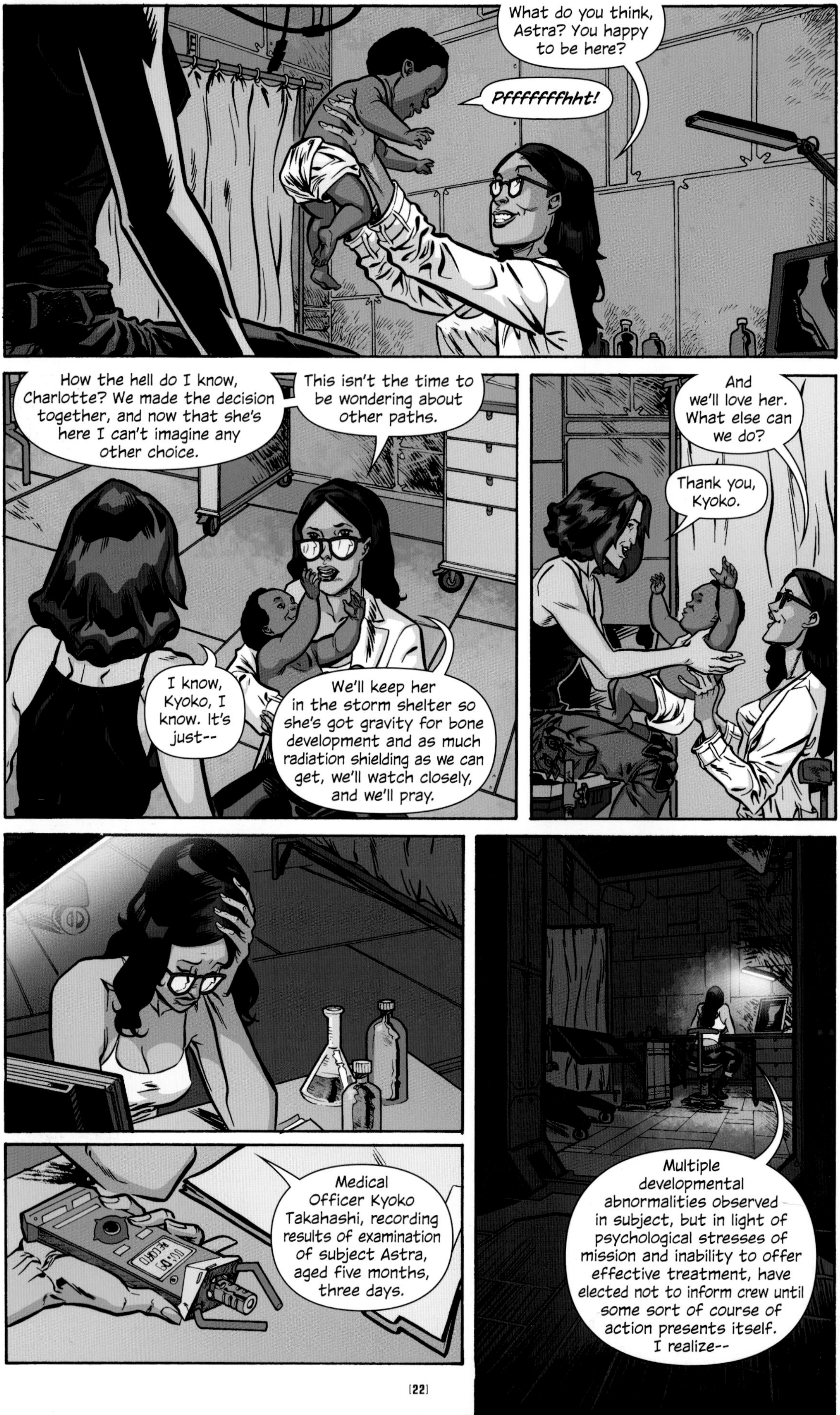
What do you think, Astra? You happy to be here?
Pfffffffhht!
How the hell do I know, Charlotte? We made the decision together, and now that she's here I can't imagine any other choice.
This isn't the time to be wondering about other paths.
I know, Kyoko, I know. It's just--
We'll keep her in the storm shelter so she's got gravity for bone development and as much radiation shielding as we can get, we'll watch closely, and we'll pray.
And we'll love her. What else can we do?
Thank you, Kyoko.
Medical Officer Kyoko Takahashi, recording results of examination of subject Astra, aged five months, three days.
Multiple developmental abnormalities observed in subject, but in light of psychological stresses of mission and inability to offer effective treatment, have elected not to inform crew until some sort of course of action presents itself. I realize--

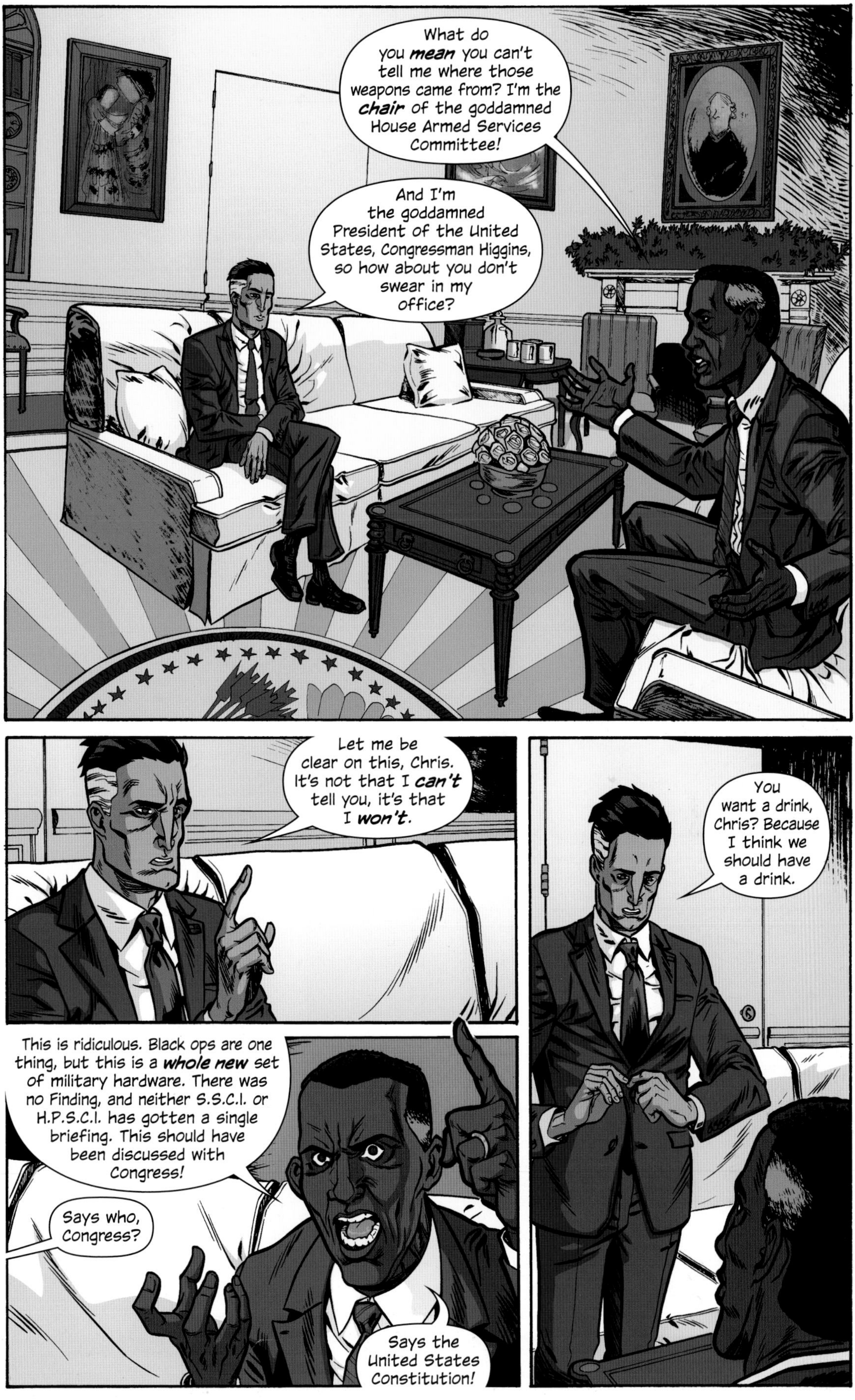
What do you *mean* you can't tell me where those weapons came from? I'm the *chair* of the goddamned House Armed Services Committee!
And I'm the goddamned President of the United States, Congressman Higgins, so how about you don't swear in my office?
Let me be clear on this, Chris. It's not that I *can't* tell you, it's that I *won't*.
This is ridiculous. Black ops are one thing, but this is a *whole new* set of military hardware. There was no Finding, and neither S.S.C.I. or H.P.S.C.I. has gotten a single briefing. This should have been discussed with Congress!
Says who, Congress?
Says the United States Constitution!
You want a drink, Chris? Because I think we should have a drink.

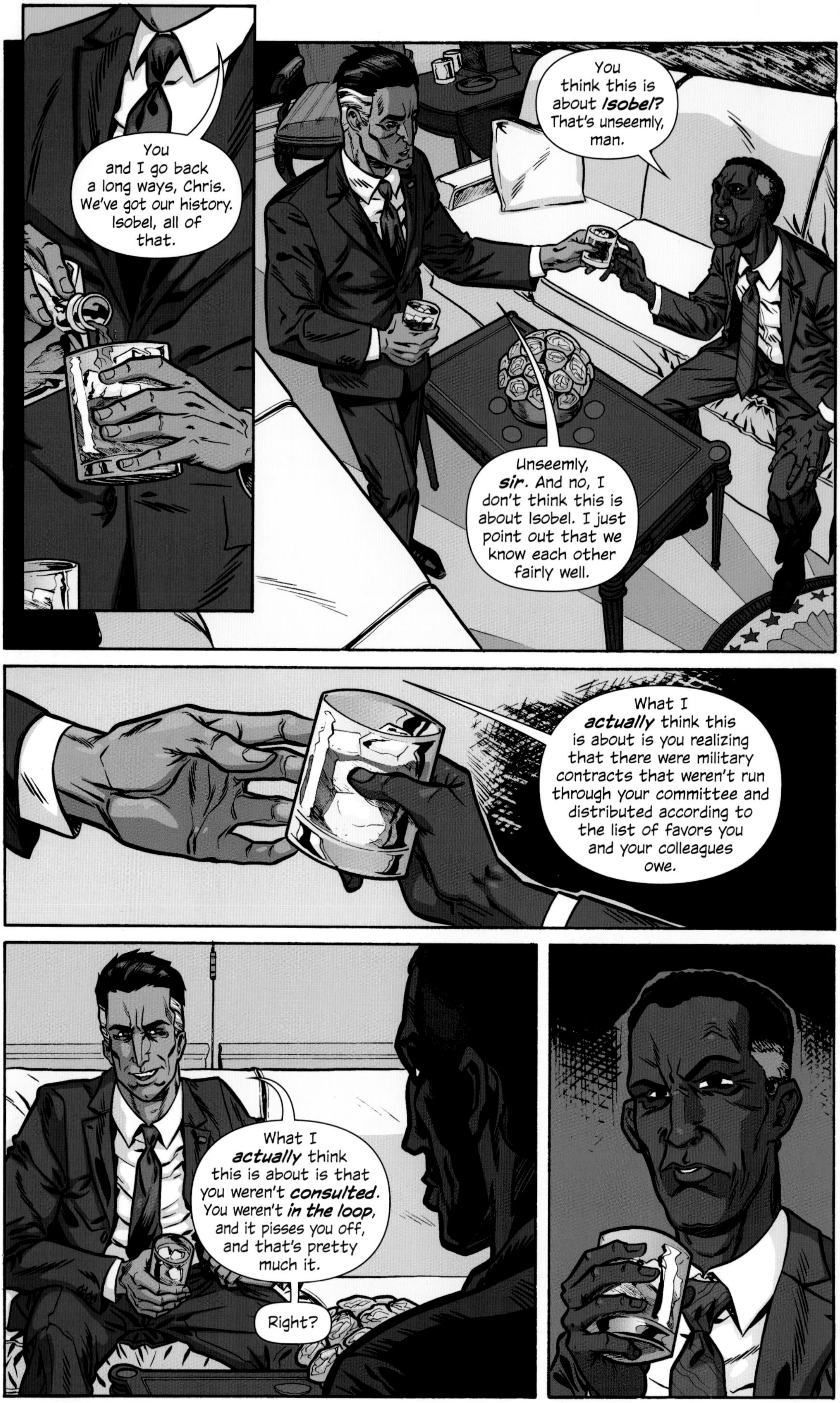

You and I go back a long ways, Chris. We've got our history. Isobel, all of that.
You think this is about *Isobel?* That's unseemly, man.
Unseemly, ***sir***. And no, I don't think this is about Isobel. I just point out that we know each other fairly well.
What I ***actually*** think this is about is you realizing that there were military contracts that weren't run through your committee and distributed according to the list of favors you and your colleagues owe.
What I ***actually*** think this is about is that you weren't ***consulted***. You weren't ***in the loop***, and it pisses you off, and that's pretty much it.
Right?

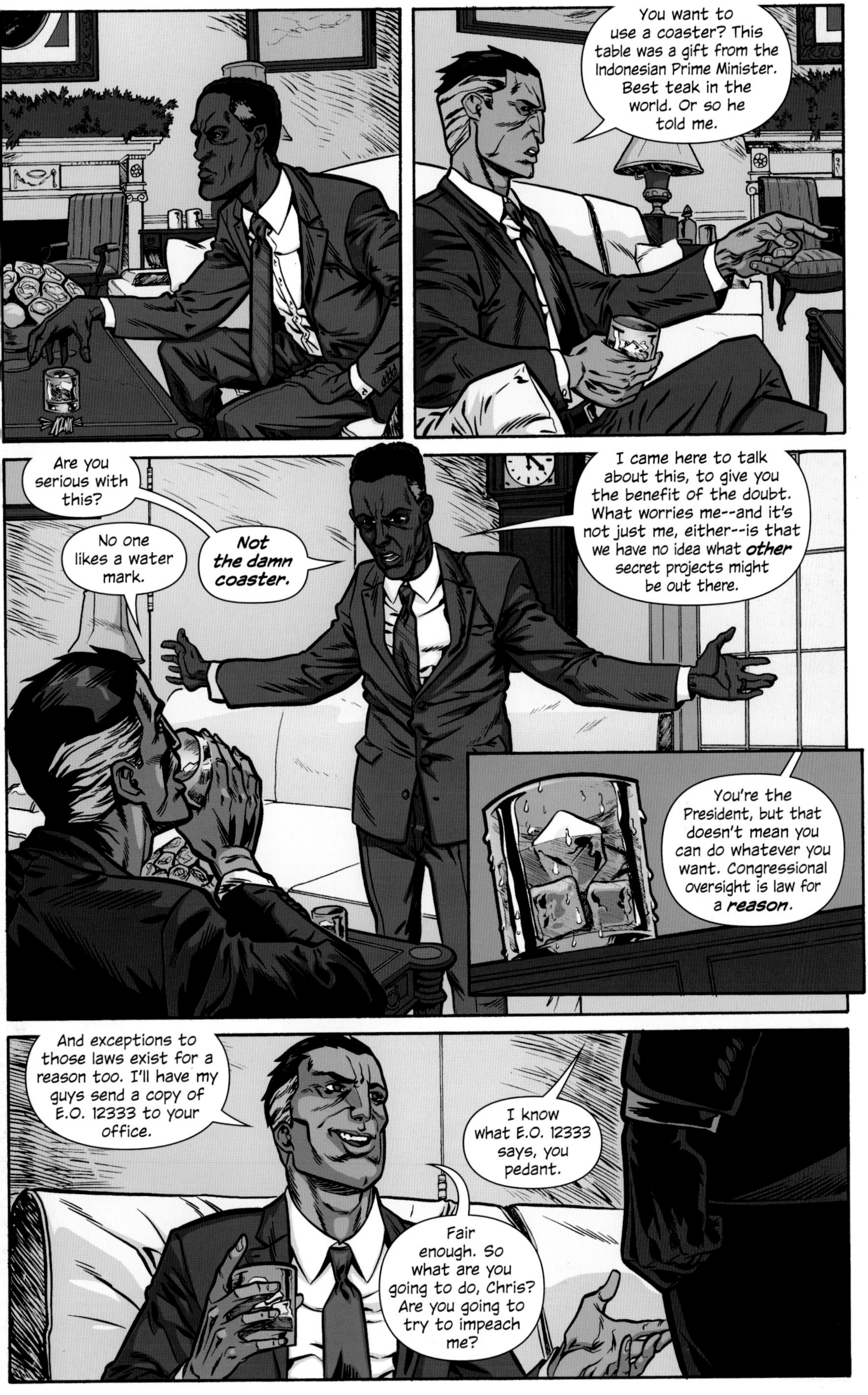
You want to use a coaster? This table was a gift from the Indonesian Prime Minister. Best teak in the world. Or so he told me.
Are you serious with this?
No one likes a water mark.
Not the damn coaster.
I came here to talk about this, to give you the benefit of the doubt. What worries me--and it's not just me, either--is that we have no idea what other secret projects might be out there.
You're the President, but that doesn't mean you can do whatever you want. Congressional oversight is law for a reason.
And exceptions to those laws exist for a reason too. I'll have my guys send a copy of E.O. 12333 to your office.
I know what E.O. 12333 says, you pedant.
Fair enough. So what are you going to do, Chris? Are you going to try to impeach me?

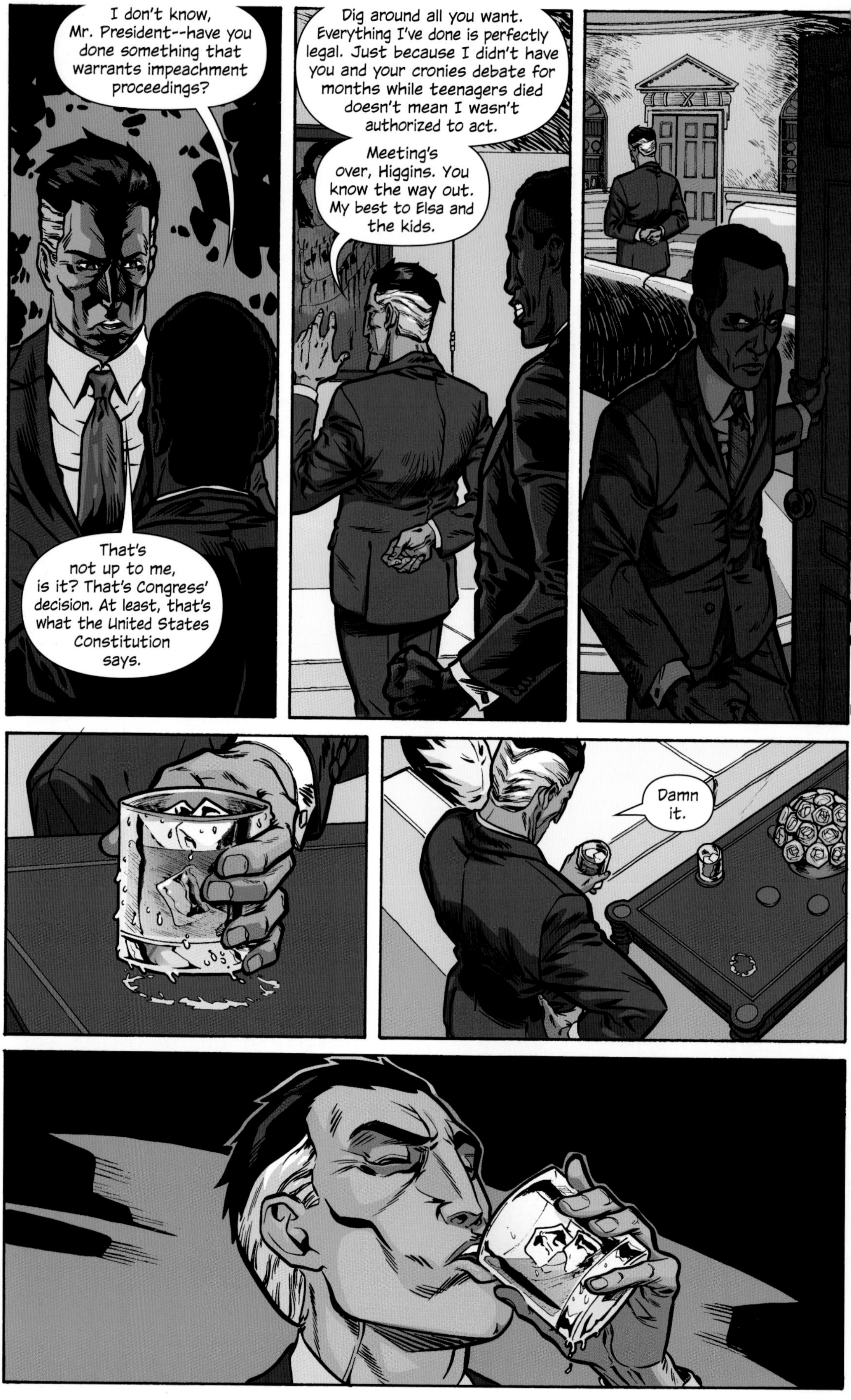

I don't know, Mr. President--have you done something that warrants impeachment proceedings?
That's not up to me, is it? That's Congress' decision. At least, that's what the United States Constitution says.
Dig around all you want. Everything I've done is perfectly legal. Just because I didn't have you and your cronies debate for months while teenagers died doesn't mean I wasn't authorized to act.
Meeting's over, Higgins. You know the way out. My best to Elsa and the kids.
Damn it.

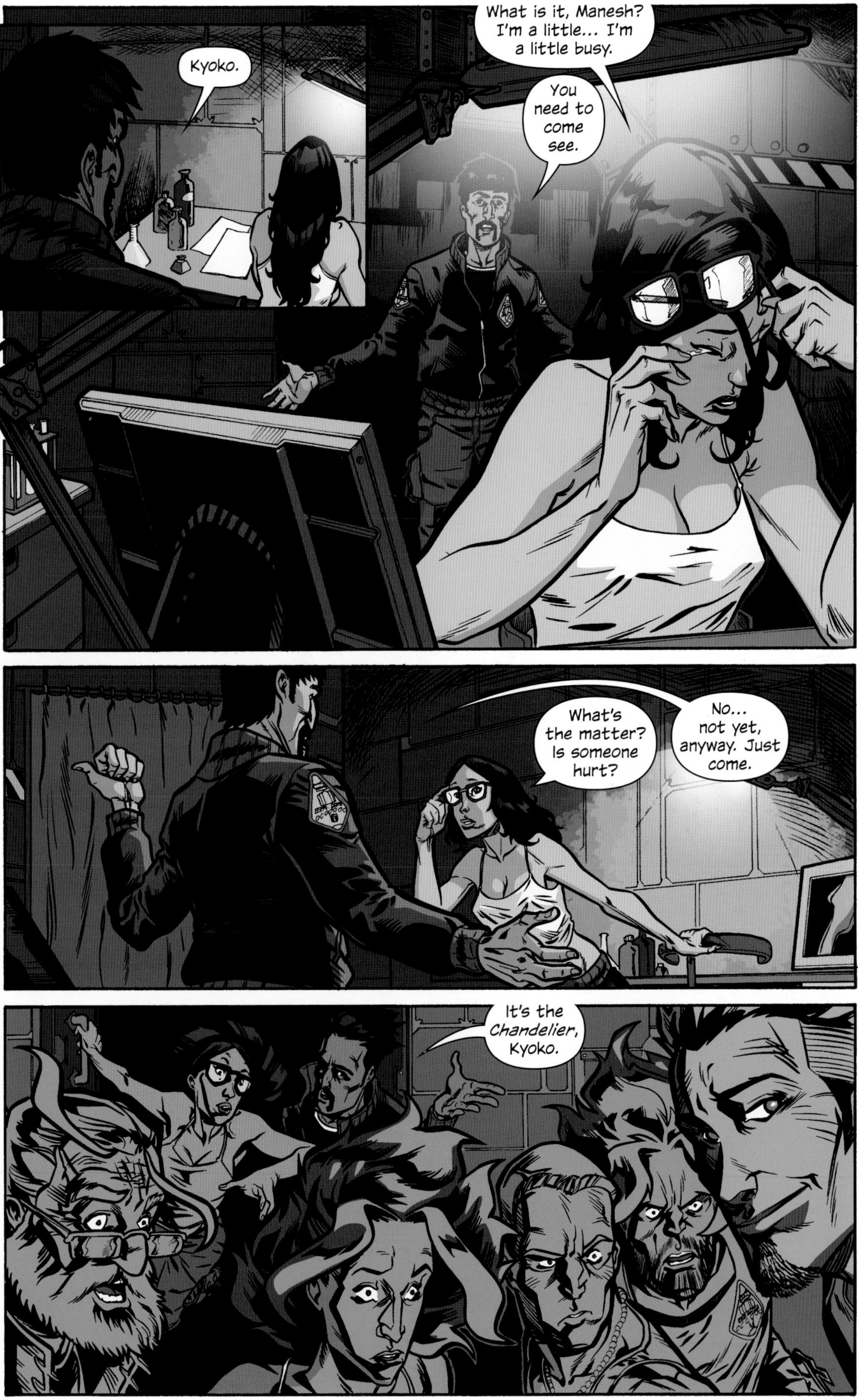
Kyoko.
What is it, Manesh? I'm a little... I'm a little busy.
You need to come see.
What's the matter? Is someone hurt?
No... not yet, anyway. Just come.
It's the *Chandelier*, Kyoko.

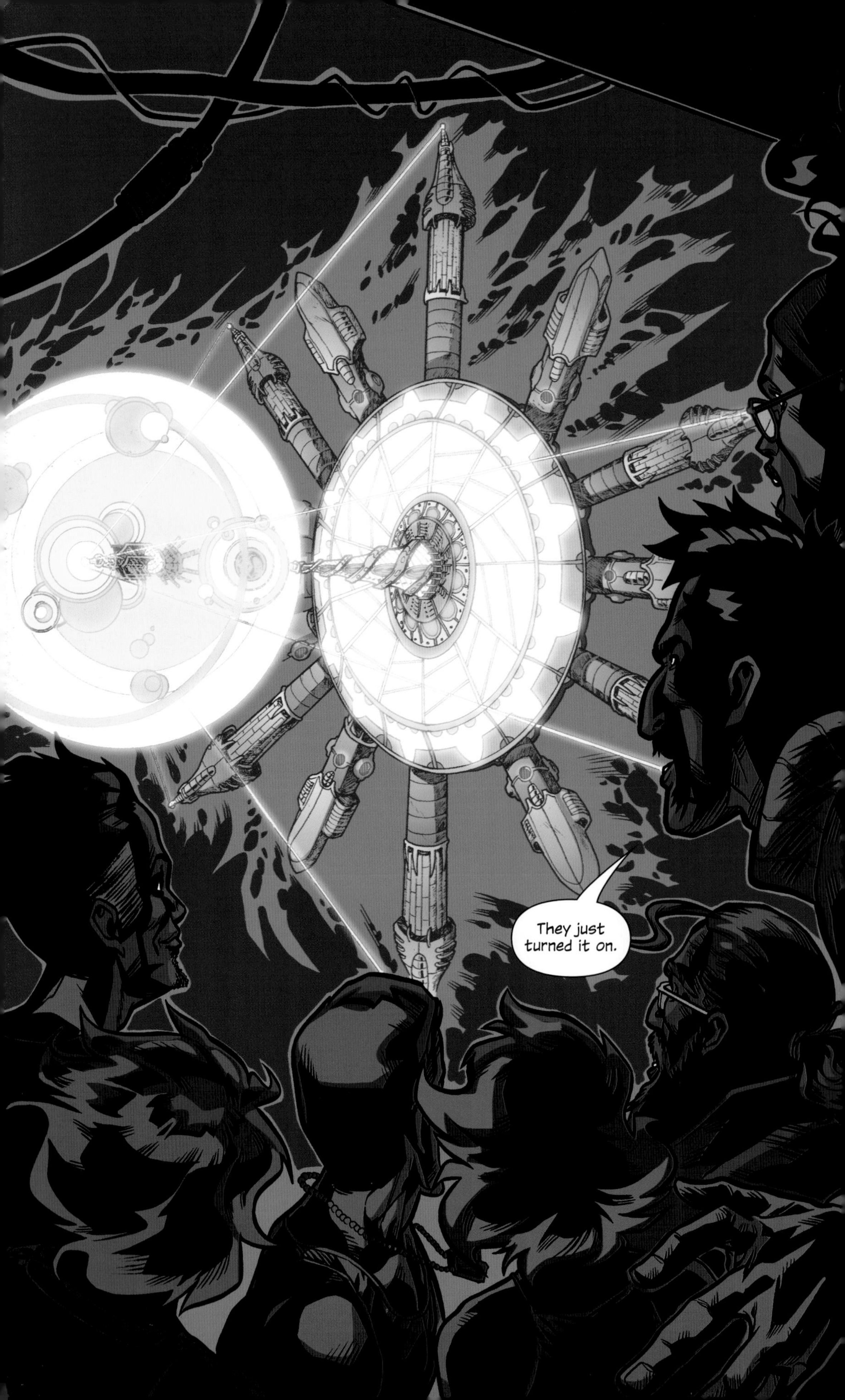
They just turned it on.

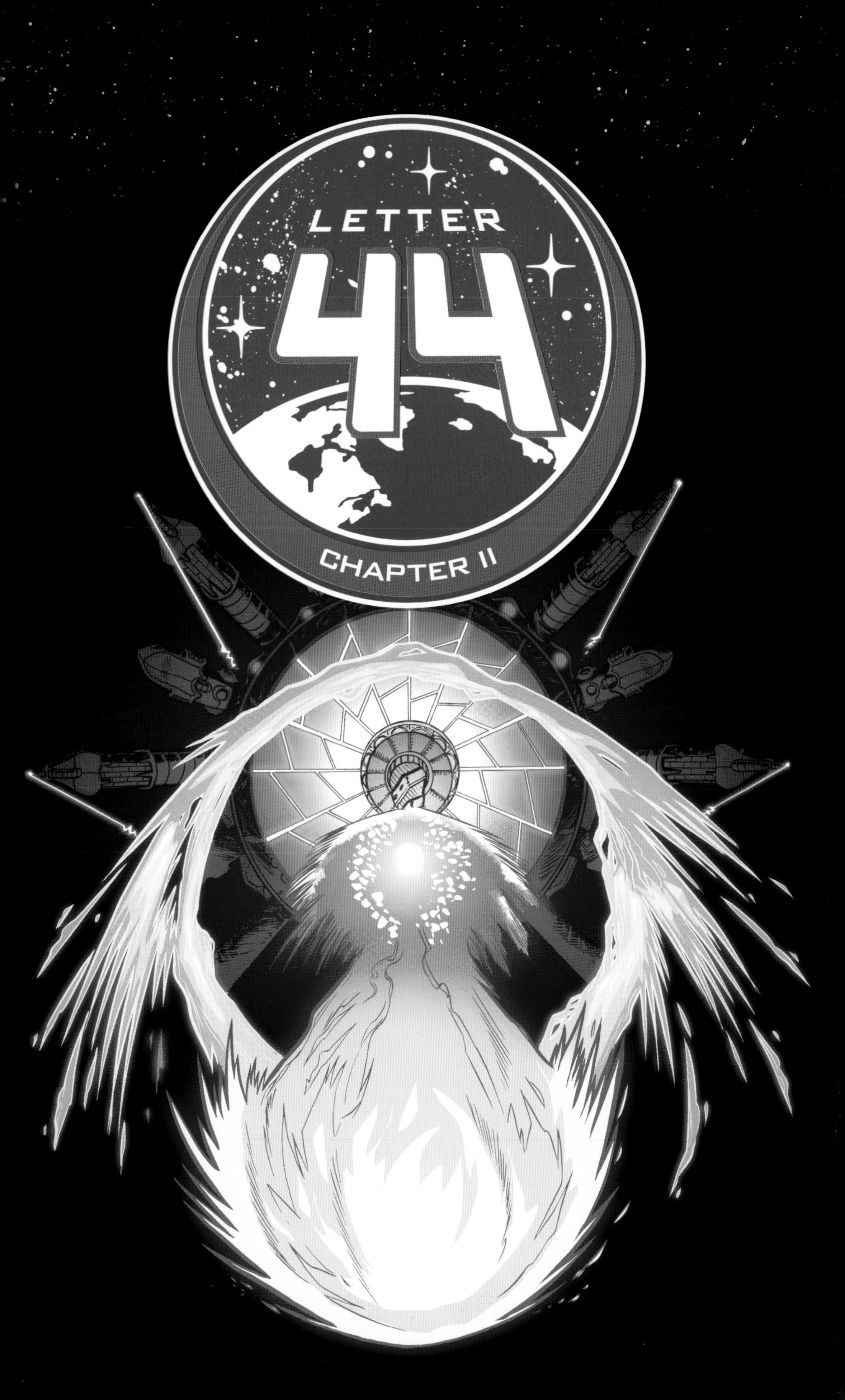
LETTER
44
CHAPTER II

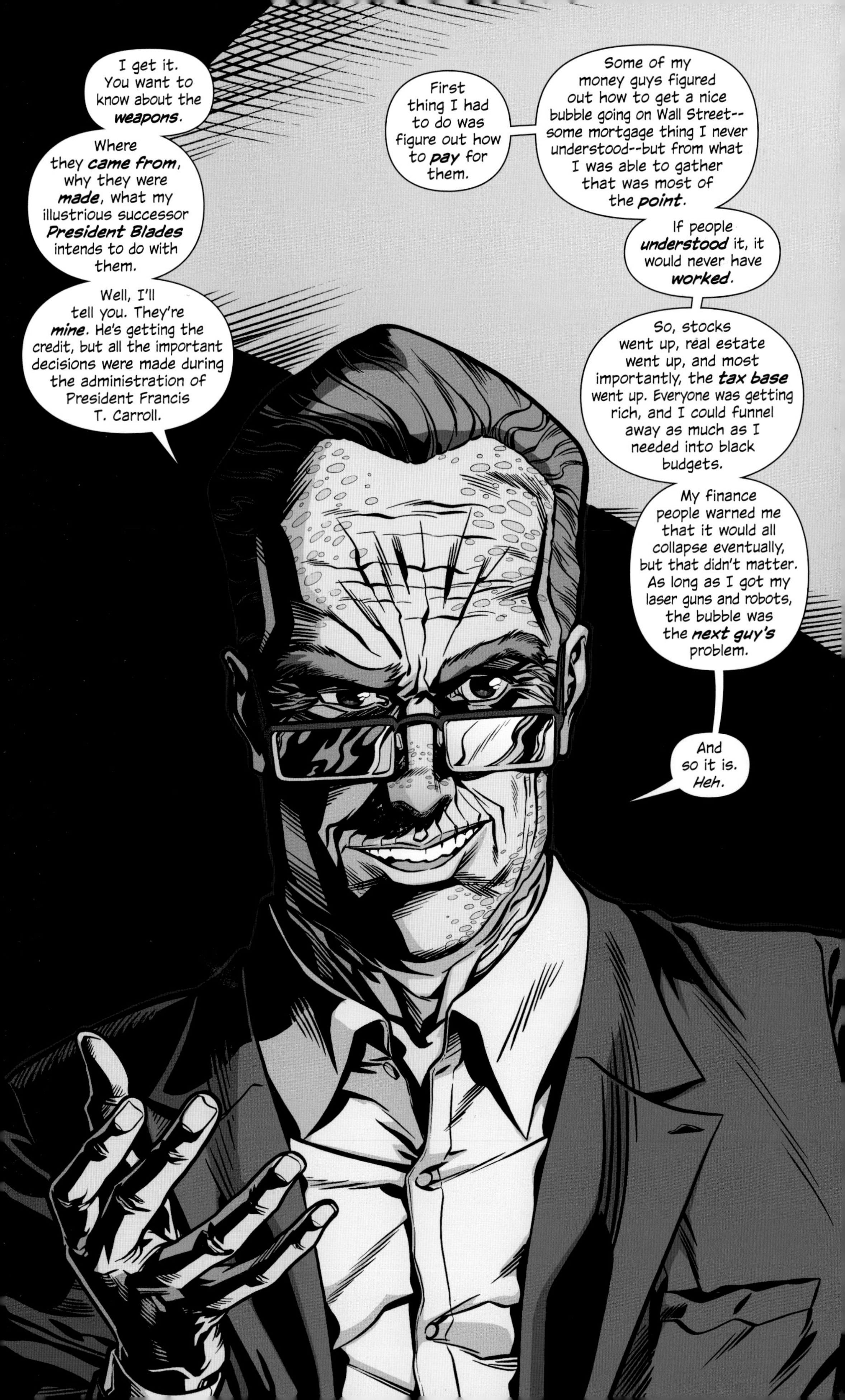
I get it. You want to know about the ***weapons***.
Where they ***came from***, why they were ***made***, what my illustrious successor ***President Blades*** intends to do with them.
Well, I'll tell you. They're ***mine***. He's getting the credit, but all the important decisions were made during the administration of President Francis T. Carroll.
First thing I had to do was figure out how to ***pay*** for them.
Some of my money guys figured out how to get a nice bubble going on Wall Street--some mortgage thing I never understood--but from what I was able to gather that was most of the ***point***.
If people ***understood*** it, it would never have ***worked***.
So, stocks went up, real estate went up, and most importantly, the ***tax base*** went up. Everyone was getting rich, and I could funnel away as much as I needed into black budgets.
My finance people warned me that it would all collapse eventually, but that didn't matter. As long as I got my laser guns and robots, the bubble was the ***next guy's*** problem.
And so it is. *Heh*.

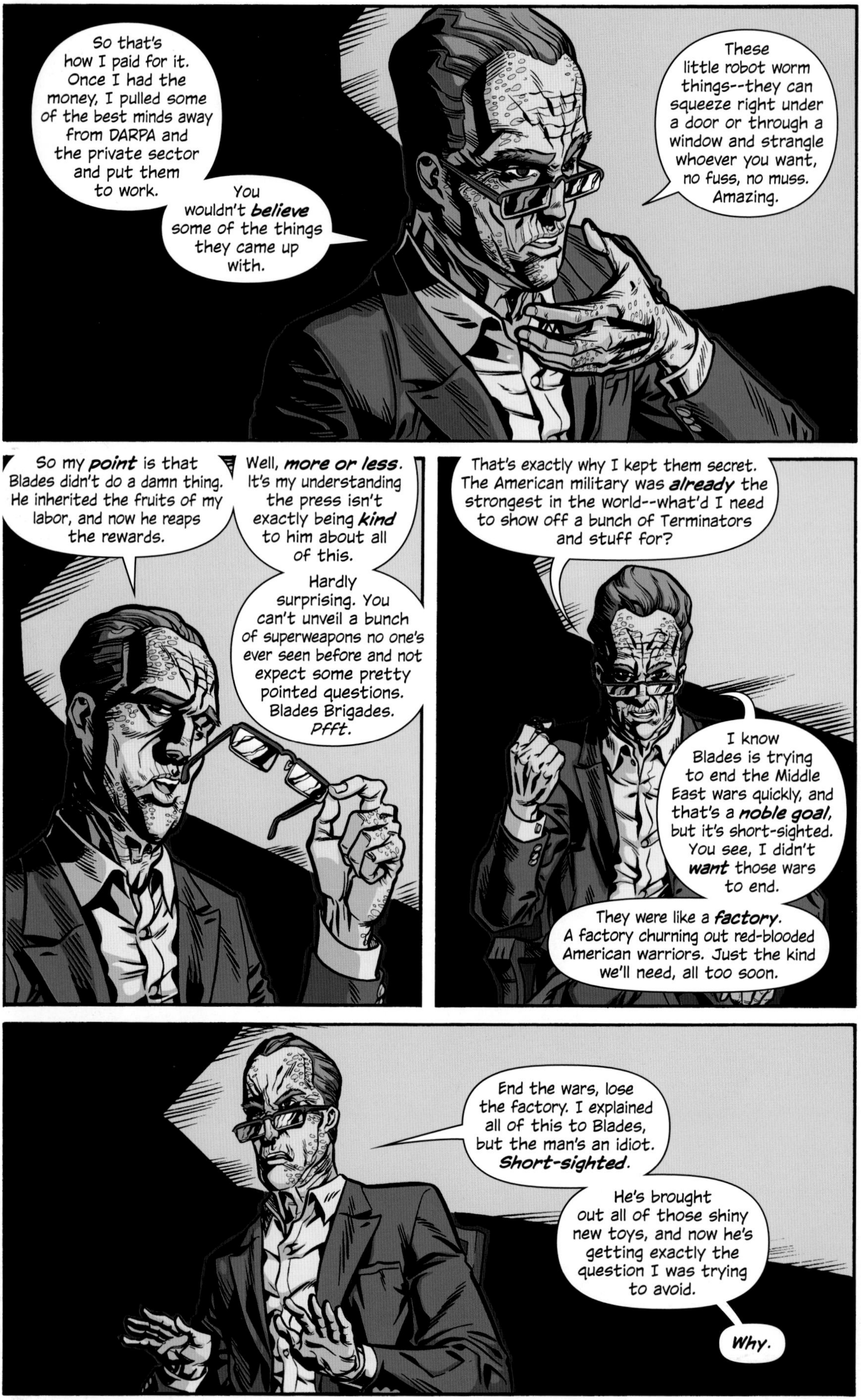

So that's how I paid for it. Once I had the money, I pulled some of the best minds away from DARPA and the private sector and put them to work.
You wouldn't believe some of the things they came up with.
These little robot worm things--they can squeeze right under a door or through a window and strangle whoever you want, no fuss, no muss. Amazing.
So my point is that Blades didn't do a damn thing. He inherited the fruits of my labor, and now he reaps the rewards.
Well, more or less. It's my understanding the press isn't exactly being kind to him about all of this.
Hardly surprising. You can't unveil a bunch of superweapons no one's ever seen before and not expect some pretty pointed questions. Blades Brigades. Pfft.
That's exactly why I kept them secret. The American military was already the strongest in the world--what'd I need to show off a bunch of Terminators and stuff for?
I know Blades is trying to end the Middle East wars quickly, and that's a noble goal, but it's short-sighted. You see, I didn't want those wars to end.
They were like a factory. A factory churning out red-blooded American warriors. Just the kind we'll need, all too soon.
End the wars, lose the factory. I explained all of this to Blades, but the man's an idiot. Short-sighted.
He's brought out all of those shiny new toys, and now he's getting exactly the question I was trying to avoid.
Why.

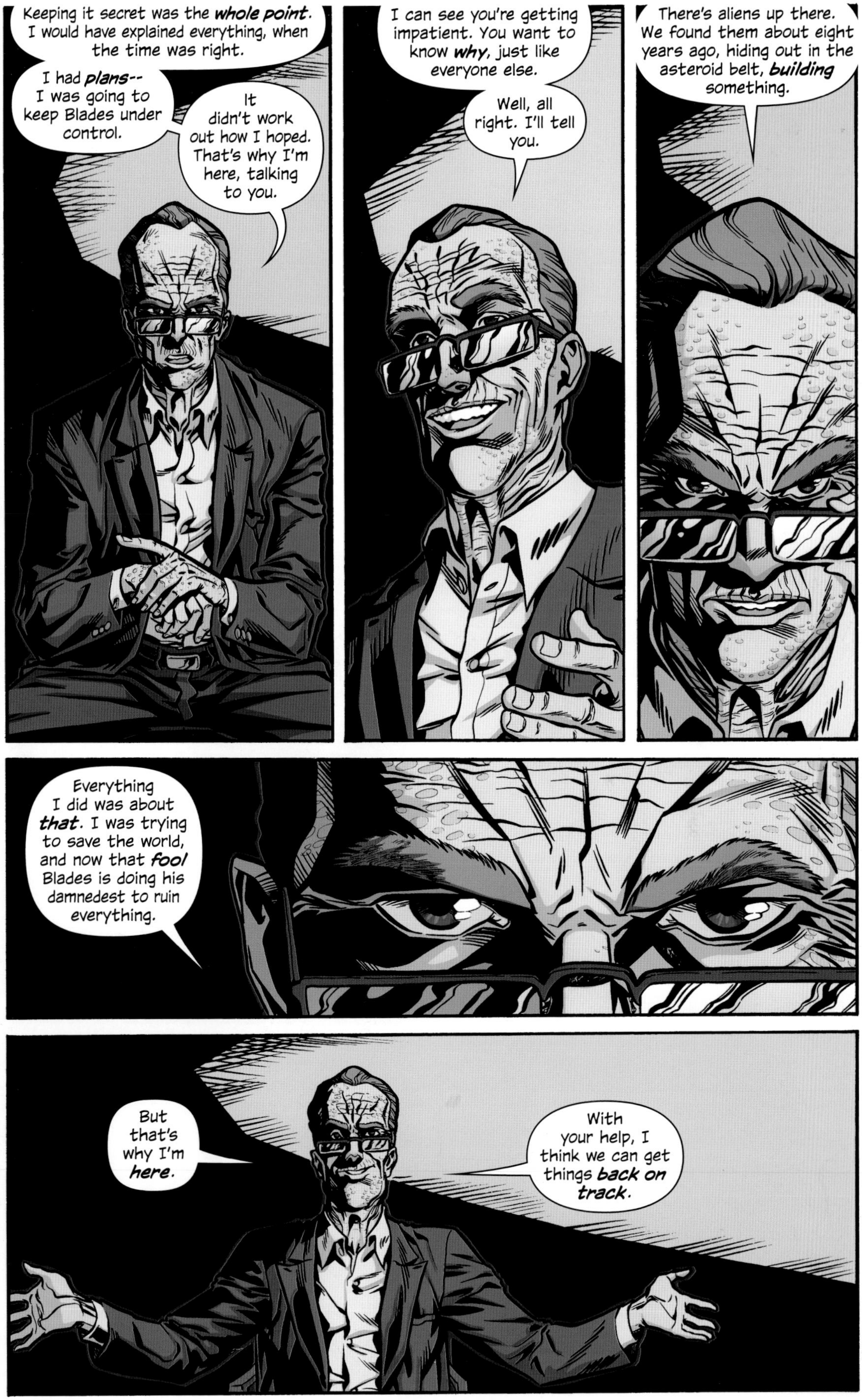
Keeping it secret was the *whole point*. I would have explained everything, when the time was right.
I had *plans*-- I was going to keep Blades under control.
It didn't work out how I hoped. That's why I'm here, talking to you.
I can see you're getting impatient. You want to know *why*, just like everyone else.
Well, all right. I'll tell you.
There's aliens up there. We found them about eight years ago, hiding out in the asteroid belt, *building* something.
Everything I did was about *that*. I was trying to save the world, and now that *fool* Blades is doing his damnedest to ruin everything.
But that's why I'm *here*.
With your help, I think we can get things *back on track*.

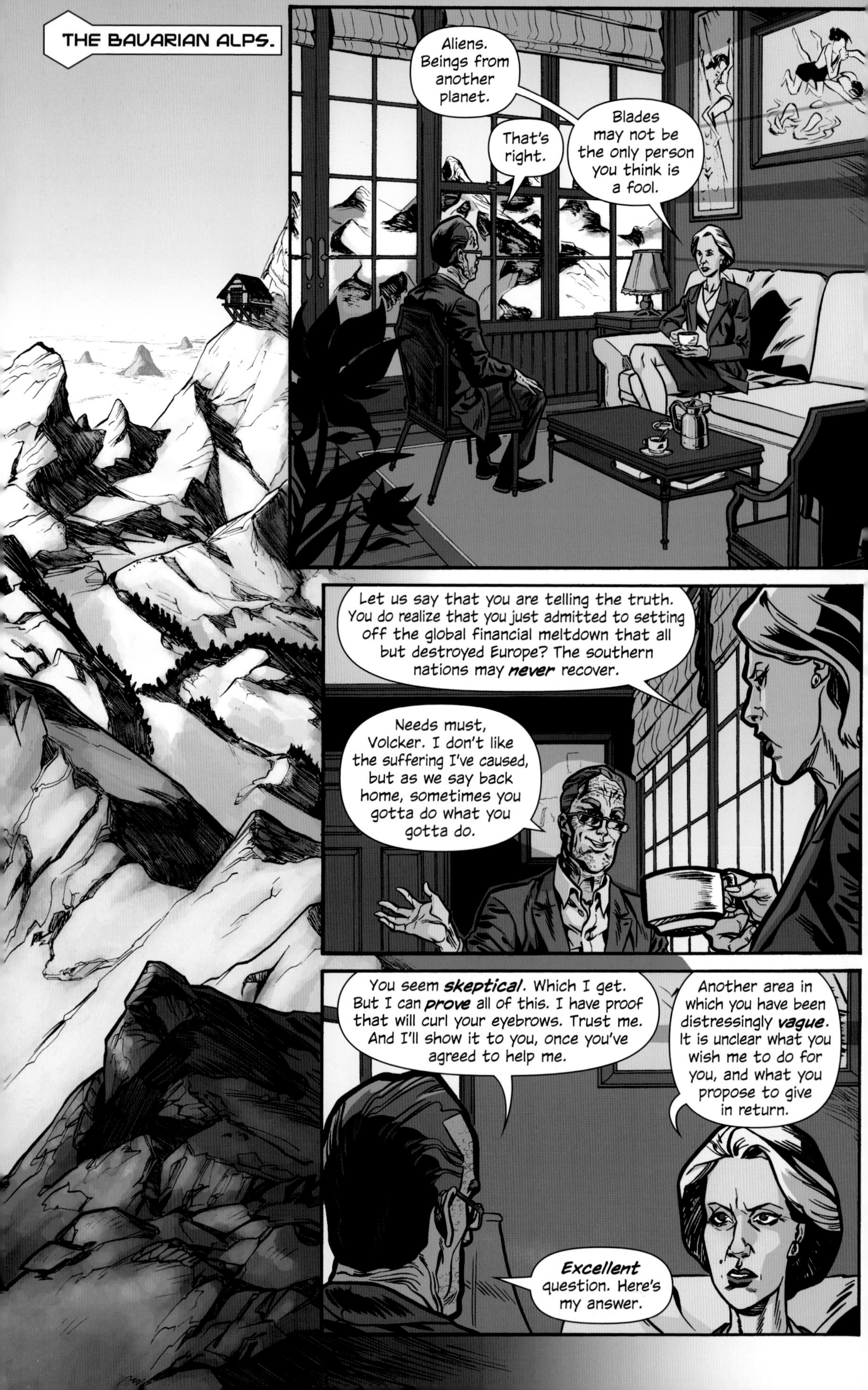
THE BAVARIAN ALPS.
Aliens. Beings from another planet.
That's right.
Blades may not be the only person you think is a fool.
Let us say that you are telling the truth. You do realize that you just admitted to setting off the global financial meltdown that all but destroyed Europe? The southern nations may never recover.
Needs must, Volcker. I don't like the suffering I've caused, but as we say back home, sometimes you gotta do what you gotta do.
You seem skeptical. Which I get. But I can prove all of this. I have proof that will curl your eyebrows. Trust me. And I'll show it to you, once you've agreed to help me.
Another area in which you have been distressingly vague. It is unclear what you wish me to do for you, and what you propose to give in return.
Excellent question. Here's my answer.

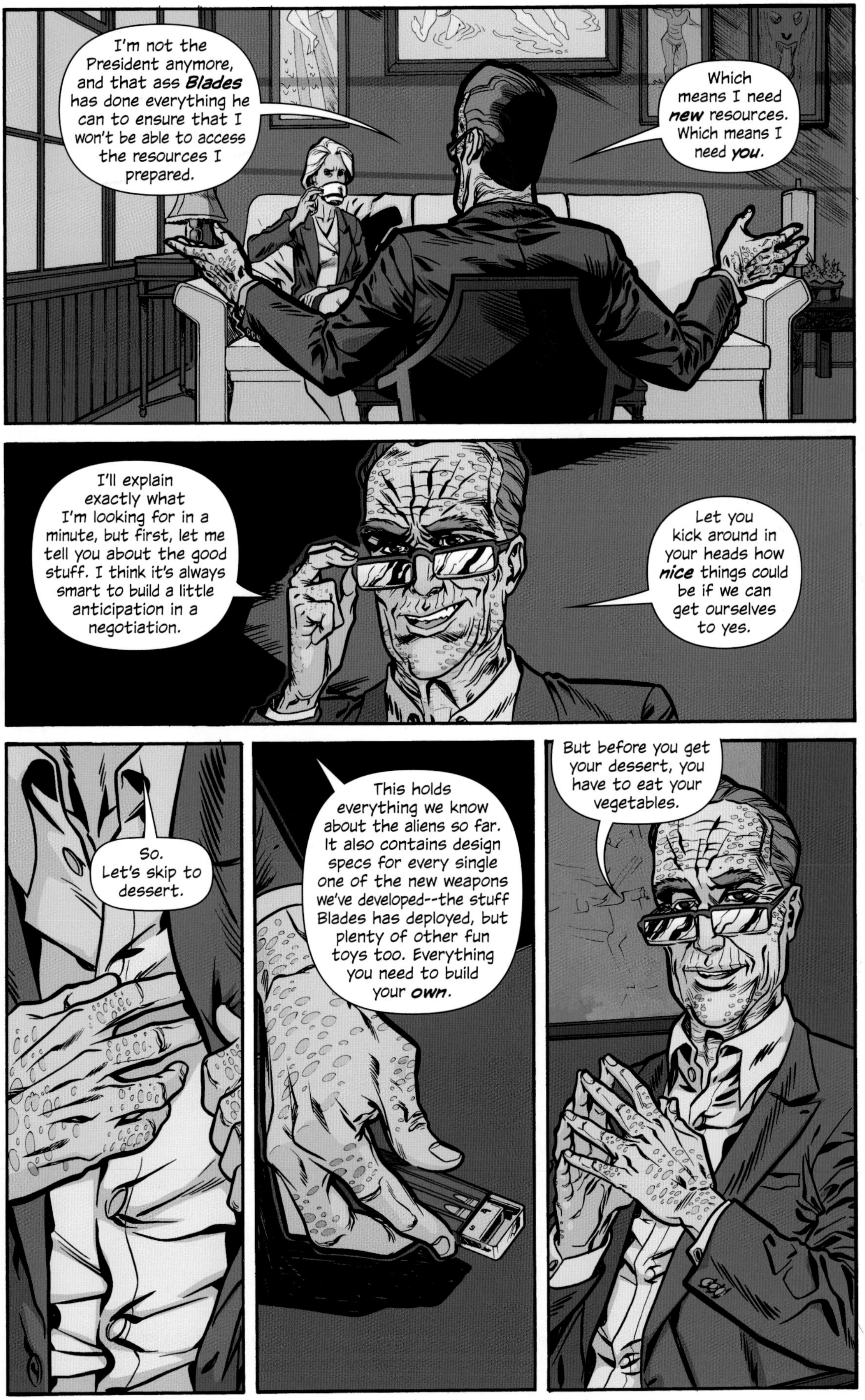
I'm not the President anymore, and that ass ***Blades*** has done everything he can to ensure that I won't be able to access the resources I prepared.
Which means I need ***new*** resources. Which means I need ***you***.
I'll explain exactly what I'm looking for in a minute, but first, let me tell you about the good stuff. I think it's always smart to build a little anticipation in a negotiation.
Let you kick around in your heads how ***nice*** things could be if we can get ourselves to yes.
So. Let's skip to dessert.
This holds everything we know about the aliens so far. It also contains design specs for every single one of the new weapons we've developed--the stuff Blades has deployed, but plenty of other fun toys too. Everything you need to build your ***own***.
But before you get your dessert, you have to eat your vegetables.

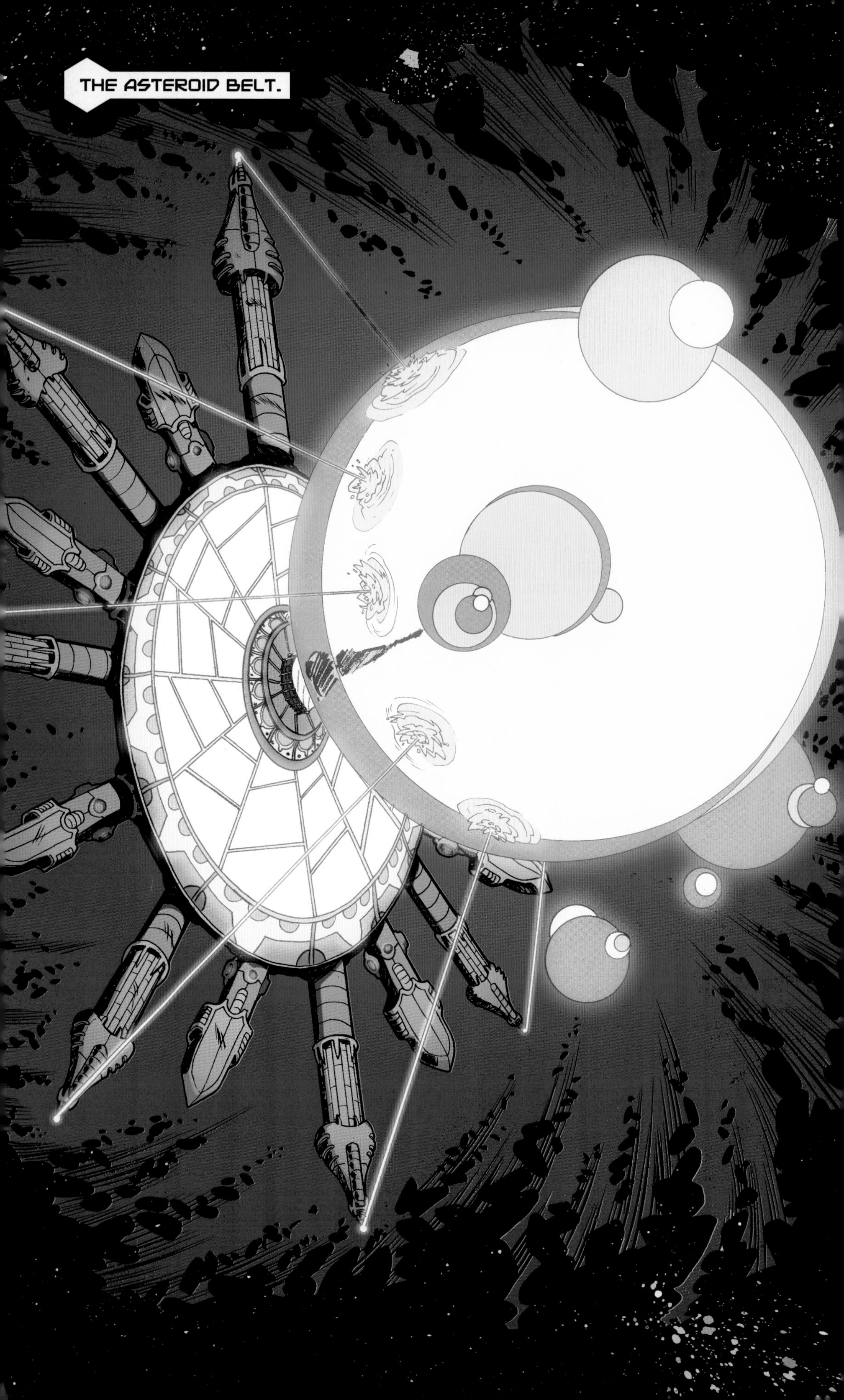
THE ASTEROID BELT.

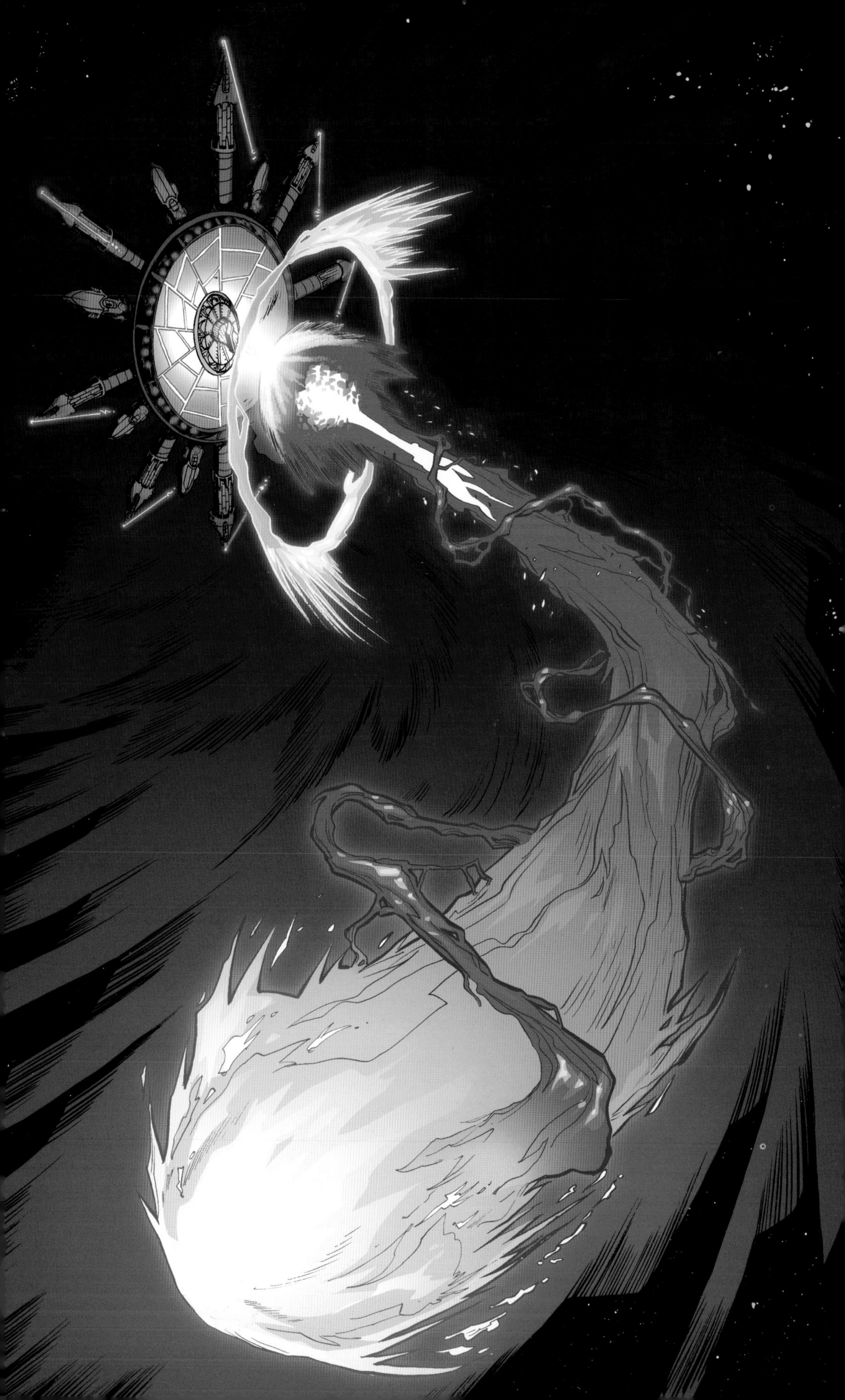

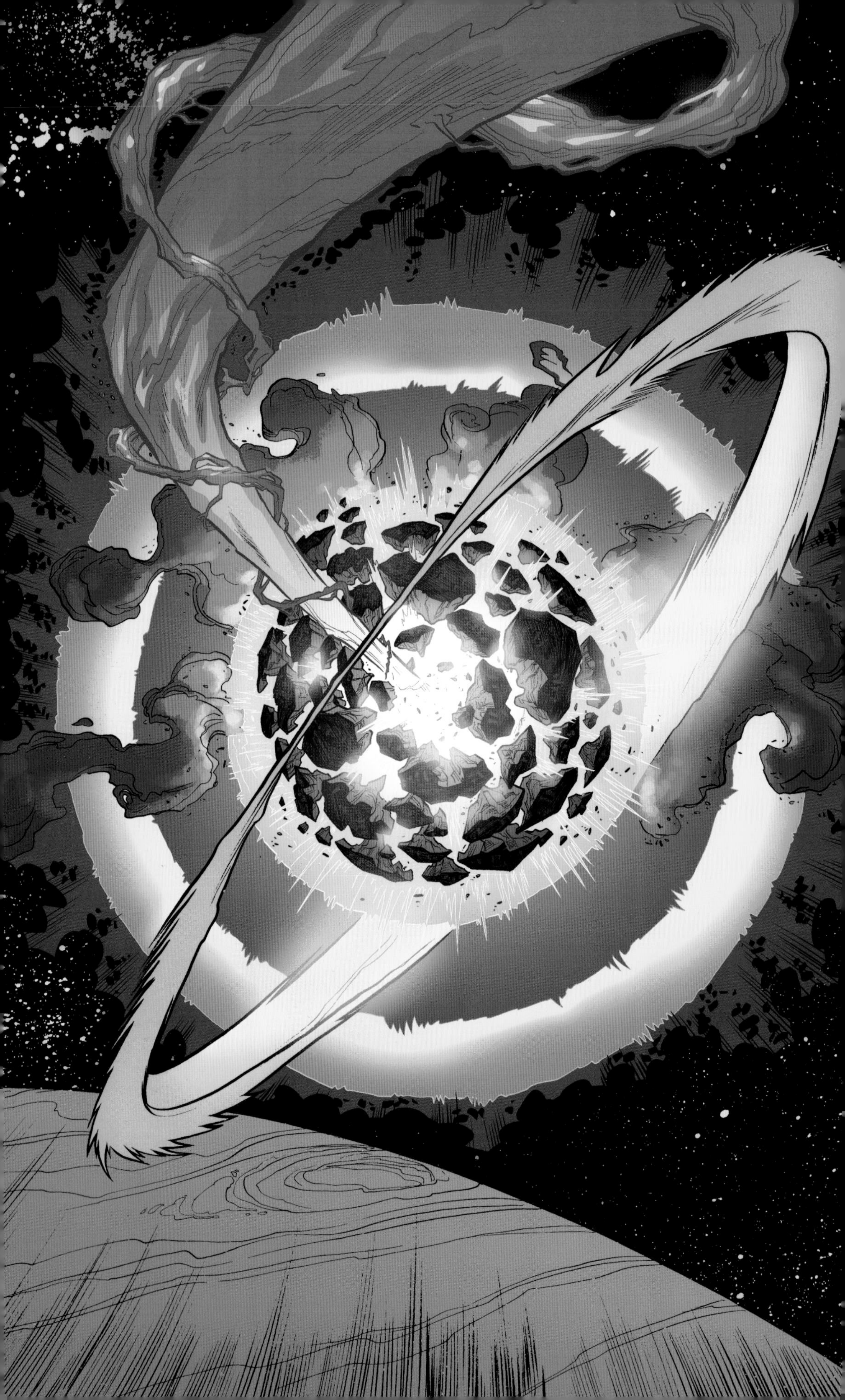

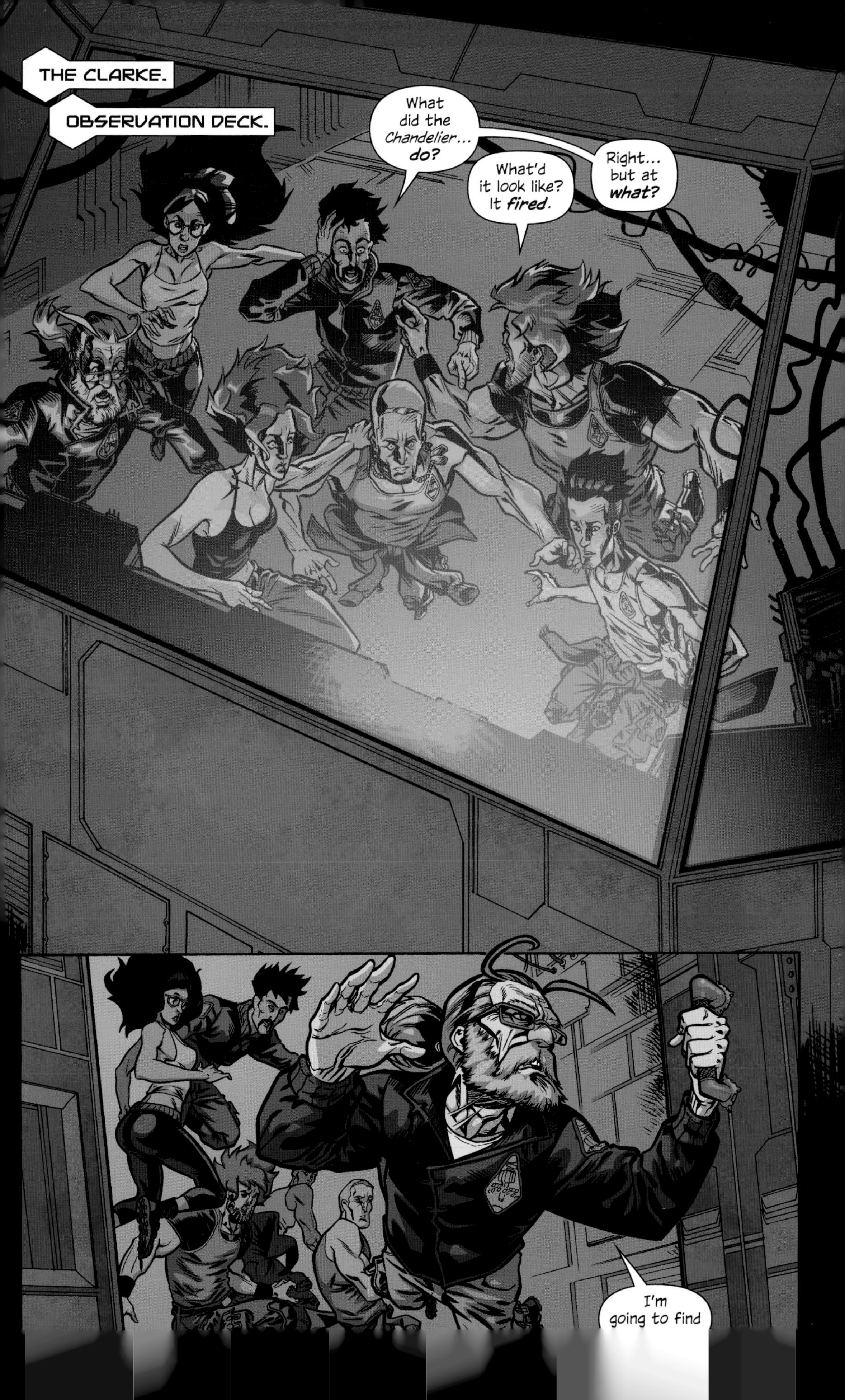
THE CLARKE.
OBSERVATION DECK.
What did the Chandelier... do?
What'd it look like? It fired.
Right... but at what?
I'm going to find

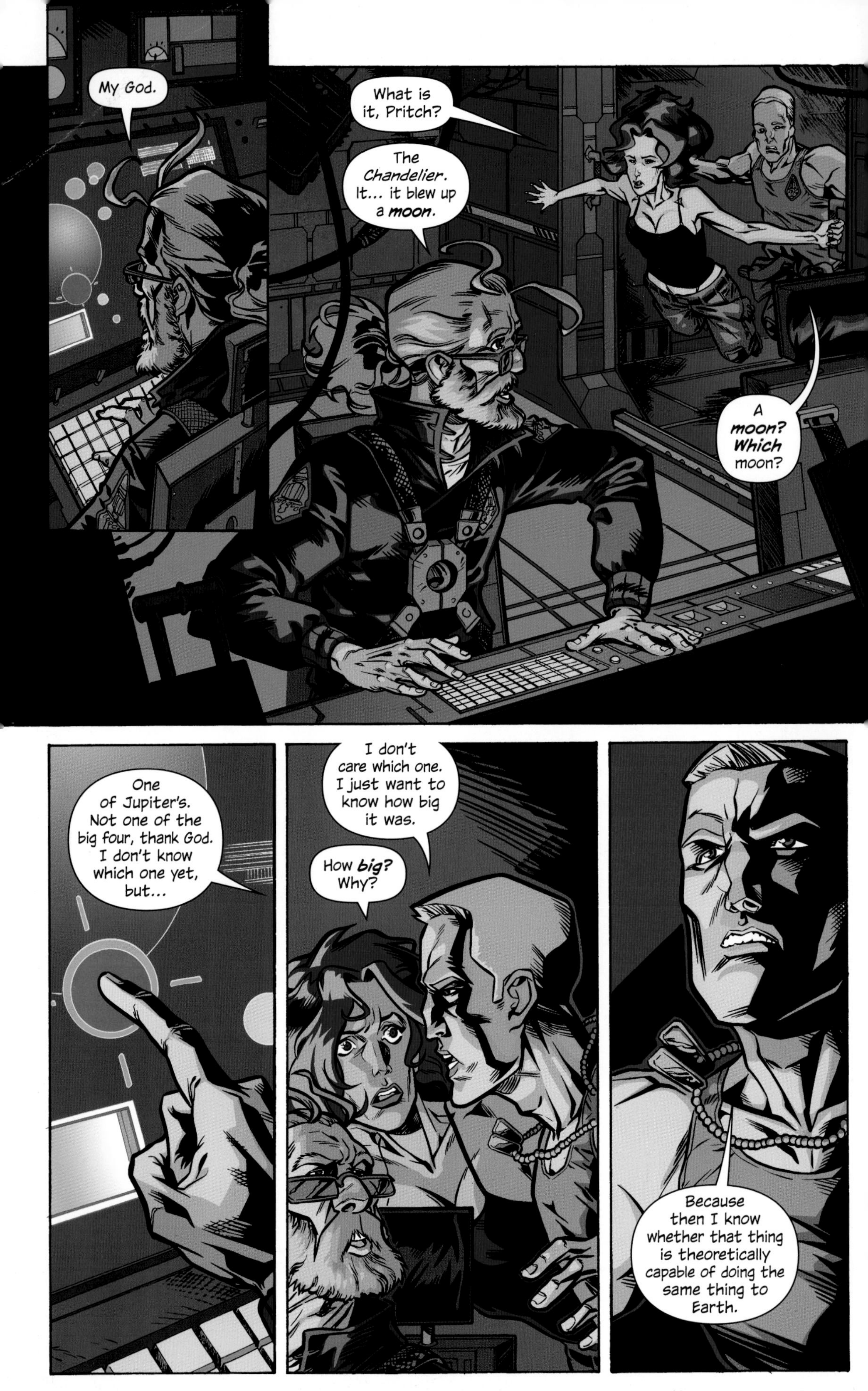
My God.
What is it, Pritch?
The *Chandelier*. It... it blew up a ***moon***.
A ***moon? Which*** moon?
One of Jupiter's. Not one of the big four, thank God. I don't know which one yet, but...
I don't care which one. I just want to know how big it was.
How ***big?*** Why?
Because then I know whether that thing is theoretically capable of doing the same thing to Earth.

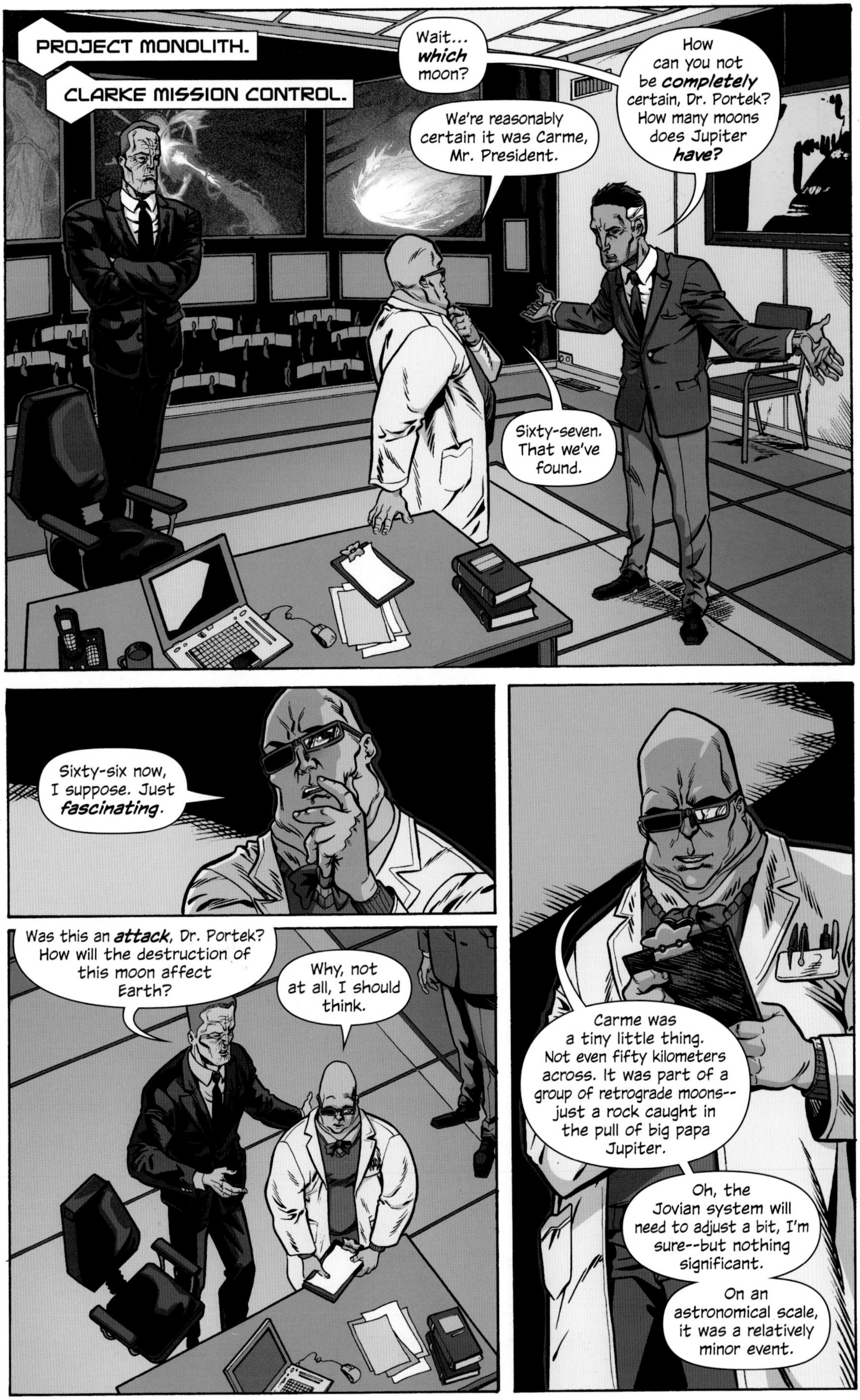
PROJECT MONOLITH.
CLARKE MISSION CONTROL.
We're reasonably certain it was Carme, Mr. President.
Wait... *which* moon?
How can you not be *completely* certain, Dr. Portek? How many moons does Jupiter *have?*
Sixty-seven. That we've found.
Sixty-six now, I suppose. Just *fascinating*.
Was this an *attack*, Dr. Portek? How will the destruction of this moon affect Earth?
Why, not at all, I should think.
Carme was a tiny little thing. Not even fifty kilometers across. It was part of a group of retrograde moons--just a rock caught in the pull of big papa Jupiter.
Oh, the Jovian system will need to adjust a bit, I'm sure--but nothing significant.
On an astronomical scale, it was a relatively minor event.

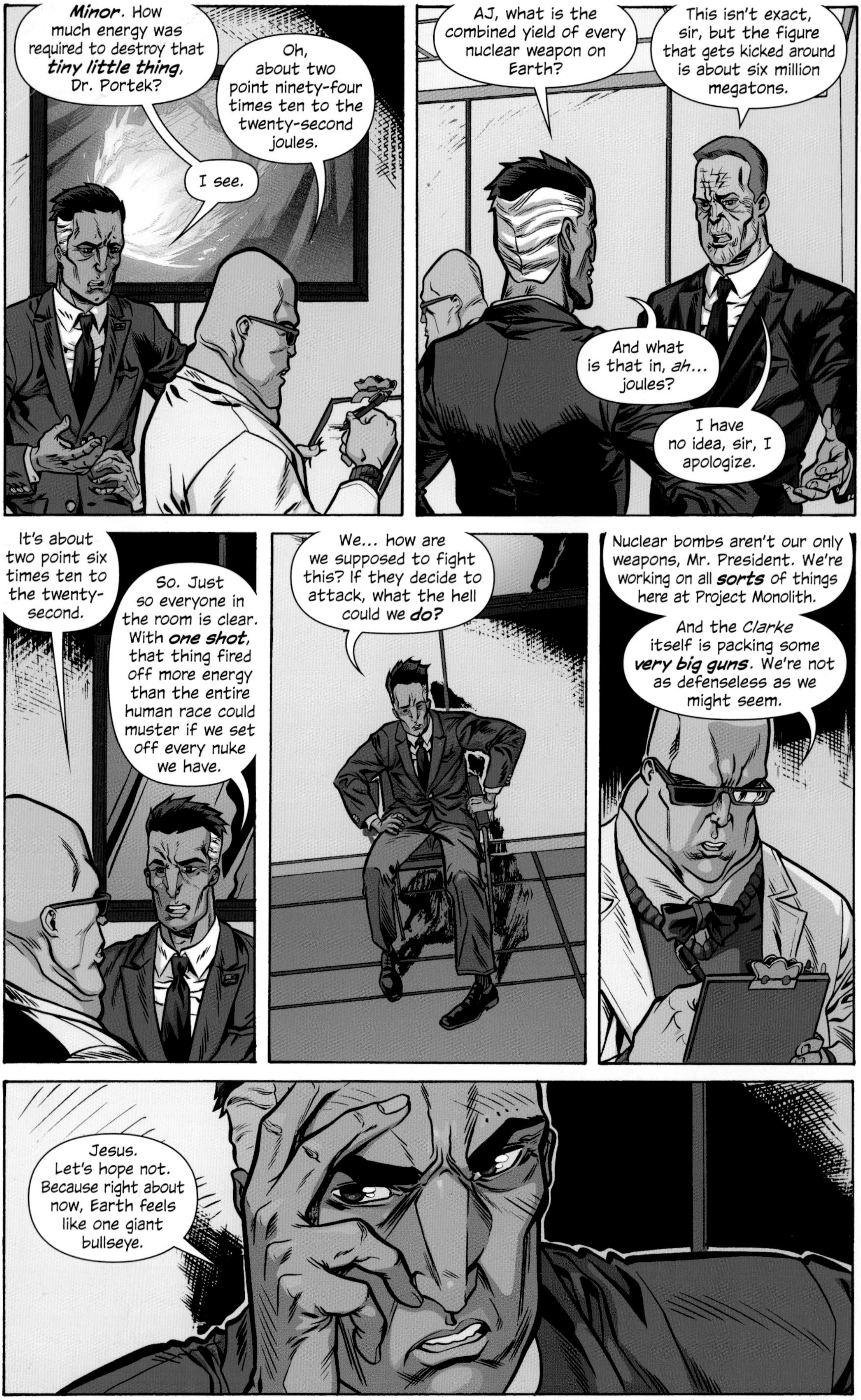

Minor. How much energy was required to destroy that *tiny little thing*, Dr. Portek?
Oh, about two point ninety-four times ten to the twenty-second joules.
I see.
AJ, what is the combined yield of every nuclear weapon on Earth?
This isn't exact, sir, but the figure that gets kicked around is about six million megatons.
And what is that in, *ah*... joules?
I have no idea, sir, I apologize.
It's about two point six times ten to the twenty-second.
So. Just so everyone in the room is clear. With *one shot*, that thing fired off more energy than the entire human race could muster if we set off every nuke we have.
We... how are we supposed to fight this? If they decide to attack, what the hell could we *do?*
Nuclear bombs aren't our only weapons, Mr. President. We're working on all *sorts* of things here at Project Monolith.
And the *Clarke* itself is packing some *very big guns*. We're not as defenseless as we might seem.
Jesus. Let's hope not. Because right about now, Earth feels like one giant bullseye.

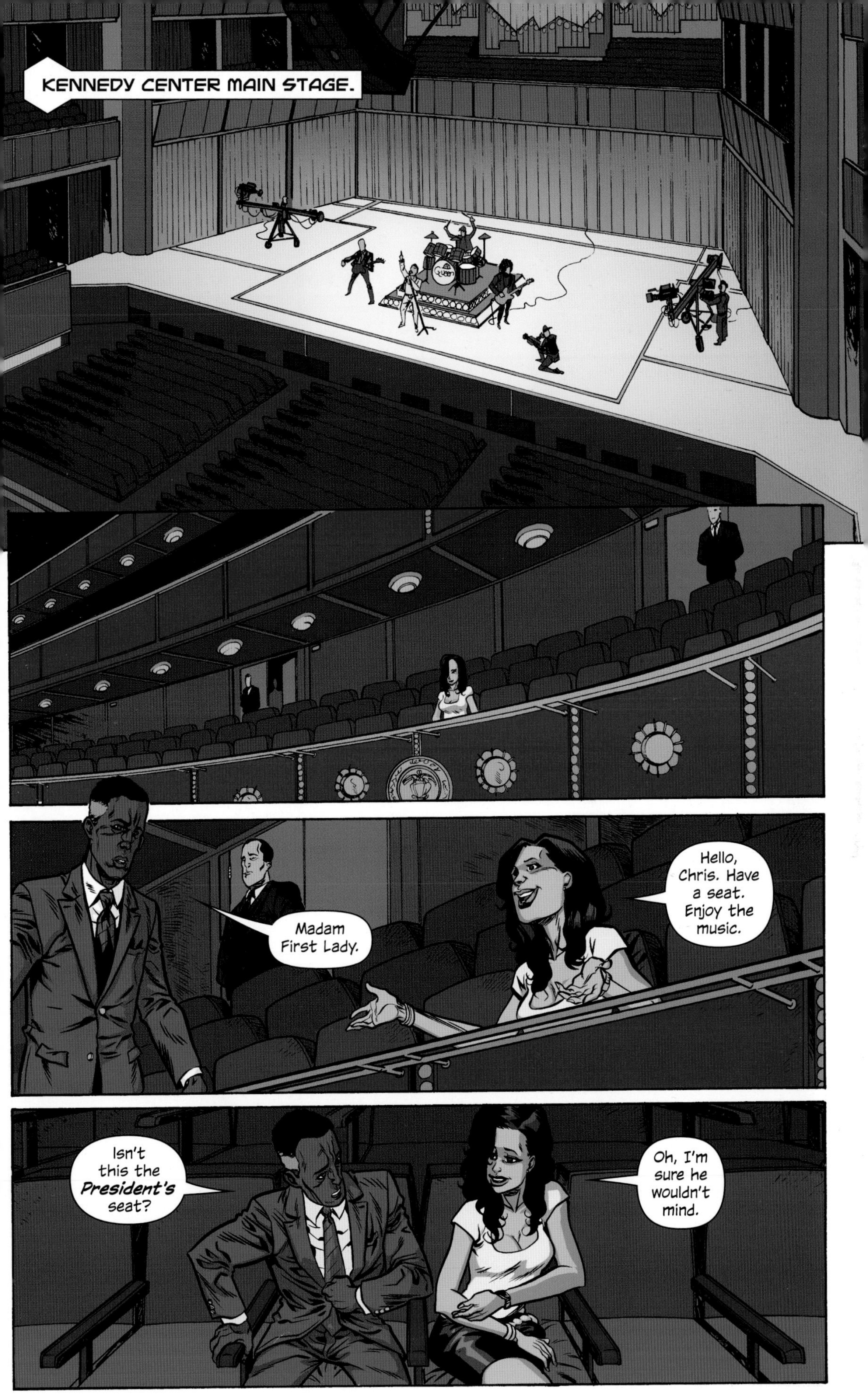
KENNEDY CENTER MAIN STAGE.
Madam First Lady.
Hello, Chris. Have a seat. Enjoy the music.
Isn't this the *President's* seat?
Oh, I'm sure he wouldn't mind.

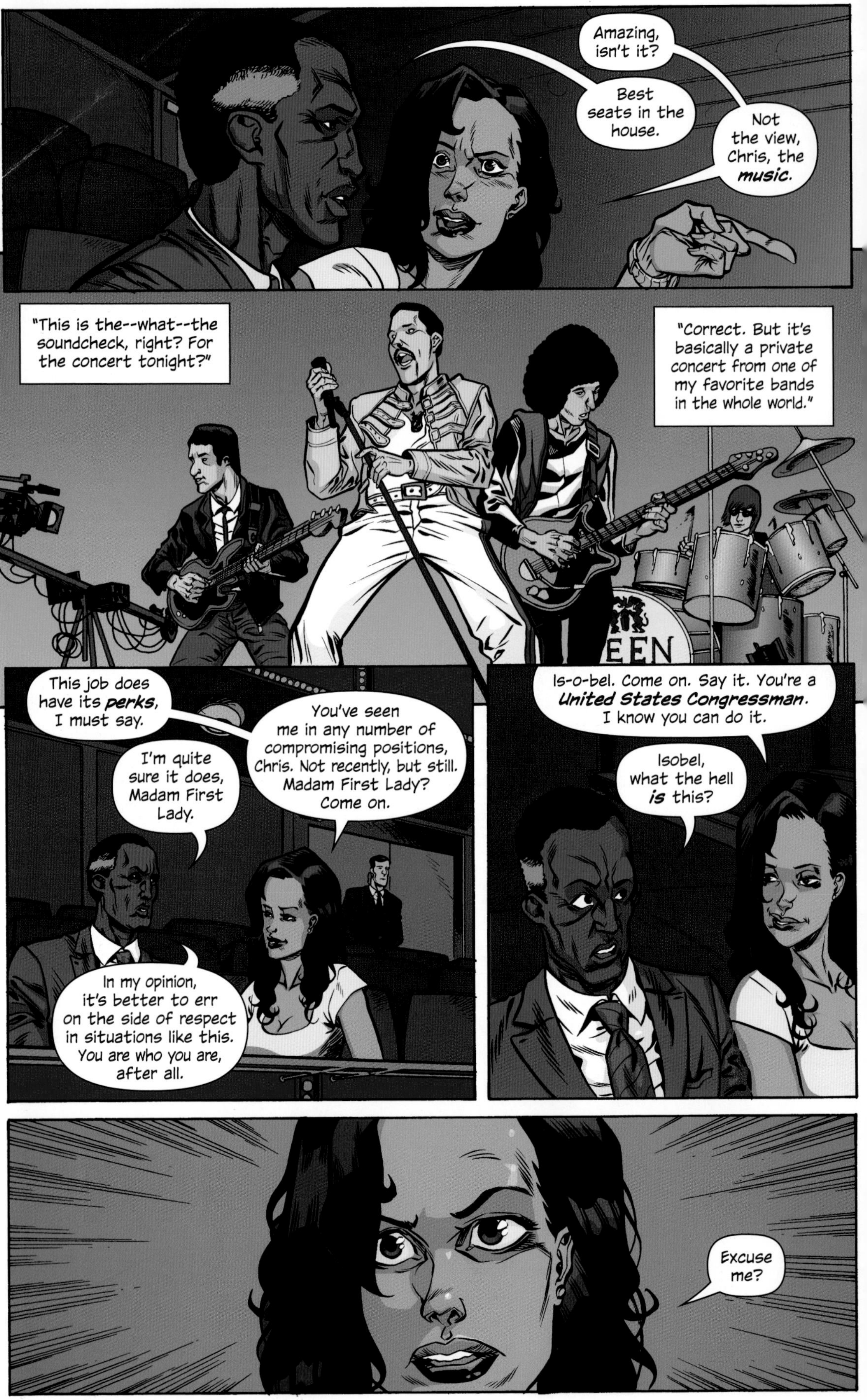

Amazing, isn't it?
Best seats in the house.
Not the view, Chris, the **music**.
"This is the--what--the soundcheck, right? For the concert tonight?"
"Correct. But it's basically a private concert from one of my favorite bands in the whole world."
EEN
This job does have its **perks**, I must say.
I'm quite sure it does, Madam First Lady.
You've seen me in any number of compromising positions, Chris. Not recently, but still. Madam First Lady? Come on.
In my opinion, it's better to err on the side of respect in situations like this. You are who you are, after all.
Is-o-bel. Come on. Say it. You're a **United States Congressman**. I know you can do it.
Isobel, what the hell **is** this?
Excuse me?

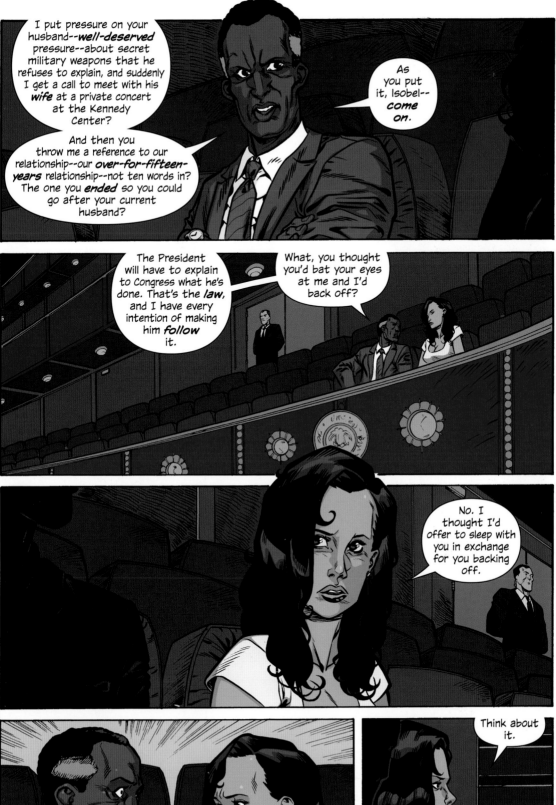

I put pressure on your husband--**well-deserved** pressure--about secret military weapons that he refuses to explain, and suddenly I get a call to meet with his *wife* at a private concert at the Kennedy Center?

And then you throw me a reference to our relationship--our **over-for-fifteen-years** relationship--not ten words in? The one you *ended* so you could go after your current husband?

As you put it, Isobel-- **come on.**

The President will have to explain to Congress what he's done. That's the *law*, and I have every intention of making him *follow* it.

What, you thought you'd bat your eyes at me and I'd back off?

No. I thought I'd offer to sleep with you in exchange for you backing off.

Think about it.

Now stop talking, all right? We're missing the show.

[45]

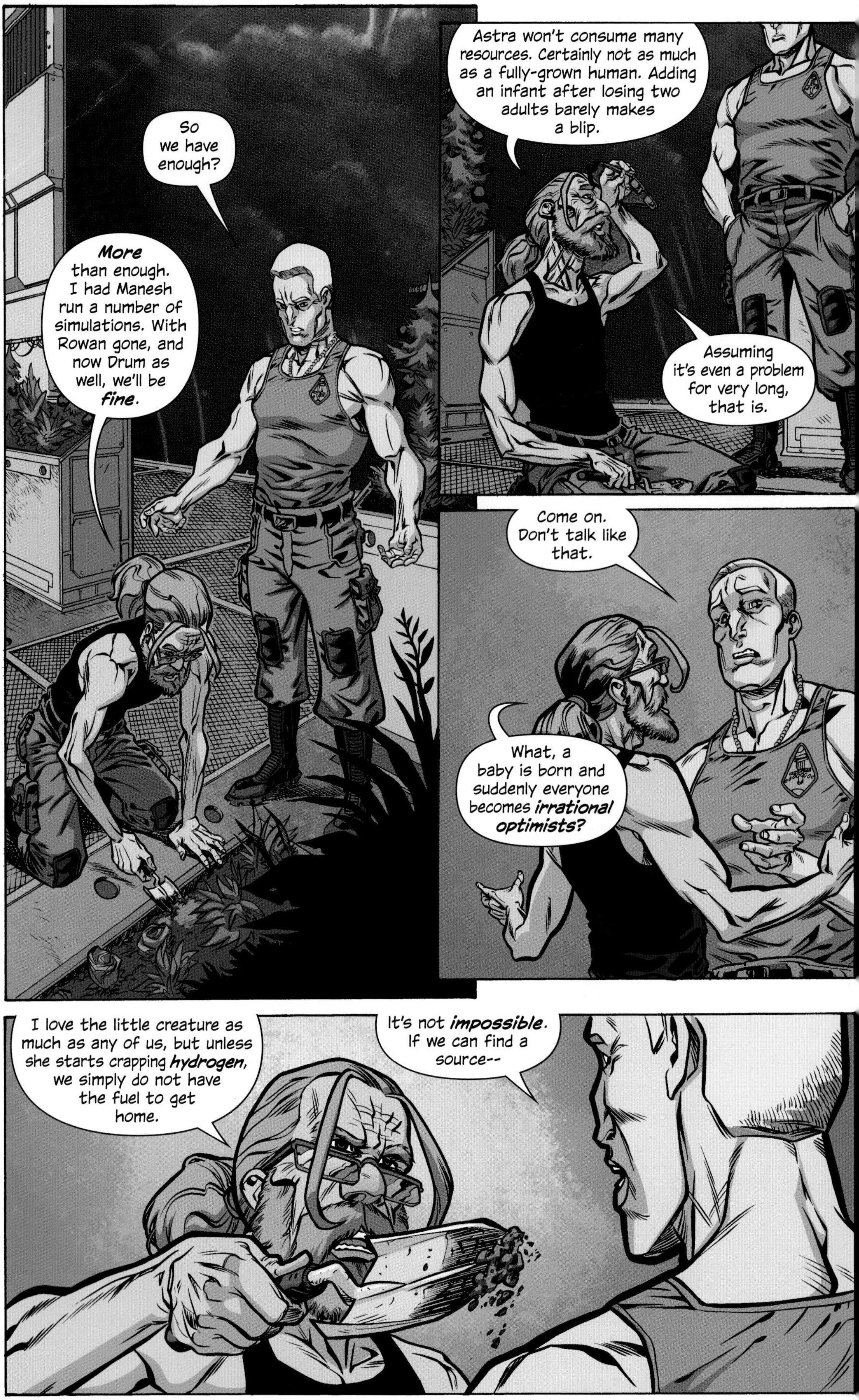
So we have enough?
More than enough. I had Manesh run a number of simulations. With Rowan gone, and now Drum as well, we'll be fine.
Astra won't consume many resources. Certainly not as much as a fully-grown human. Adding an infant after losing two adults barely makes a blip.
Assuming it's even a problem for very long, that is.
Come on. Don't talk like that.
What, a baby is born and suddenly everyone becomes irrational optimists?
I love the little creature as much as any of us, but unless she starts crapping hydrogen, we simply do not have the fuel to get home.
It's not impossible. If we can find a source--

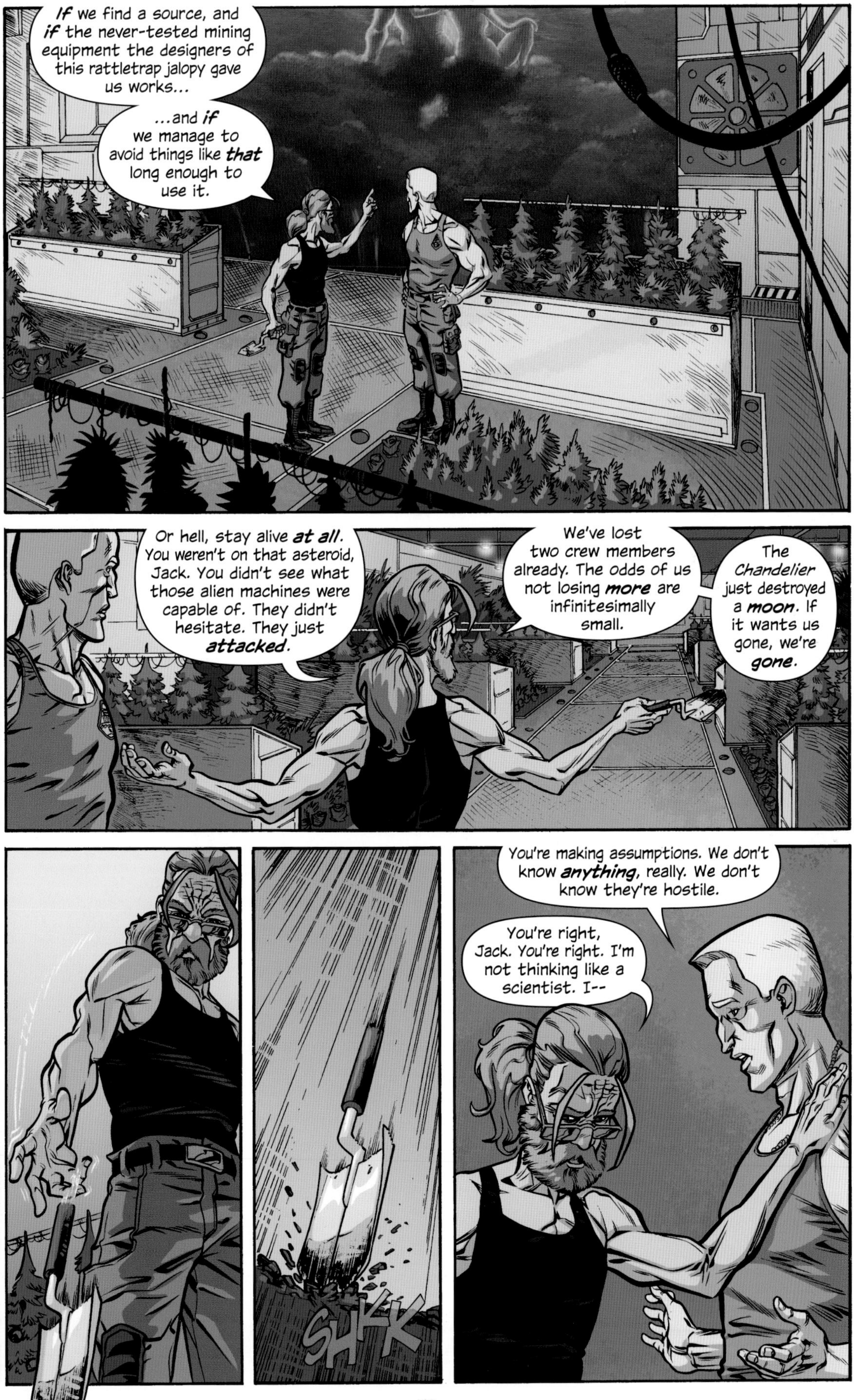
If we find a source, and if the never-tested mining equipment the designers of this rattletrap jalopy gave us works...
...and if we manage to avoid things like that long enough to use it.
Or hell, stay alive at all. You weren't on that asteroid, Jack. You didn't see what those alien machines were capable of. They didn't hesitate. They just attacked.
We've lost two crew members already. The odds of us not losing more are infinitesimally small.
The Chandelier just destroyed a moon. If it wants us gone, we're gone.
SHKK
You're making assumptions. We don't know anything, really. We don't know they're hostile.
You're right, Jack. You're right. I'm not thinking like a scientist. I--

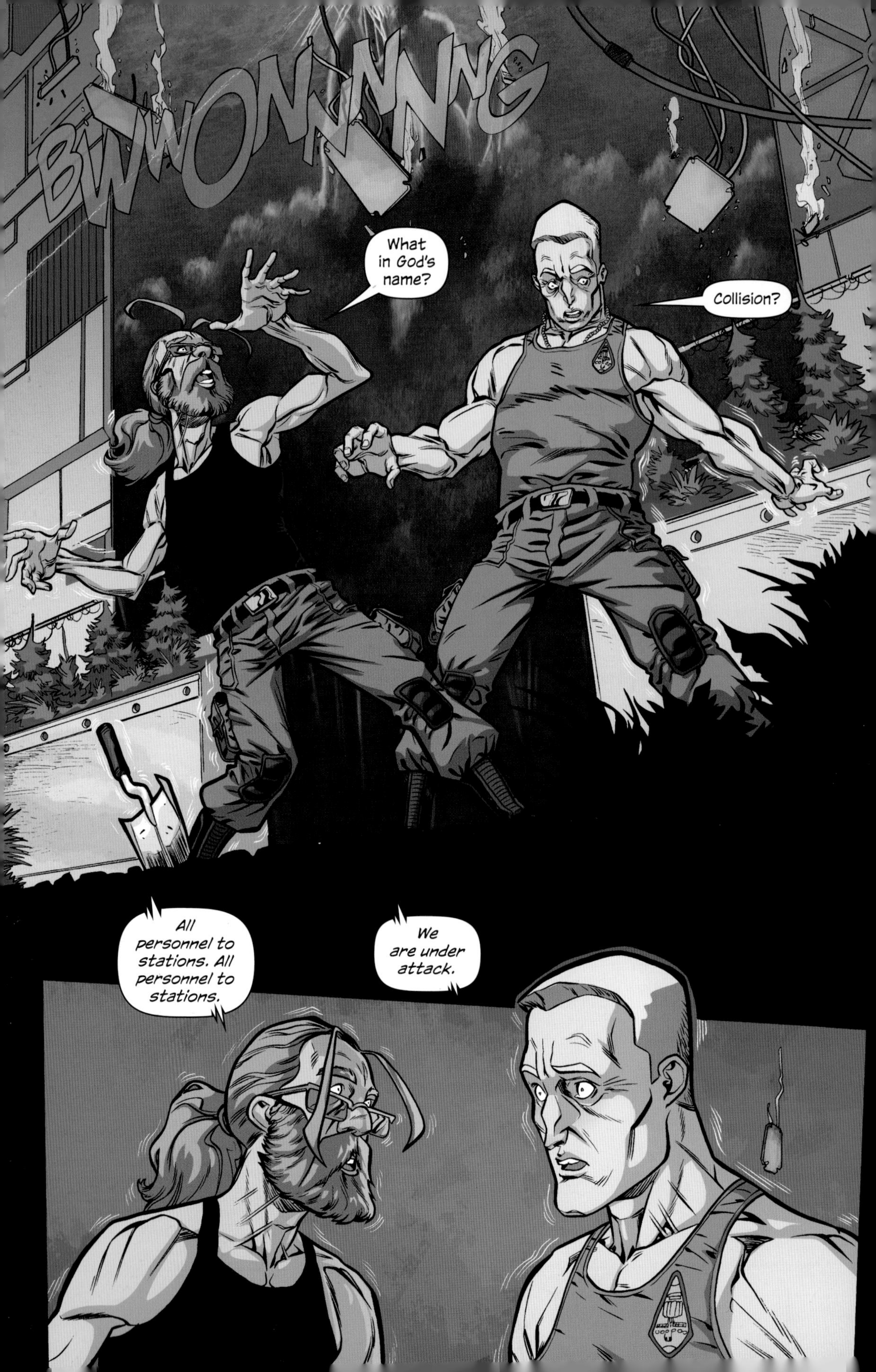
BWONNNNNG
What in God's name?
Collision?
All personnel to stations. All personnel to stations.
We are under attack.

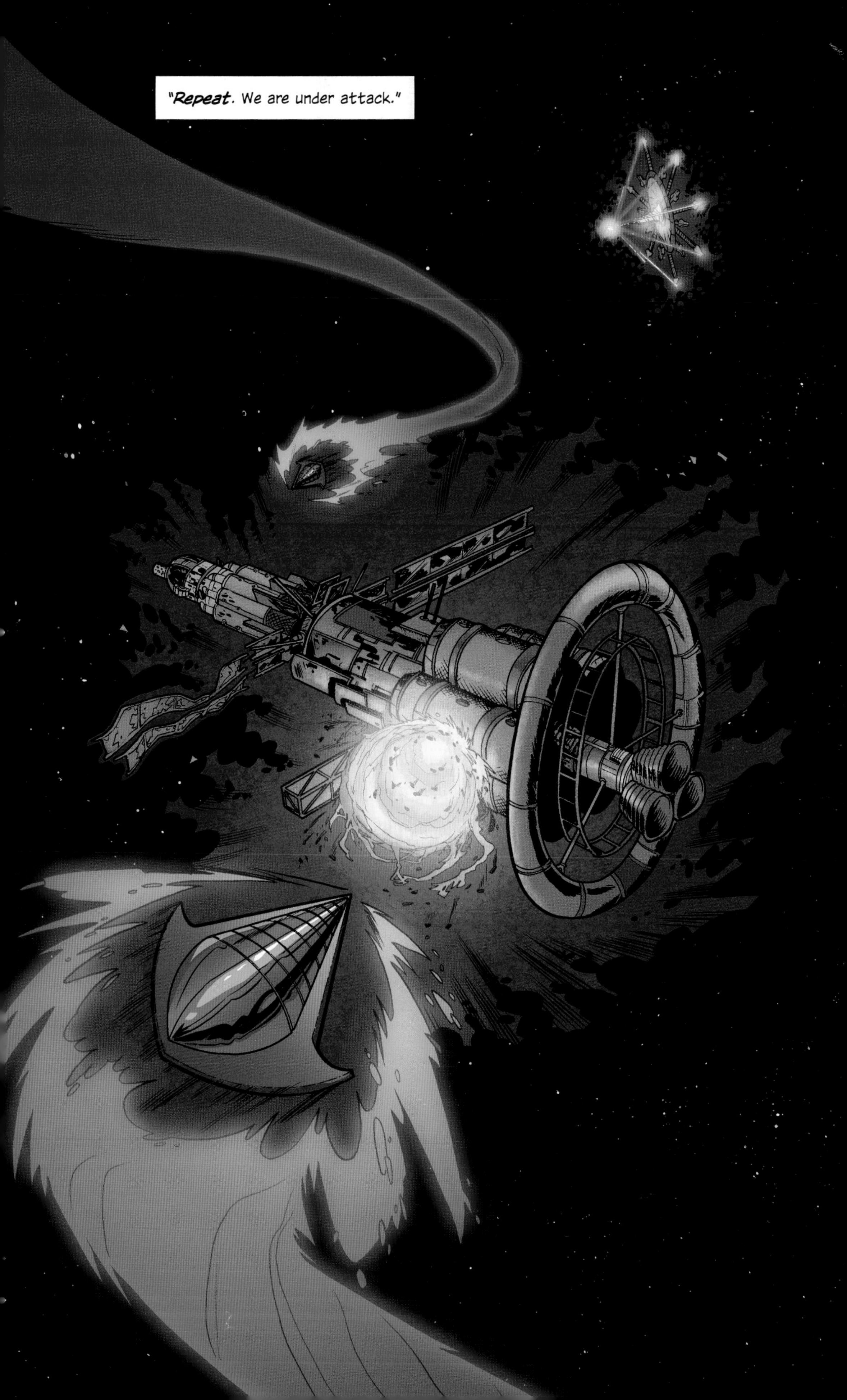
"*Repeat*. We are under attack."

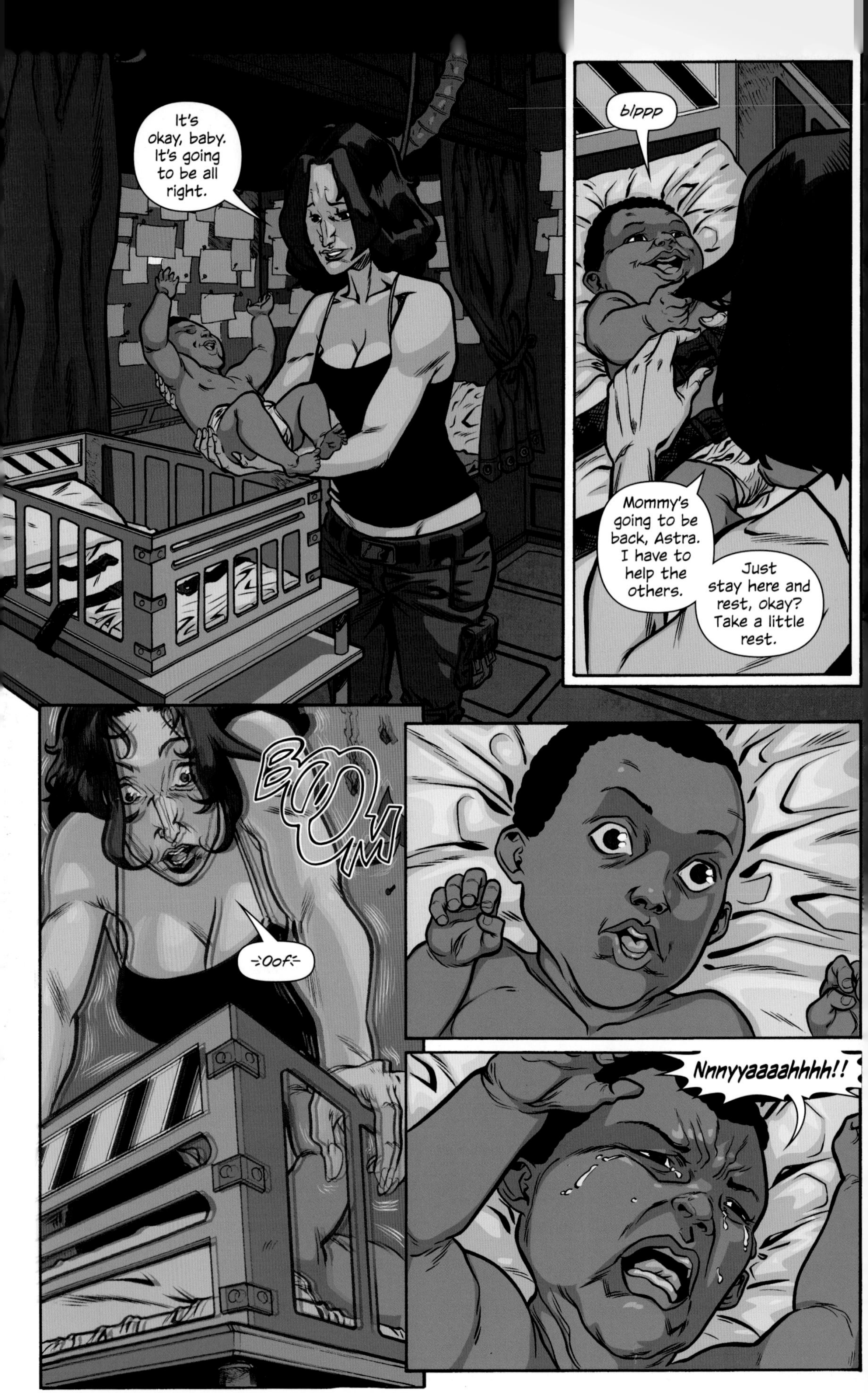
It's okay, baby. It's going to be all right.
blppp
Mommy's going to be back, Astra. I have to help the others.
Just stay here and rest, okay? Take a little rest.
BOOM
Oof
Nnnyyaaaahhhh!!

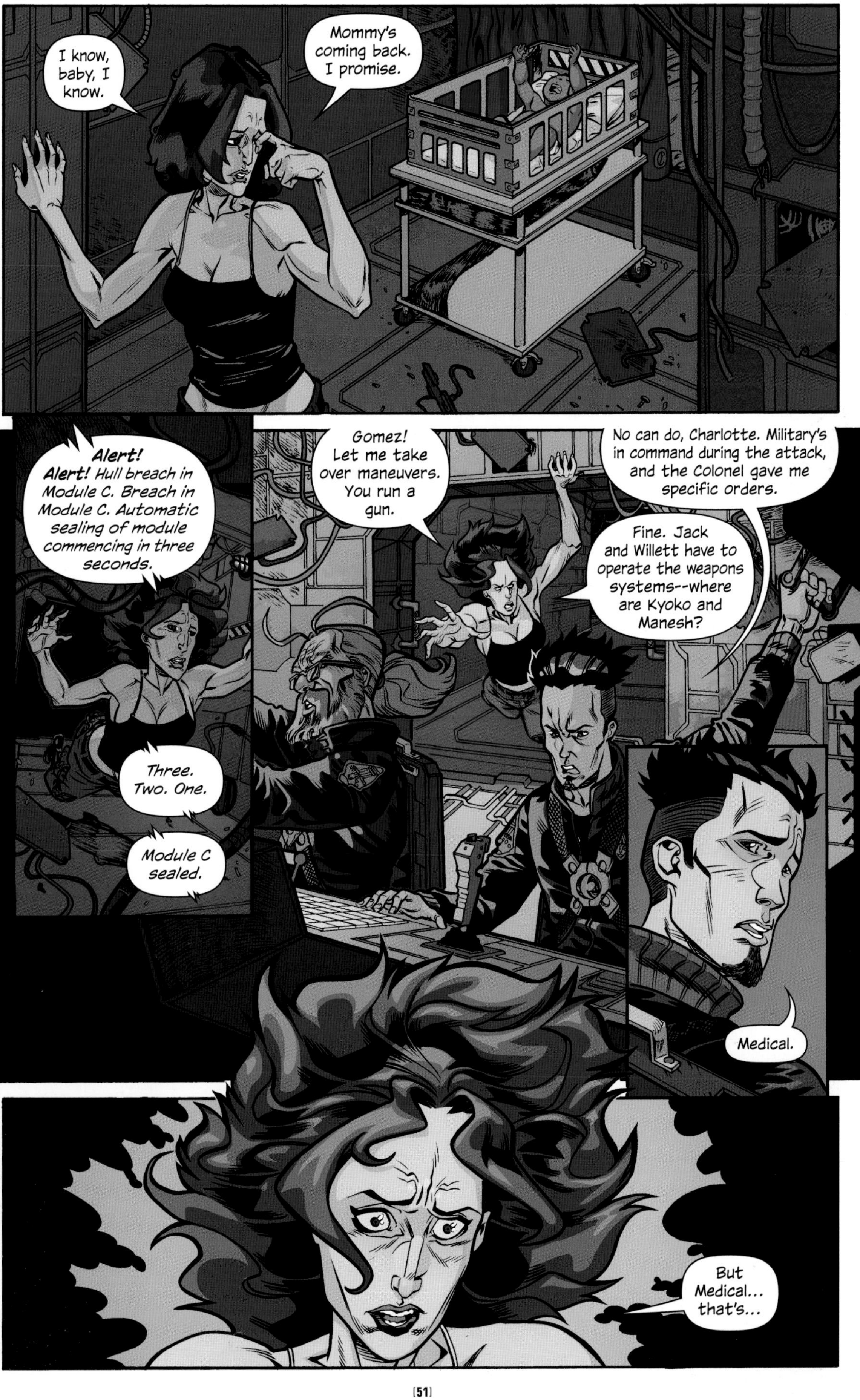
I know, baby, I know.
Mommy's coming back. I promise.
Alert! Alert! Hull breach in Module C. Breach in Module C. Automatic sealing of module commencing in three seconds.
Three. Two. One.
Module C sealed.
Gomez! Let me take over maneuvers. You run a gun.
No can do, Charlotte. Military's in command during the attack, and the Colonel gave me specific orders.
Fine. Jack and Willett have to operate the weapons systems--where are Kyoko and Manesh?
Medical.
But Medical... that's...

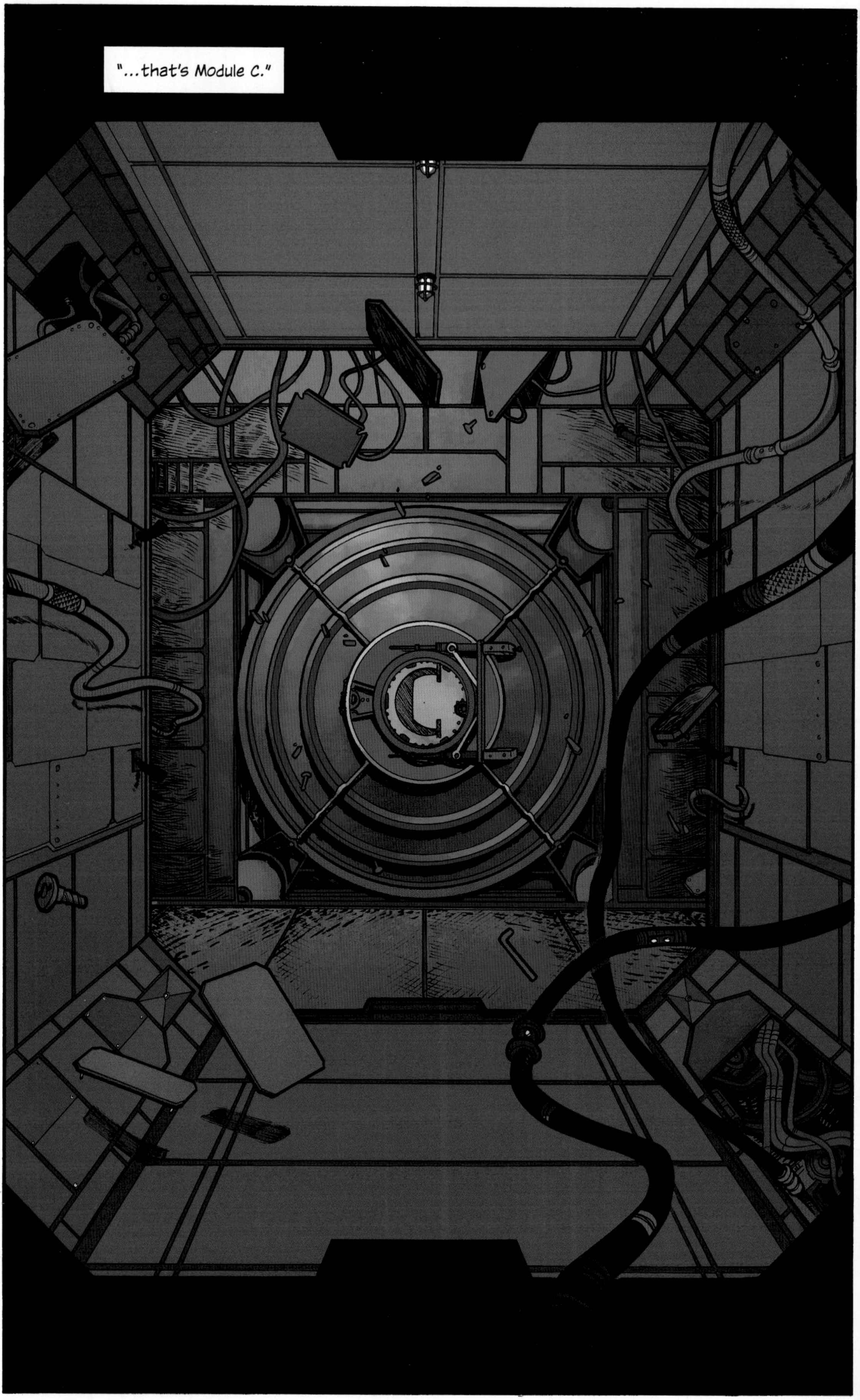
"...that's Module C."

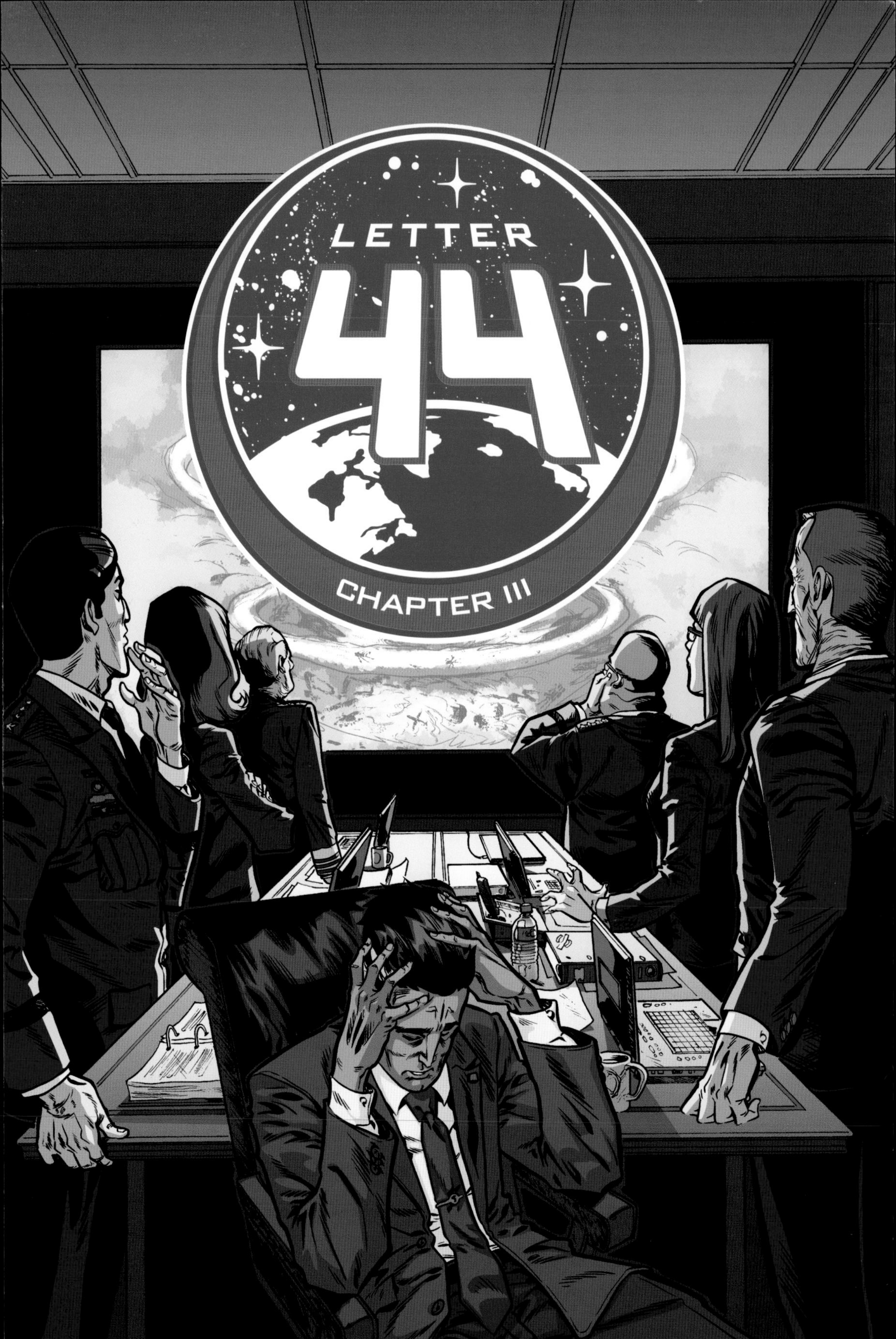
LETTER
44
CHAPTER III

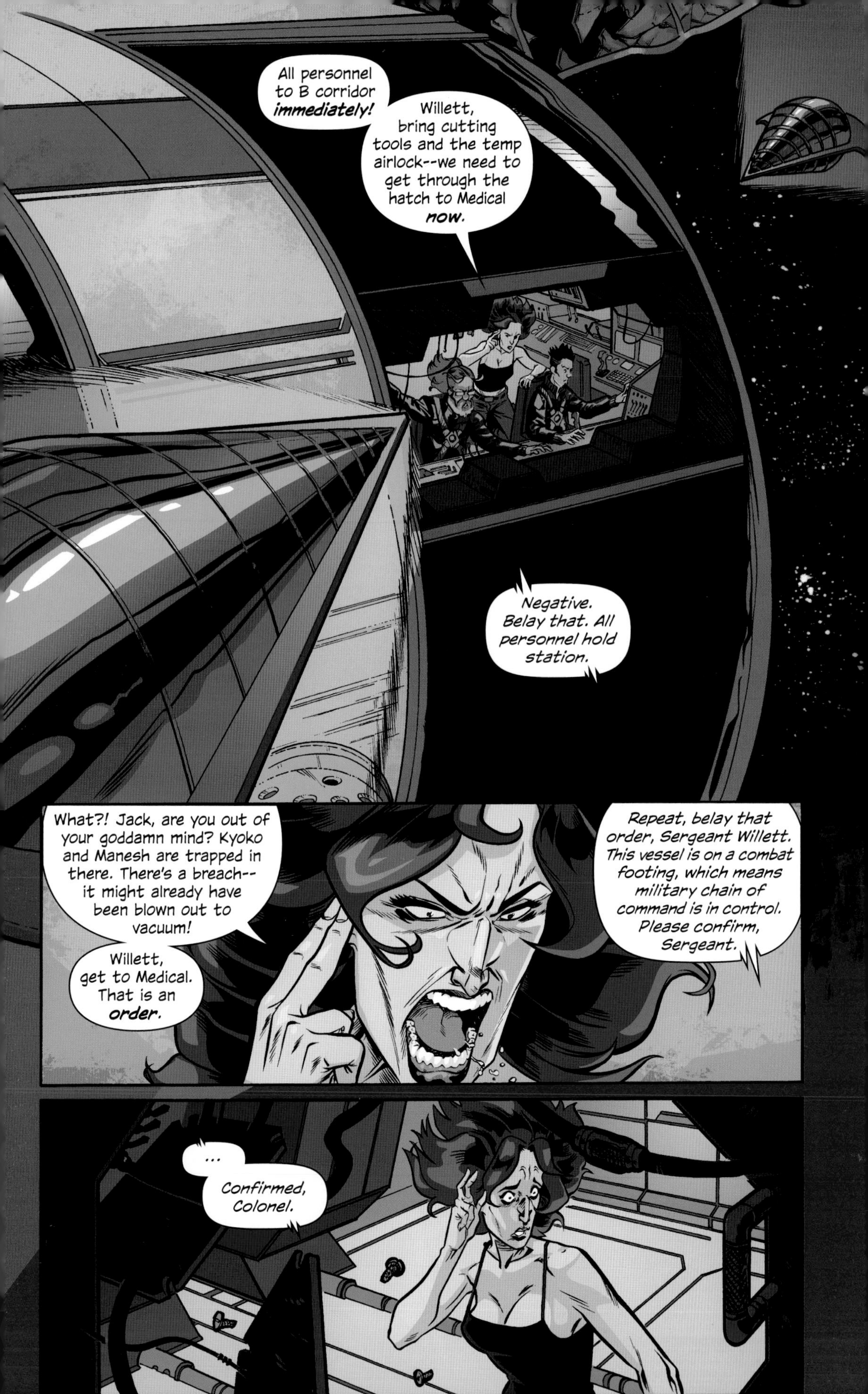
All personnel to B corridor *immediately!*
Willett, bring cutting tools and the temp airlock--we need to get through the hatch to Medical **now**.
Negative. Belay that. All personnel hold station.
What?! Jack, are you out of your goddamn mind? Kyoko and Manesh are trapped in there. There's a breach--it might already have been blown out to vacuum!
Willett, get to Medical. That is an **order**.
Repeat, belay that order, Sergeant Willett. This vessel is on a combat footing, which means military chain of command is in control. Please confirm, Sergeant.
...
Confirmed, Colonel.

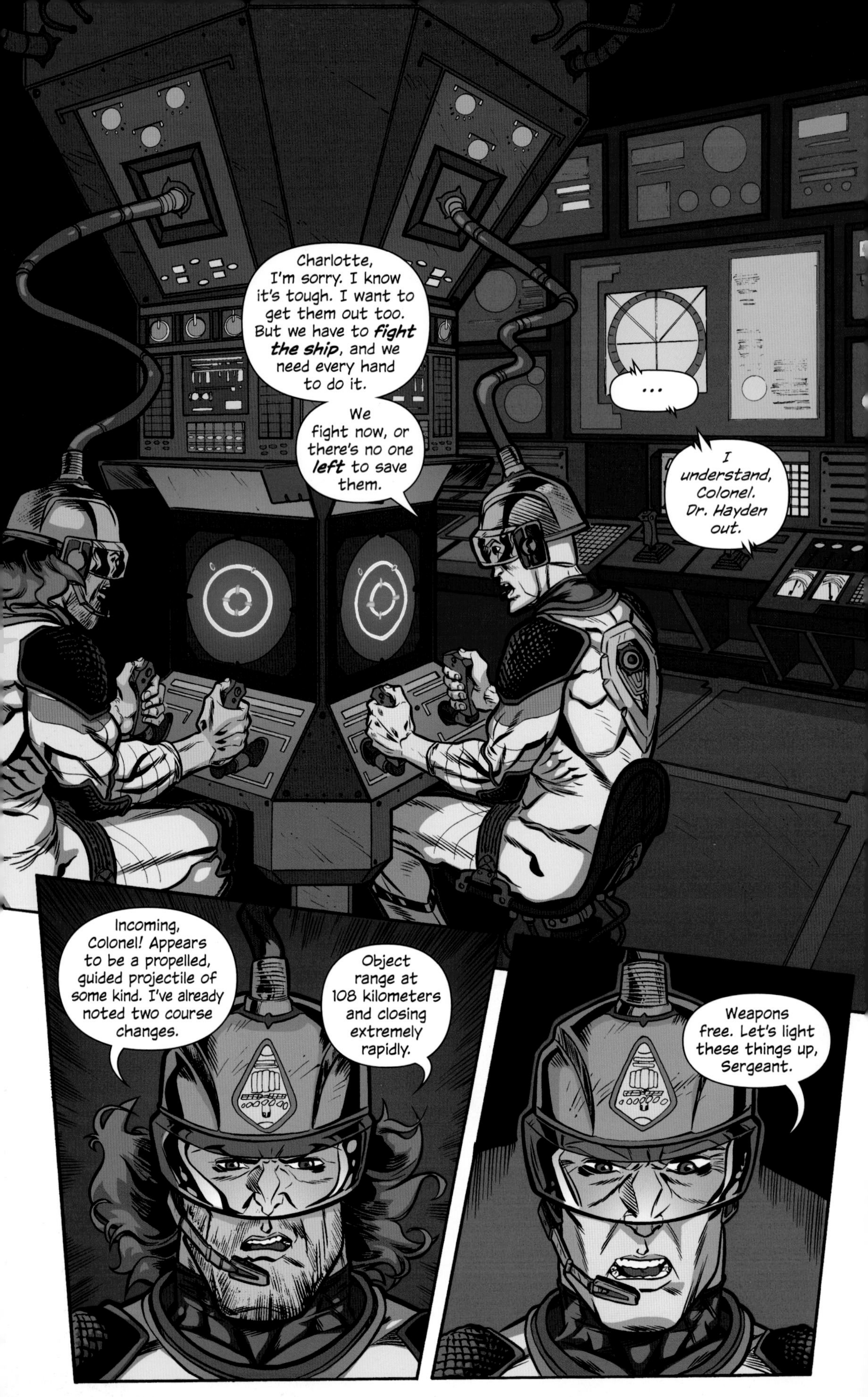
Charlotte, I'm sorry. I know it's tough. I want to get them out too. But we have to *fight the ship*, and we need every hand to do it.
We fight now, or there's no one *left* to save them.
...
I understand, Colonel. Dr. Hayden out.
Incoming, Colonel! Appears to be a propelled, guided projectile of some kind. I've already noted two course changes.
Object range at 108 kilometers and closing extremely rapidly.
Weapons free. Let's light these things up, Sergeant.

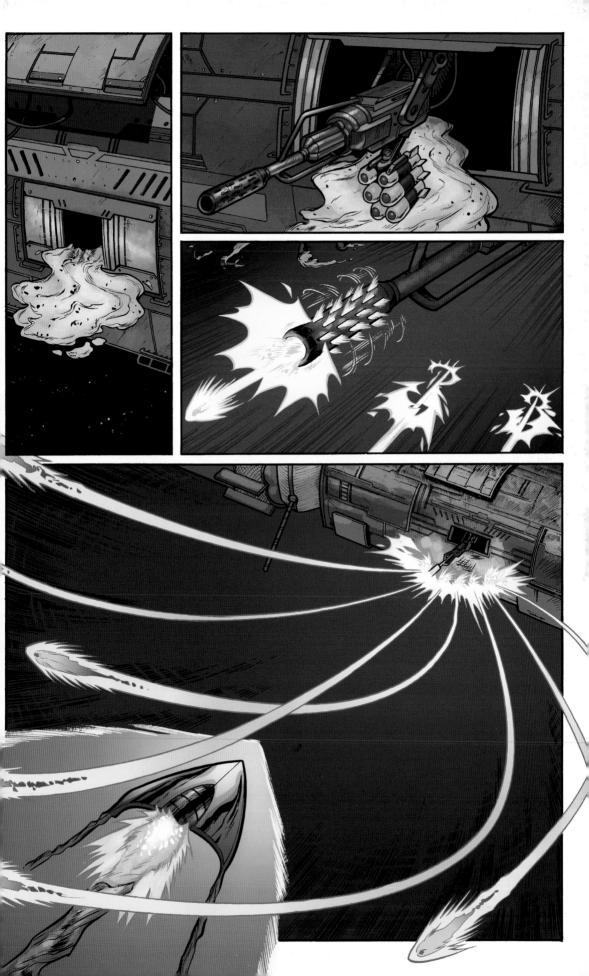

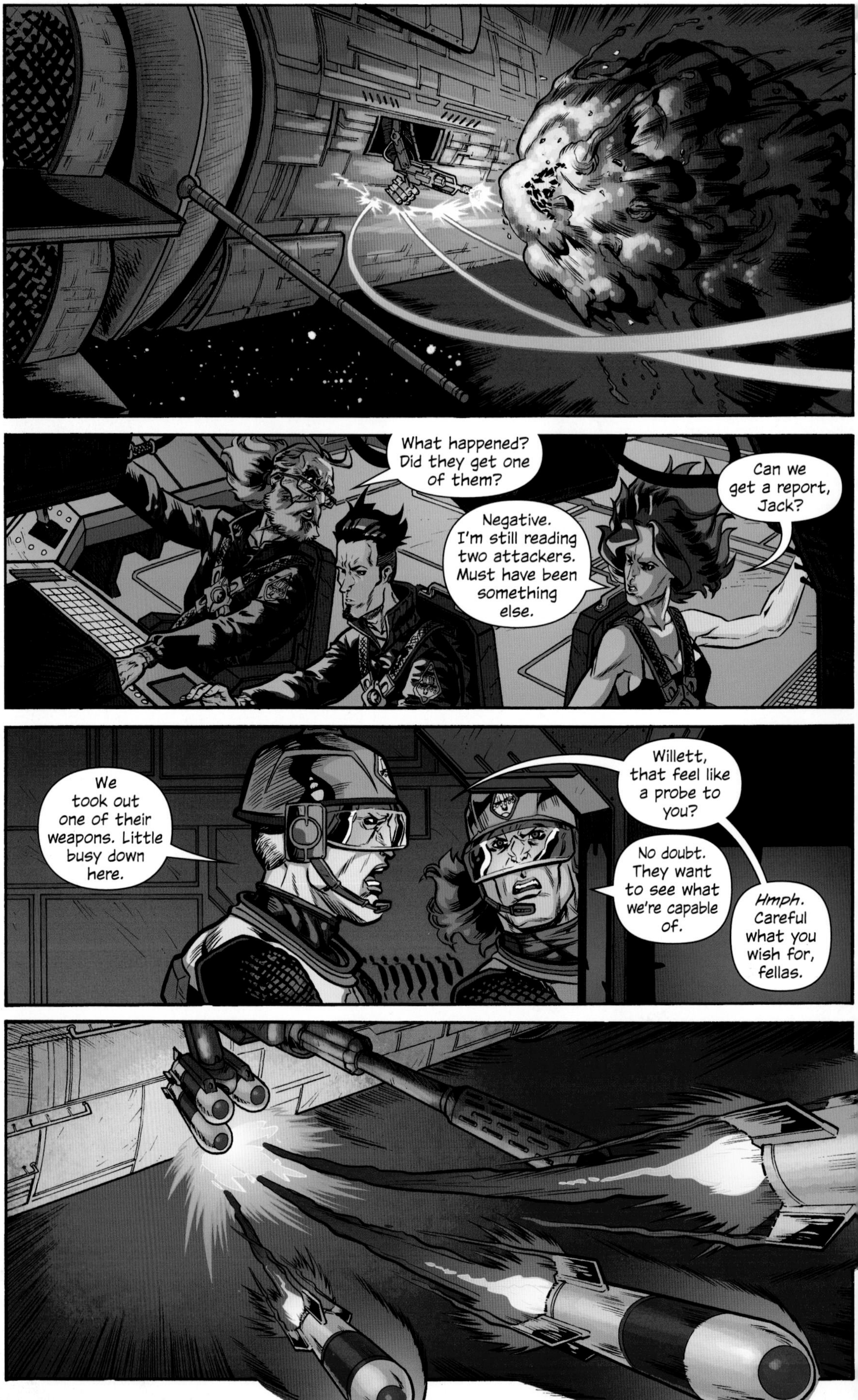
What happened? Did they get one of them?
Negative. I'm still reading two attackers. Must have been something else.
Can we get a report, Jack?
We took out one of their weapons. Little busy down here.
Willett, that feel like a probe to you?
No doubt. They want to see what we're capable of.
Hmph. Careful what you wish for, fellas.

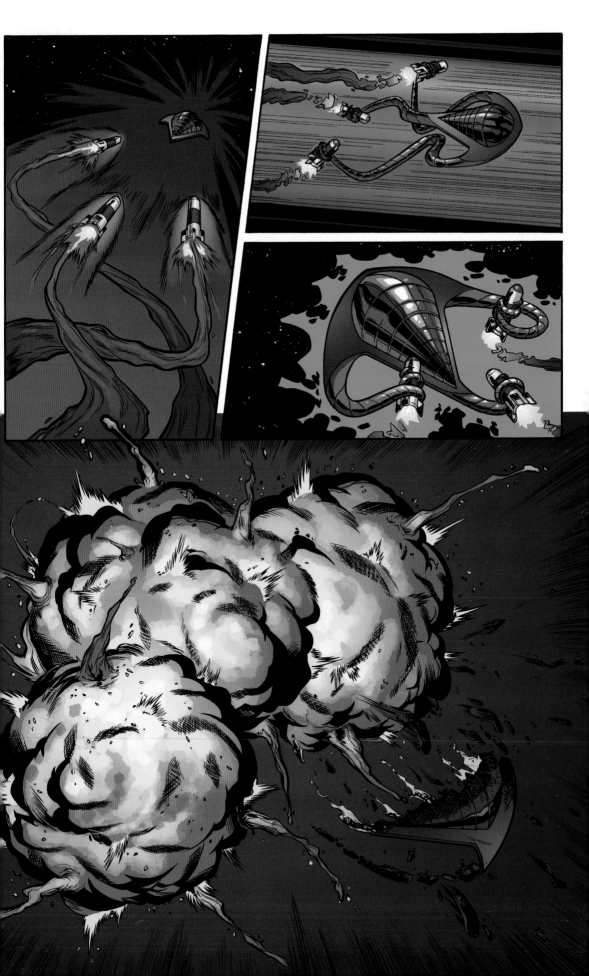

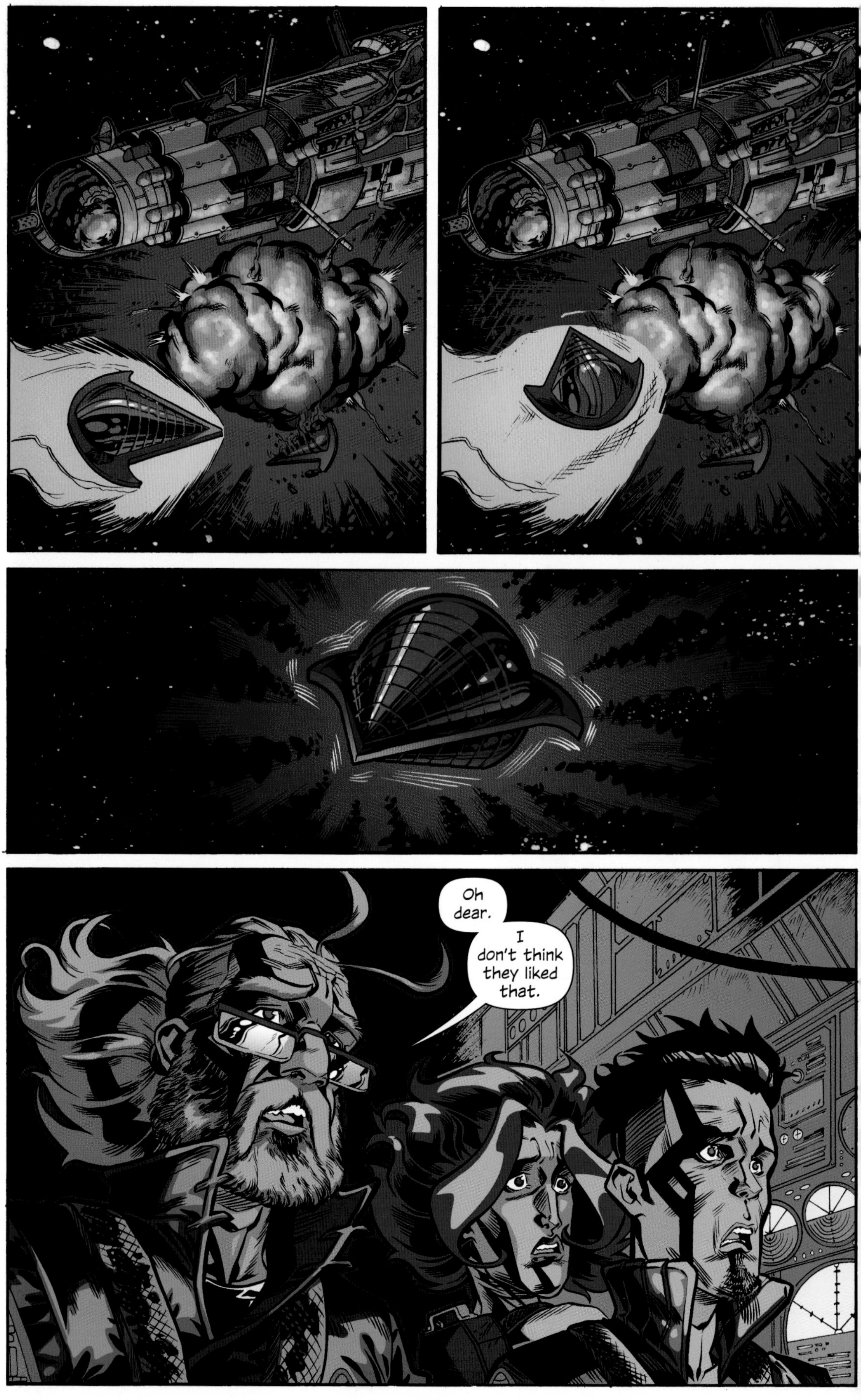
Oh dear.
I don't think they liked that.

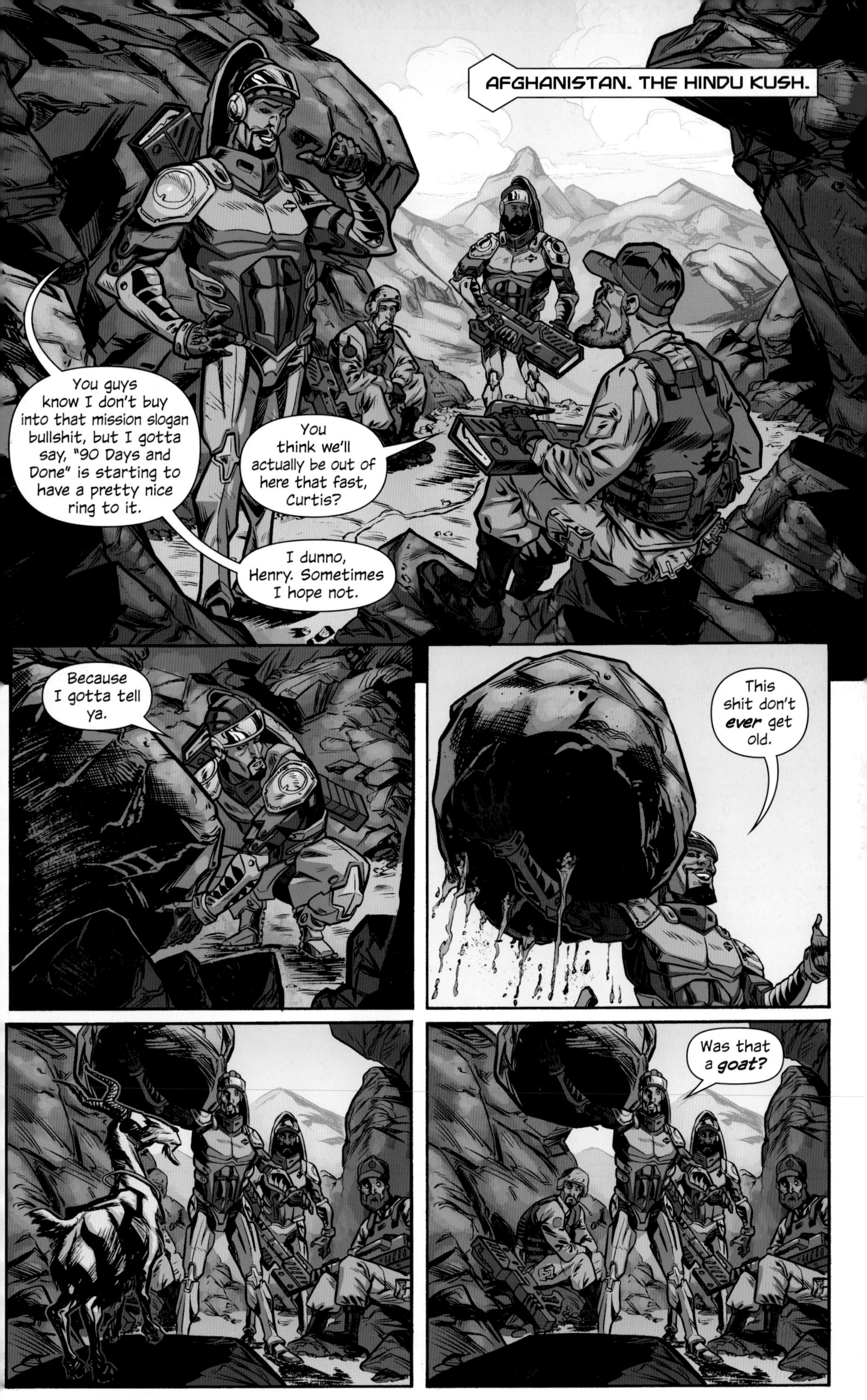

AFGHANISTAN. THE HINDU KUSH.
You guys know I don't buy into that mission slogan bullshit, but I gotta say, "90 Days and Done" is starting to have a pretty nice ring to it.
You think we'll actually be out of here that fast, Curtis?
I dunno, Henry. Sometimes I hope not.
Because I gotta tell ya.
This shit don't *ever* get old.
Was that a *goat?*

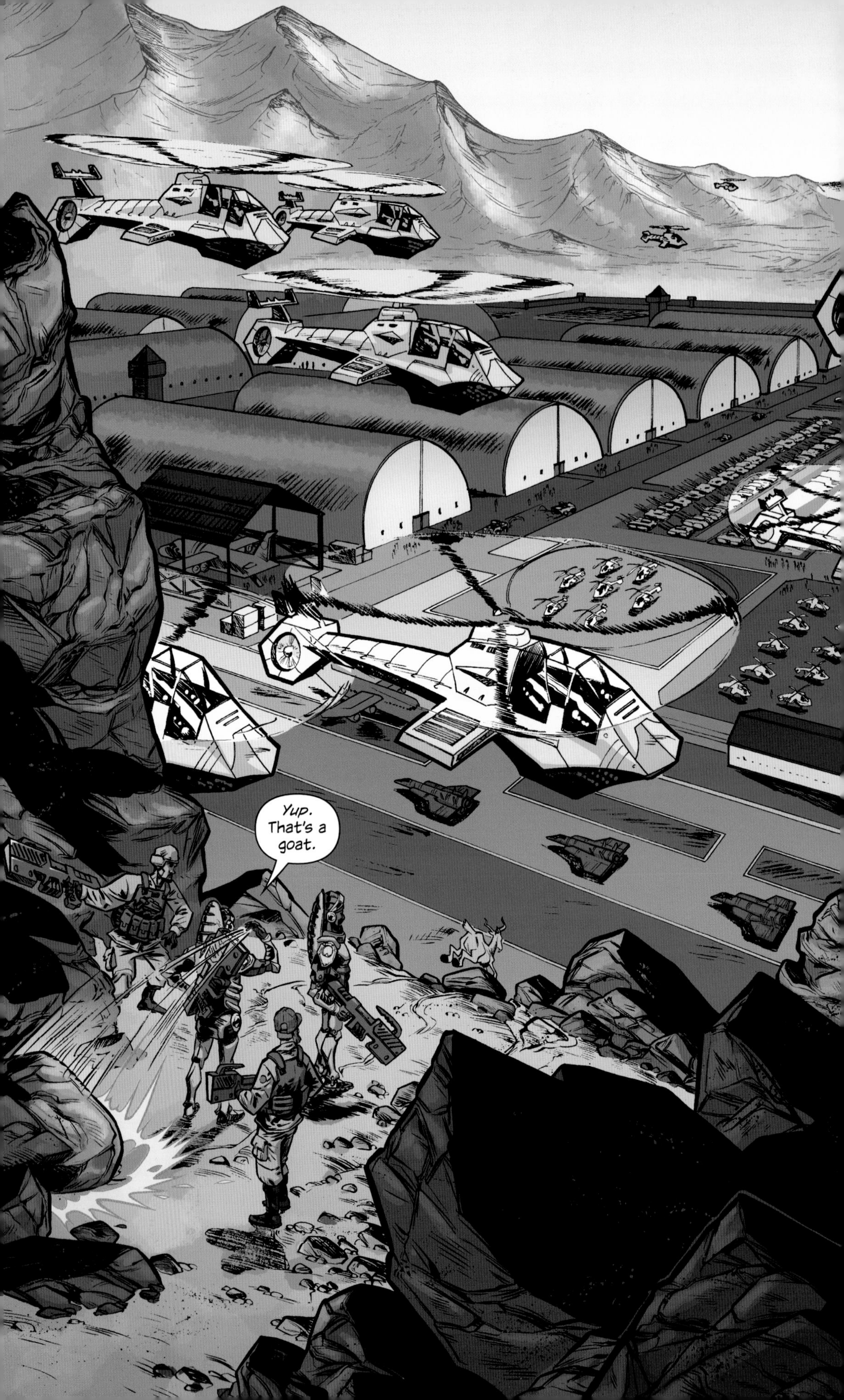
Yup. That's a goat.

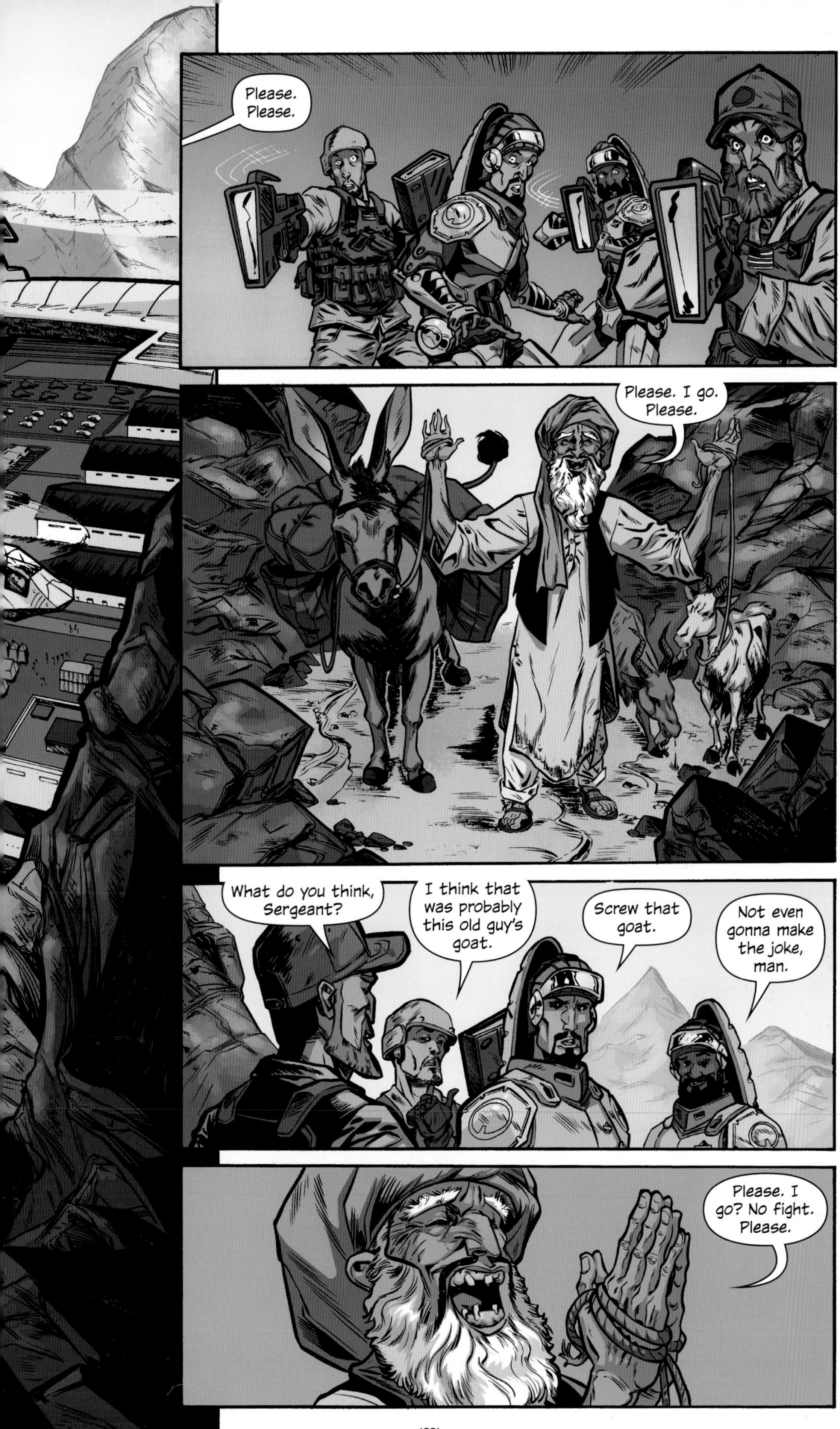
Please. Please.
Please. I go. Please.
What do you think, Sergeant?
I think that was probably this old guy's goat.
Screw that goat.
Not even gonna make the joke, man.
Please. I go? No fight. Please.

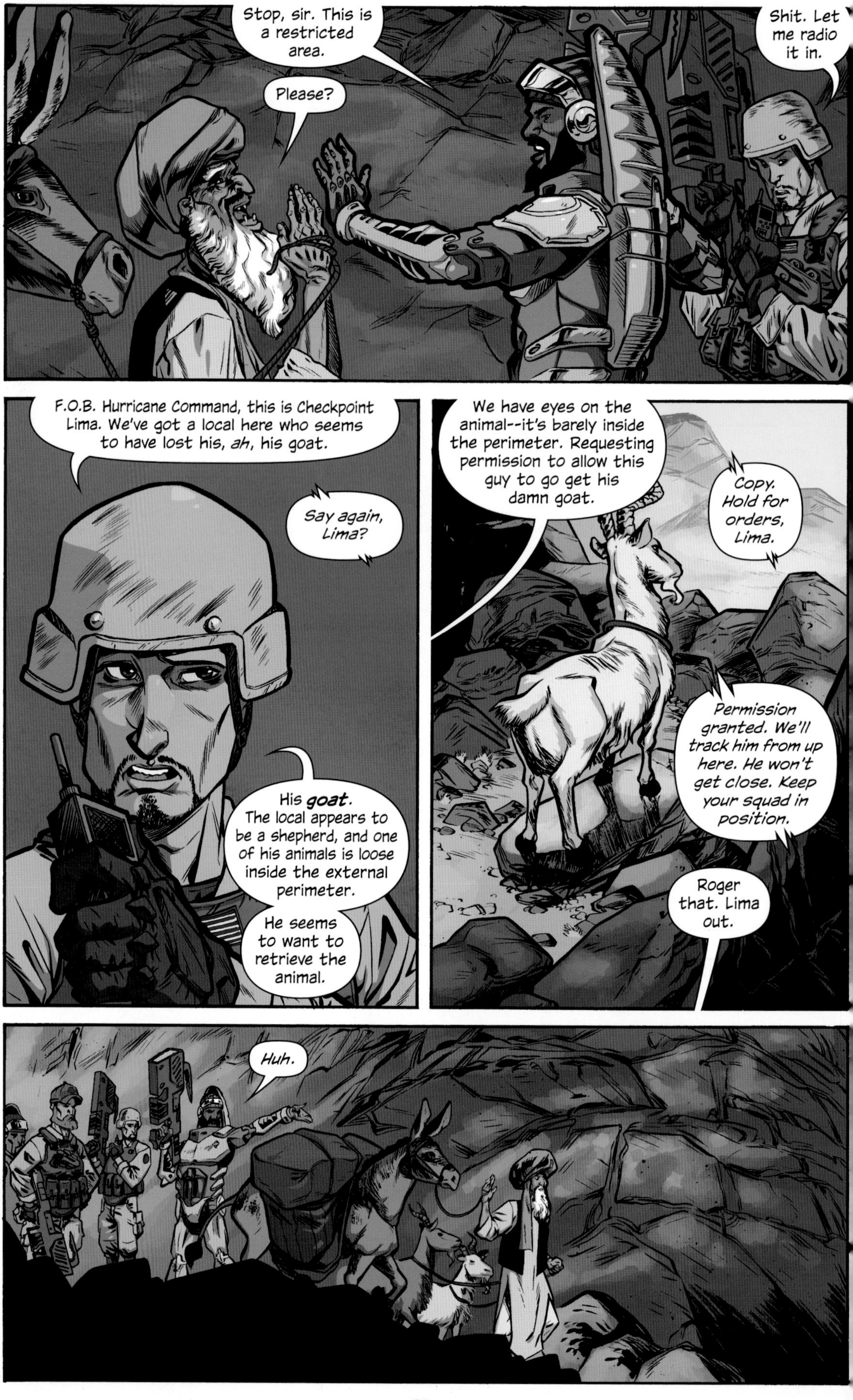
Stop, sir. This is a restricted area.
Please?
Shit. Let me radio it in.
F.O.B. Hurricane Command, this is Checkpoint Lima. We've got a local here who seems to have lost his, *ah*, his goat.
Say again, Lima?
His ***goat***. The local appears to be a shepherd, and one of his animals is loose inside the external perimeter.
He seems to want to retrieve the animal.
We have eyes on the animal--it's barely inside the perimeter. Requesting permission to allow this guy to go get his damn goat.
Copy. Hold for orders, Lima.
Permission granted. We'll track him from up here. He won't get close. Keep your squad in position.
Roger that. Lima out.
Huh.

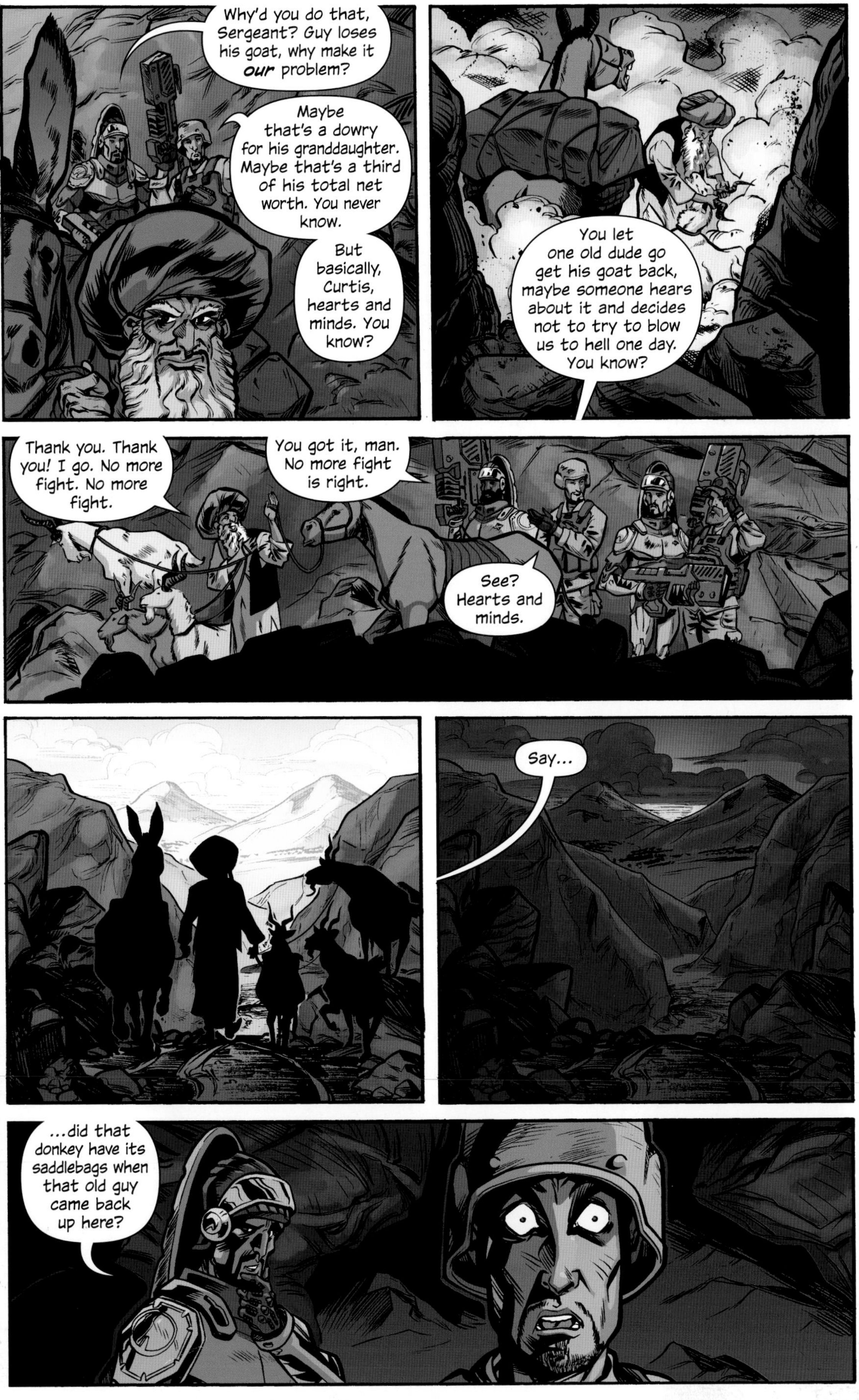
Why'd you do that, Sergeant? Guy loses his goat, why make it *our* problem?
Maybe that's a dowry for his granddaughter. Maybe that's a third of his total net worth. You never know.
But basically, Curtis, hearts and minds. You know?
You let one old dude go get his goat back, maybe someone hears about it and decides not to try to blow us to hell one day. You know?
Thank you. Thank you! I go. No more fight. No more fight.
You got it, man. No more fight is right.
See? Hearts and minds.
Say...
...did that donkey have its saddlebags when that old guy came back up here?

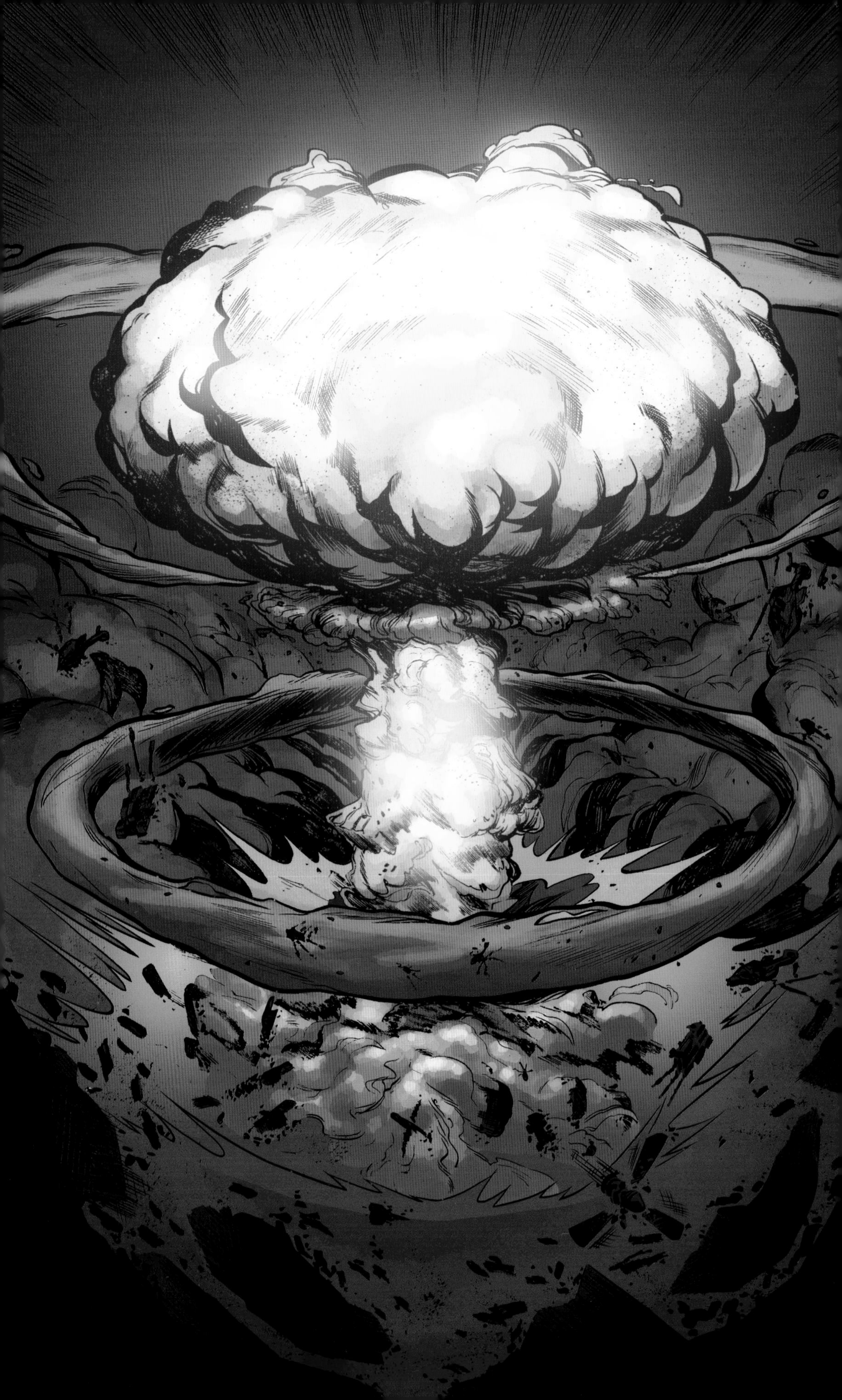

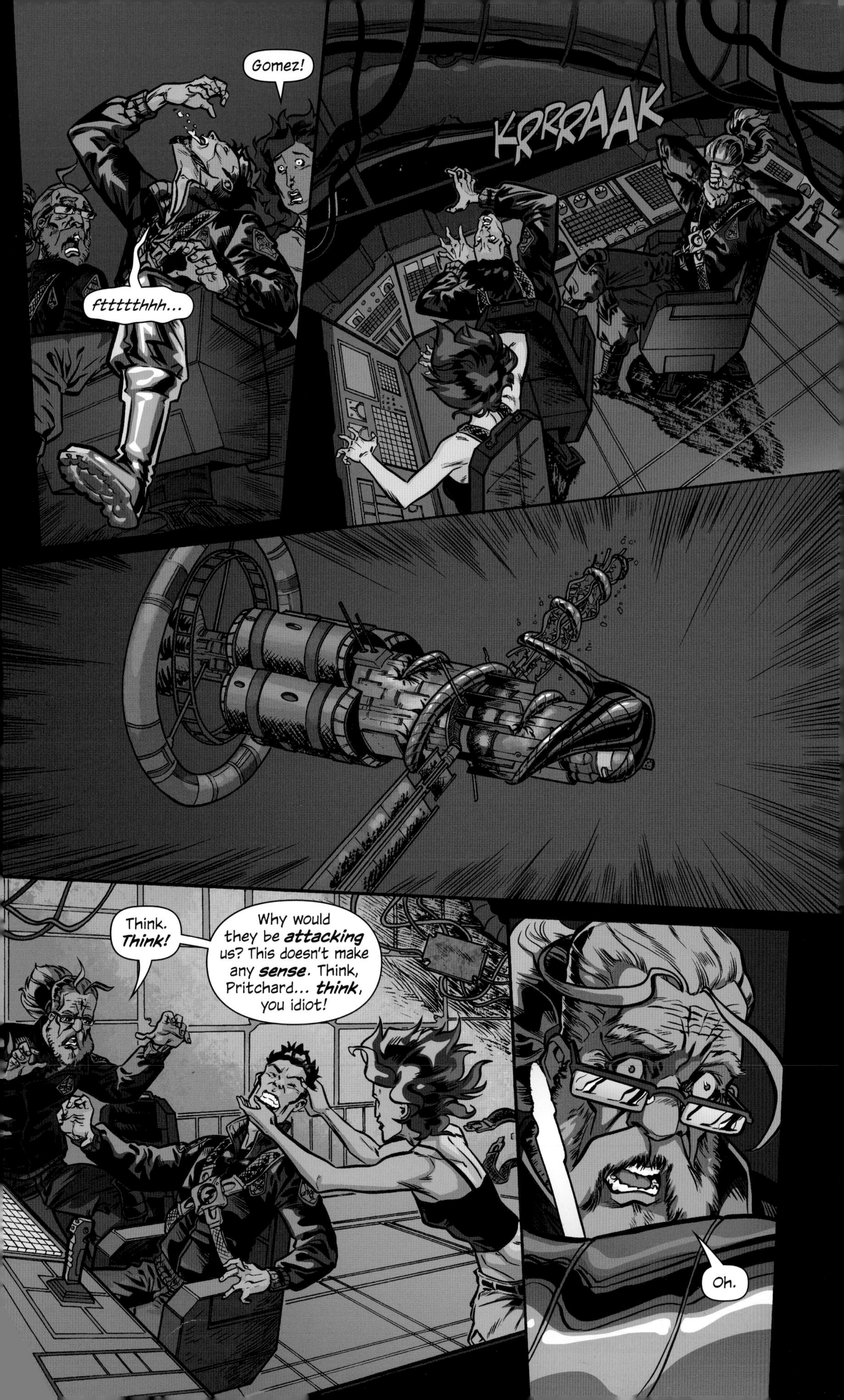
Gomez!
ftttttthhh...
KRRRAAK
Think. Think!
Why would they be attacking us? This doesn't make any sense. Think, Pritchard... think, you idiot!
Oh.

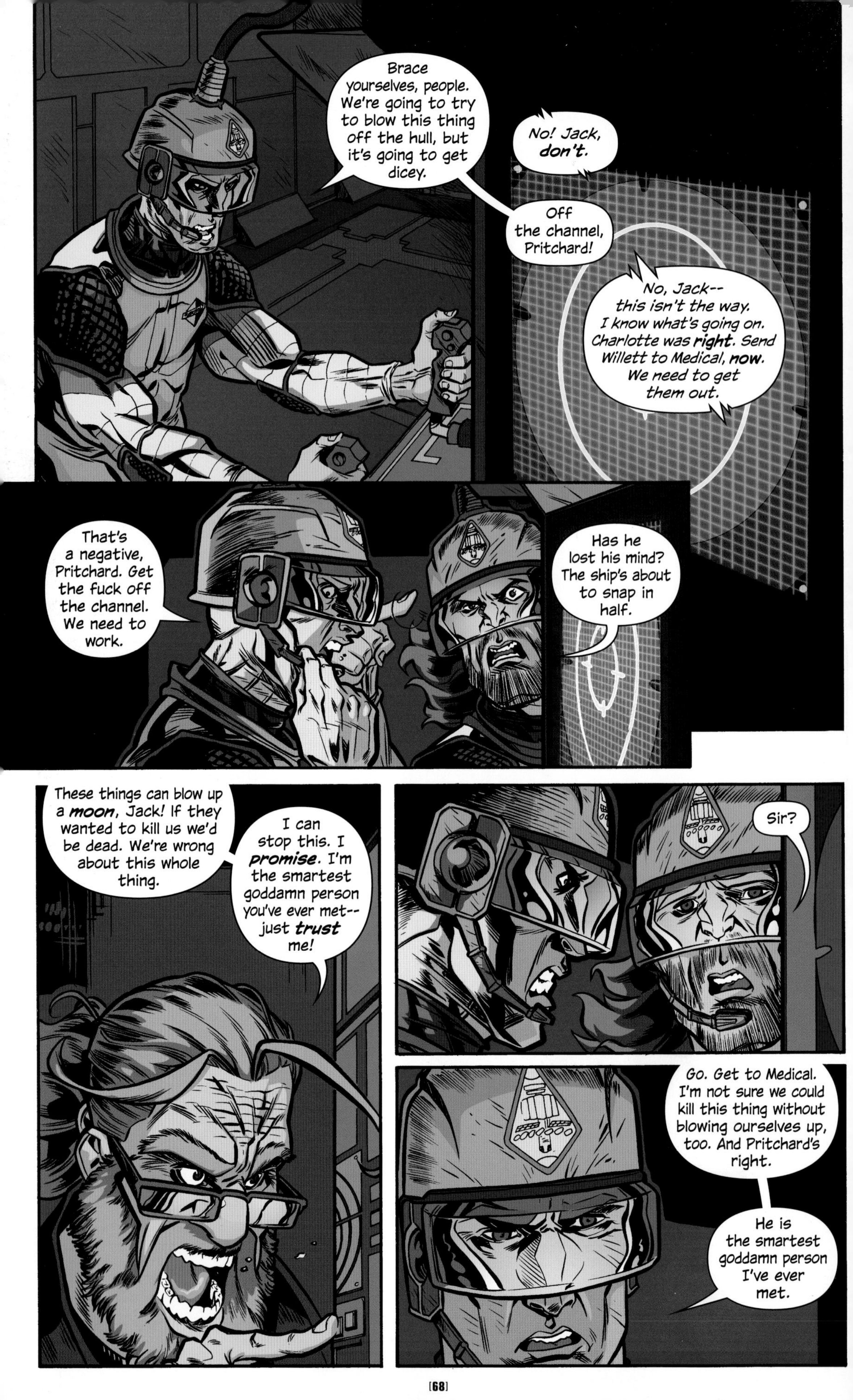
Brace yourselves, people. We're going to try to blow this thing off the hull, but it's going to get dicey.
No! Jack, **don't**.
Off the channel, Pritchard!
*No, Jack-- this isn't the way. I know what's going on. Charlotte was **right**. Send Willett to Medical, **now**. We need to get them out.*
That's a negative, Pritchard. Get the fuck off the channel. We need to work.
Has he lost his mind? The ship's about to snap in half.
These things can blow up a ***moon***, Jack! If they wanted to kill us we'd be dead. We're wrong about this whole thing.
I can stop this. I ***promise***. I'm the smartest goddamn person you've ever met-- just ***trust*** me!
Sir?
Go. Get to Medical. I'm not sure we could kill this thing without blowing ourselves up, too. And Pritchard's right.
He is the smartest goddamn person I've ever met.

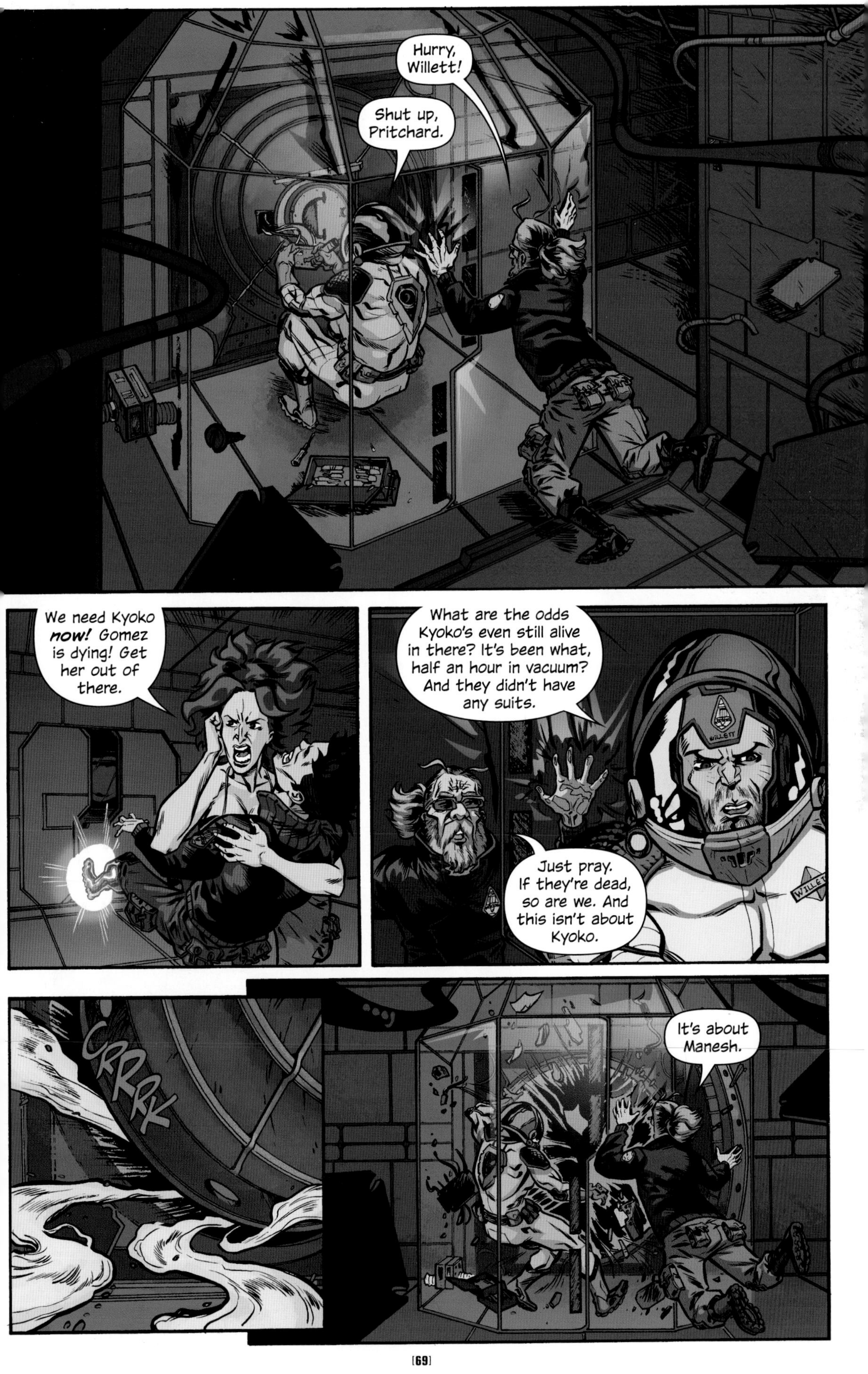
Hurry, Willett!
Shut up, Pritchard.
We need Kyoko *now!* Gomez is dying! Get her out of there.
What are the odds Kyoko's even still alive in there? It's been what, half an hour in vacuum? And they didn't have any suits.
Just pray. If they're dead, so are we. And this isn't about Kyoko.
CRRKK
It's about Manesh.

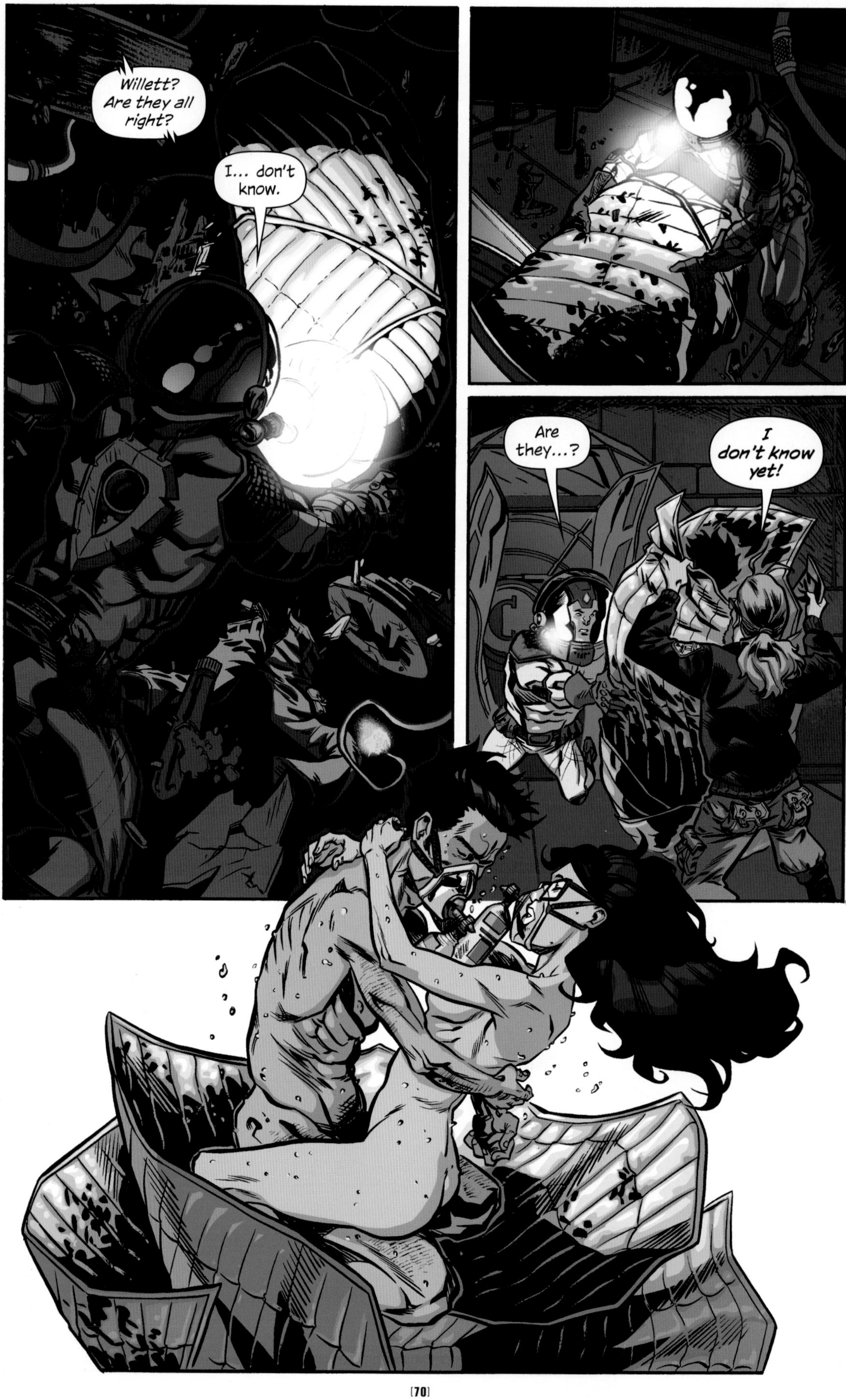
Willett? Are they all right?
I... don't know.
Are they...?
I don't know yet!

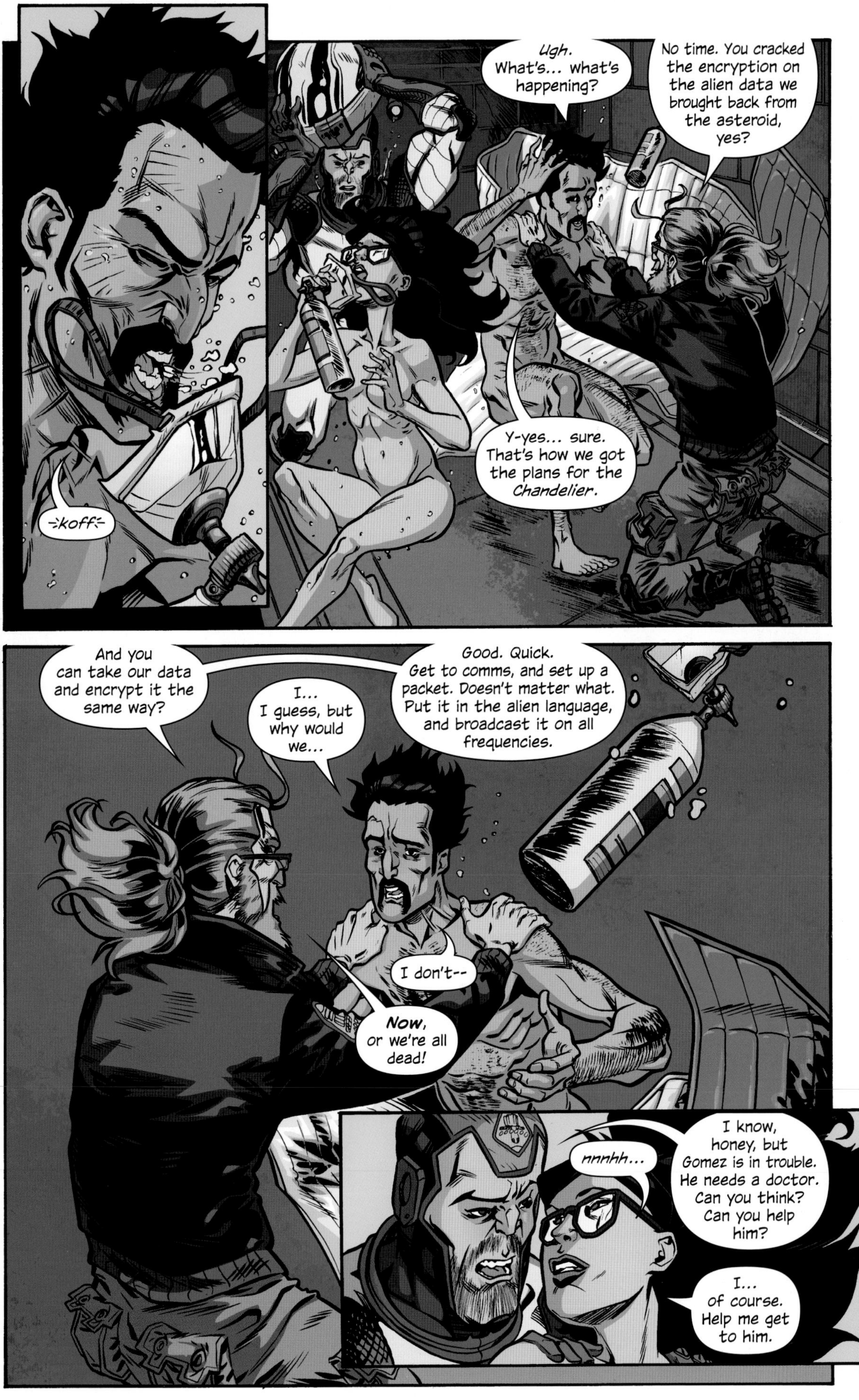

-koff-
Ugh. What's... what's happening?
No time. You cracked the encryption on the alien data we brought back from the asteroid, yes?
Y-yes... sure. That's how we got the plans for the Chandelier.
And you can take our data and encrypt it the same way?
I... I guess, but why would we...
Good. Quick. Get to comms, and set up a packet. Doesn't matter what. Put it in the alien language, and broadcast it on all frequencies.
I don't--
Now, or we're all dead!
mnhh...
I know, honey, but Gomez is in trouble. He needs a doctor. Can you think? Can you help him?
I... of course. Help me get to him.

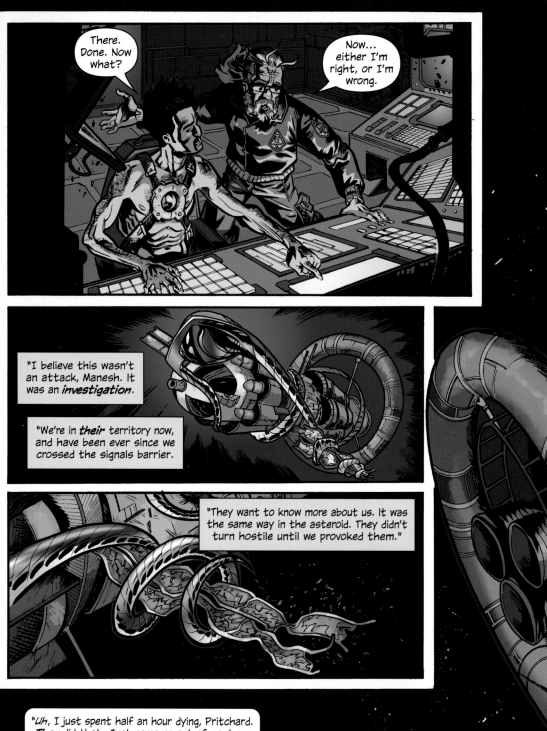

There. Done. Now what?

Now... either I'm right, or I'm wrong.

"I believe this wasn't an attack, Manesh. It was an *investigation*."

"We're in *their* territory now, and have been ever since we crossed the signals barrier."

"They want to know more about us. It was the same way in the asteroid. They didn't turn hostile until we provoked them."

"*Uh*, I just spent half an hour dying, Pritchard. *They* did that. Just came up out of nowhere and *boom*--atmo's gone, power's out, and I'm trying to convince Kyoko to get naked.

"Not that we actually got to have sex in that thing--even I have my limits--but it was the closest I've been in a while."

"The attack was a misunderstanding, Manesh. I'm sure of it. An accident.

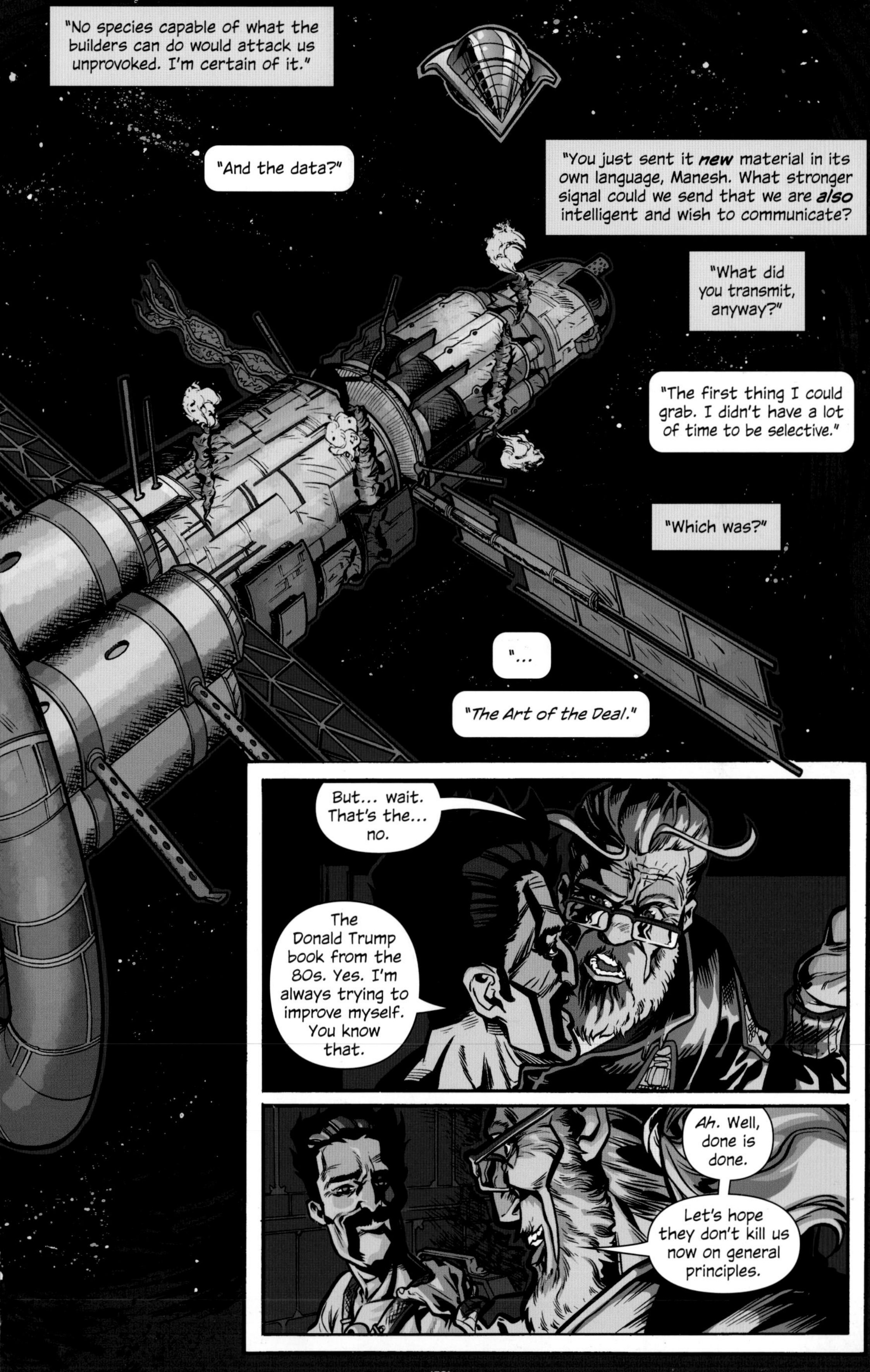

"No species capable of what the builders can do would attack us unprovoked. I'm certain of it."

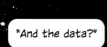

"And the data?"

"You just sent it *new* material in its own language, Manesh. What stronger signal could we send that we are *also* intelligent and wish to communicate?"

"What did you transmit, anyway?"

"The first thing I could grab. I didn't have a lot of time to be selective."

"Which was?"

"..."

"*The Art of the Deal.*"

But... wait. That's the... no.

The Donald Trump book from the 80s. Yes. I'm always trying to improve myself. You know that.

Ah. Well, done is done.

Let's hope they don't kill us now on general principles.

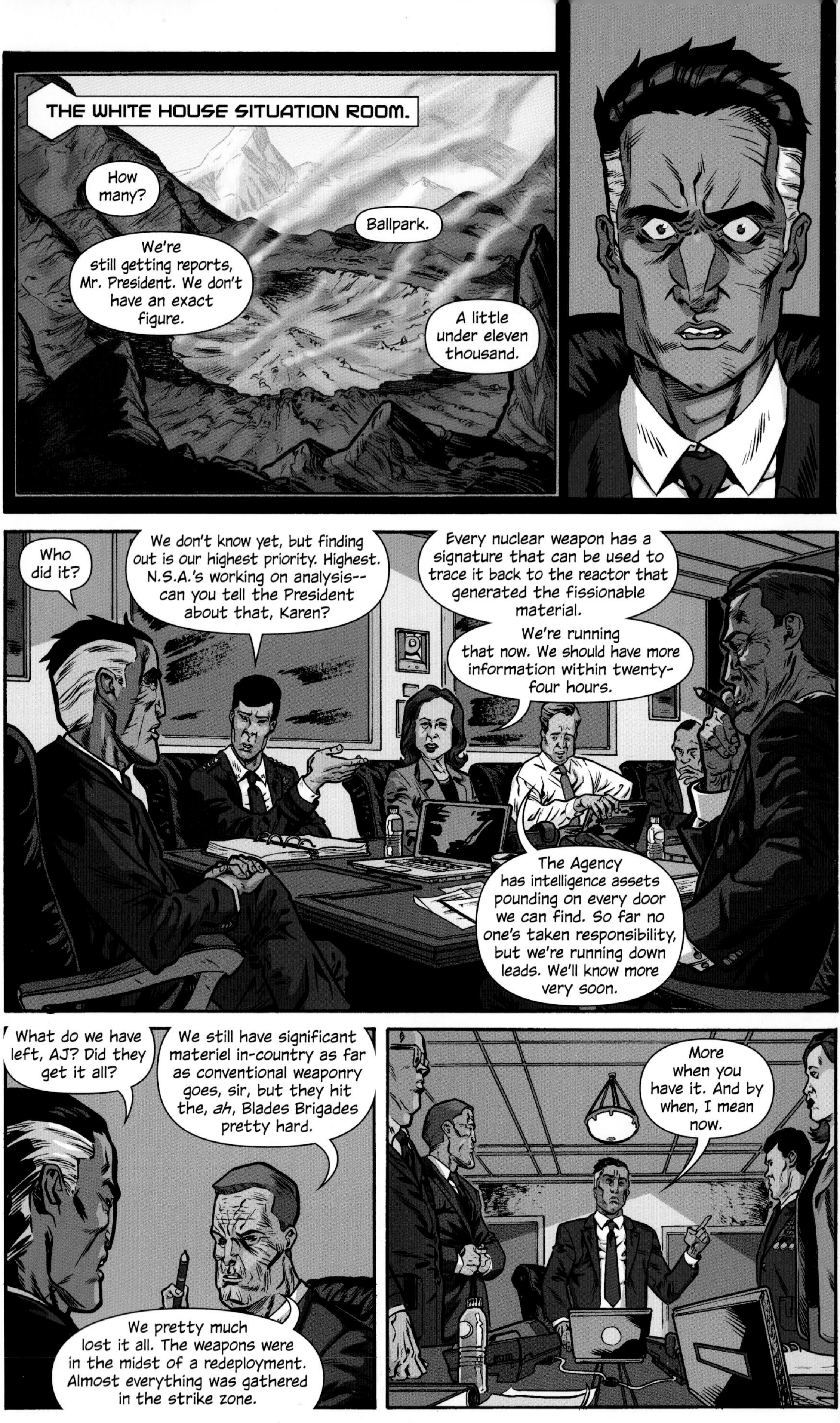
THE WHITE HOUSE SITUATION ROOM.
How many?
We're still getting reports, Mr. President. We don't have an exact figure.
Ballpark.
A little under eleven thousand.
Who did it?
We don't know yet, but finding out is our highest priority. Highest. N.S.A.'s working on analysis-- can you tell the President about that, Karen?
Every nuclear weapon has a signature that can be used to trace it back to the reactor that generated the fissionable material.
We're running that now. We should have more information within twenty-four hours.
The Agency has intelligence assets pounding on every door we can find. So far no one's taken responsibility, but we're running down leads. We'll know more very soon.
What do we have left, AJ? Did they get it all?
We still have significant materiel in-country as far as conventional weaponry goes, sir, but they hit the, *ah*, Blades Brigades pretty hard.
We pretty much lost it all. The weapons were in the midst of a redeployment. Almost everything was gathered in the strike zone.
More when you have it. And by when, I mean now.

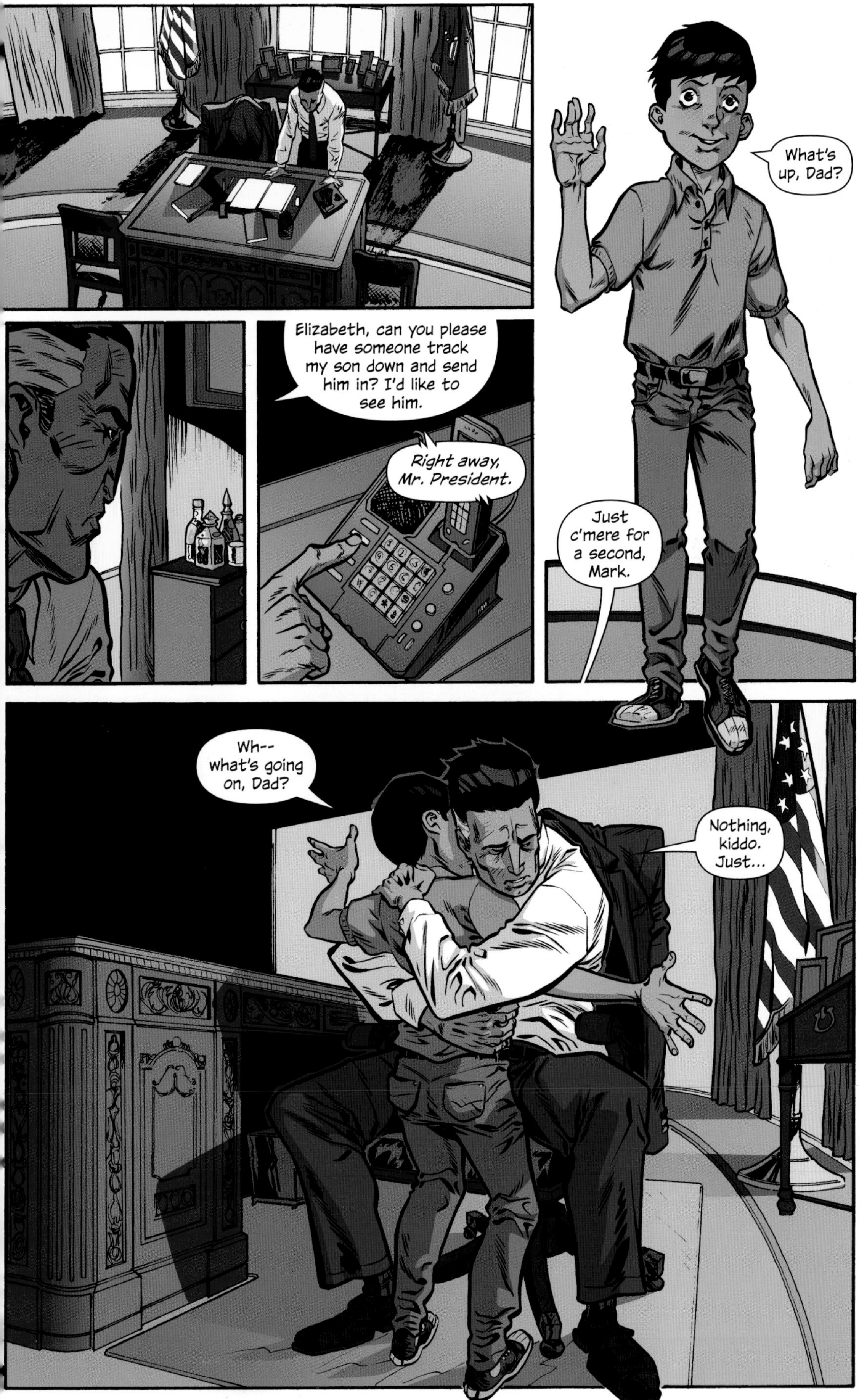
Elizabeth, can you please have someone track my son down and send him in? I'd like to see him.
Right away, Mr. President.
What's up, Dad?
Just c'mere for a second, Mark.
Wh-- what's going on, Dad?
Nothing, kiddo. Just...

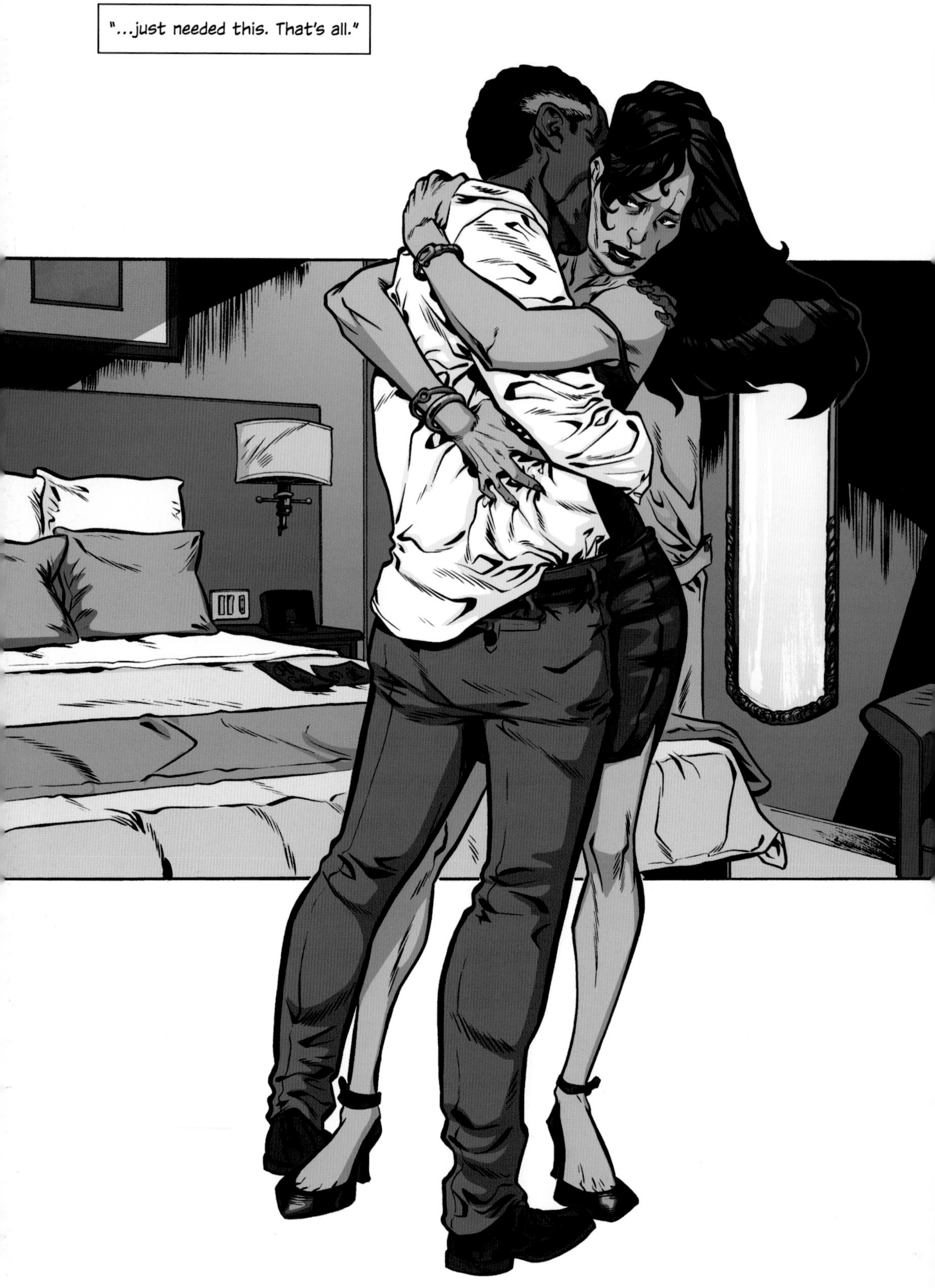
"...just needed this. That's all."

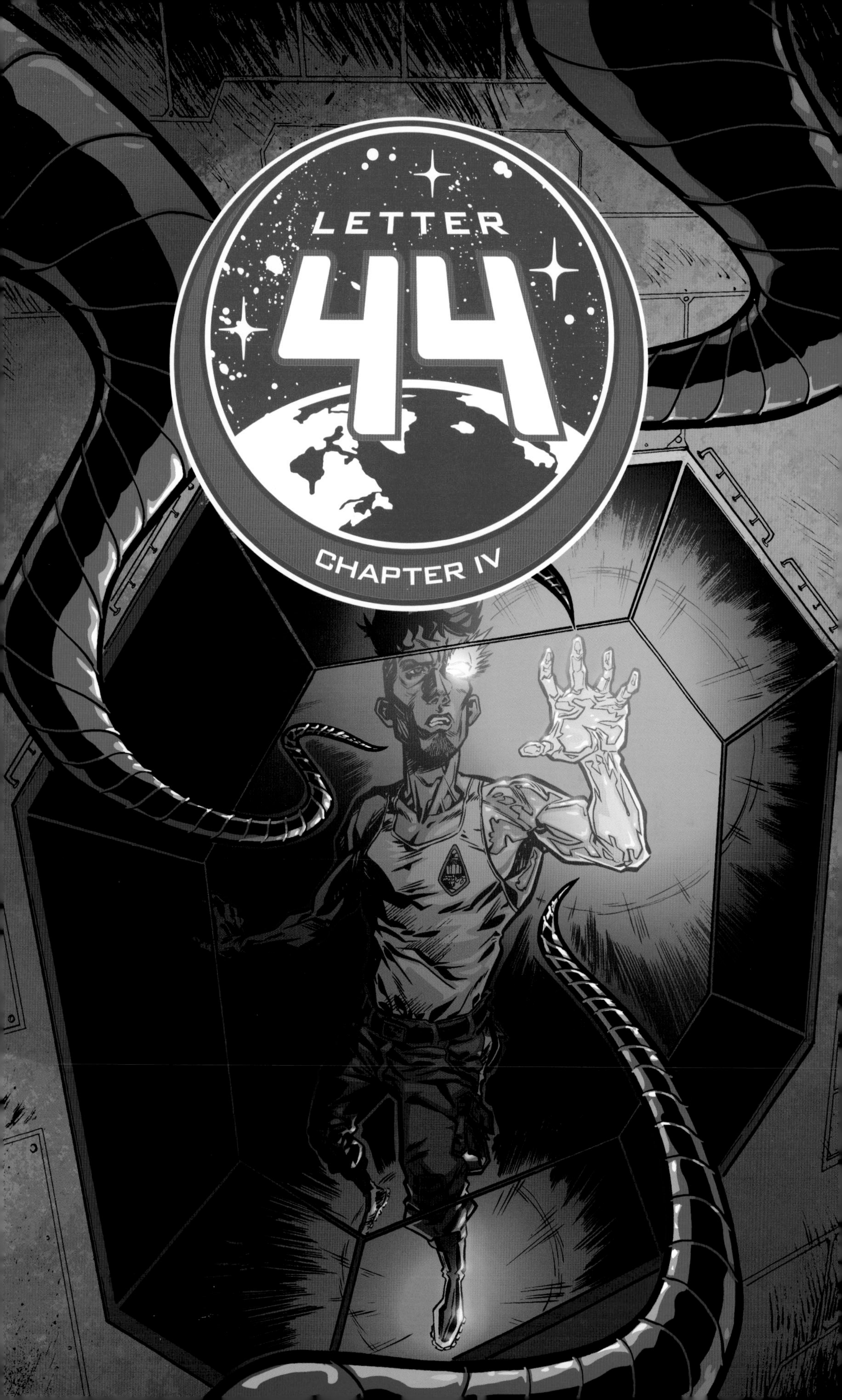
LETTER
44
CHAPTER IV

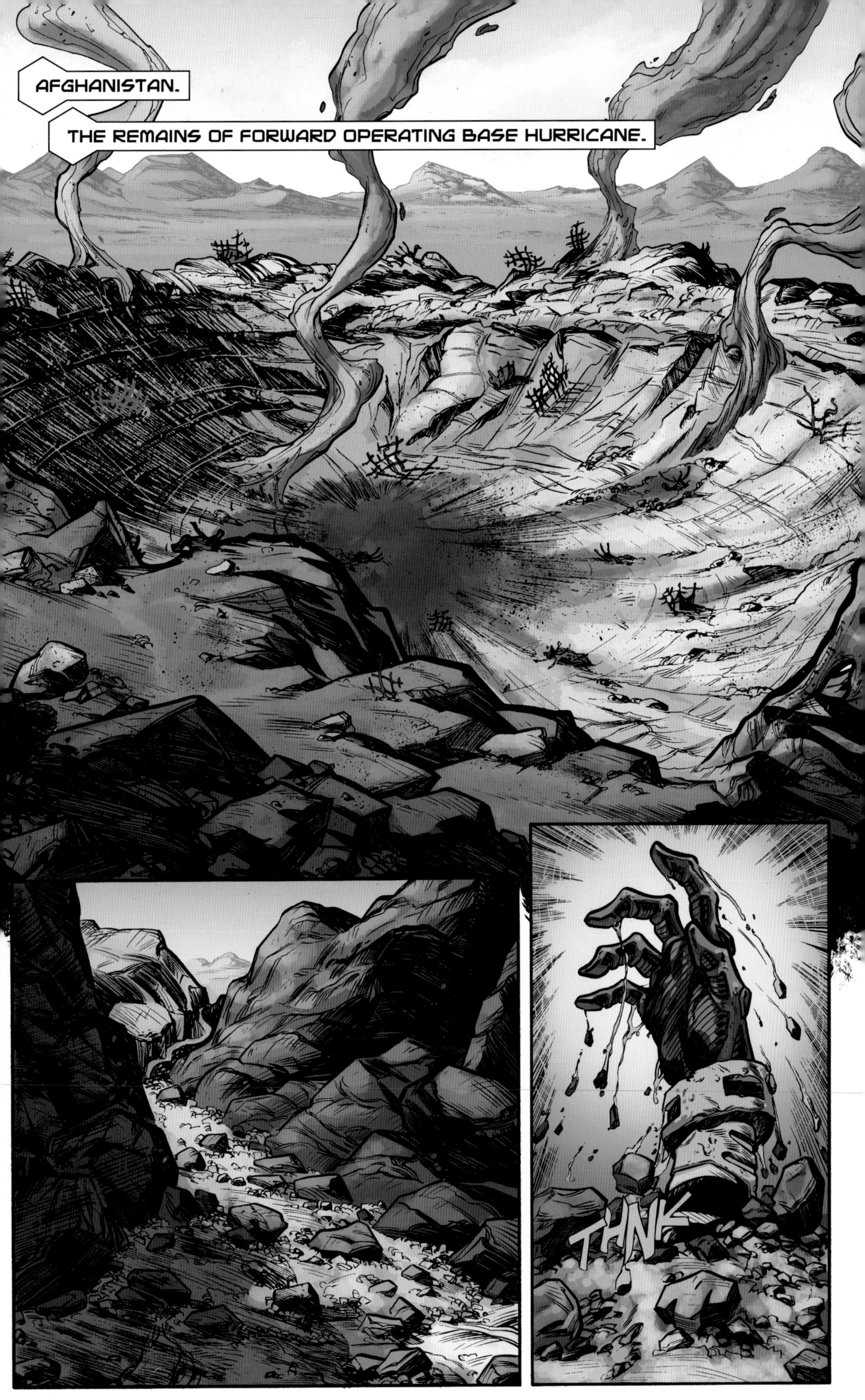
AFGHANISTAN.
THE REMAINS OF FORWARD OPERATING BASE HURRICANE.
THNK

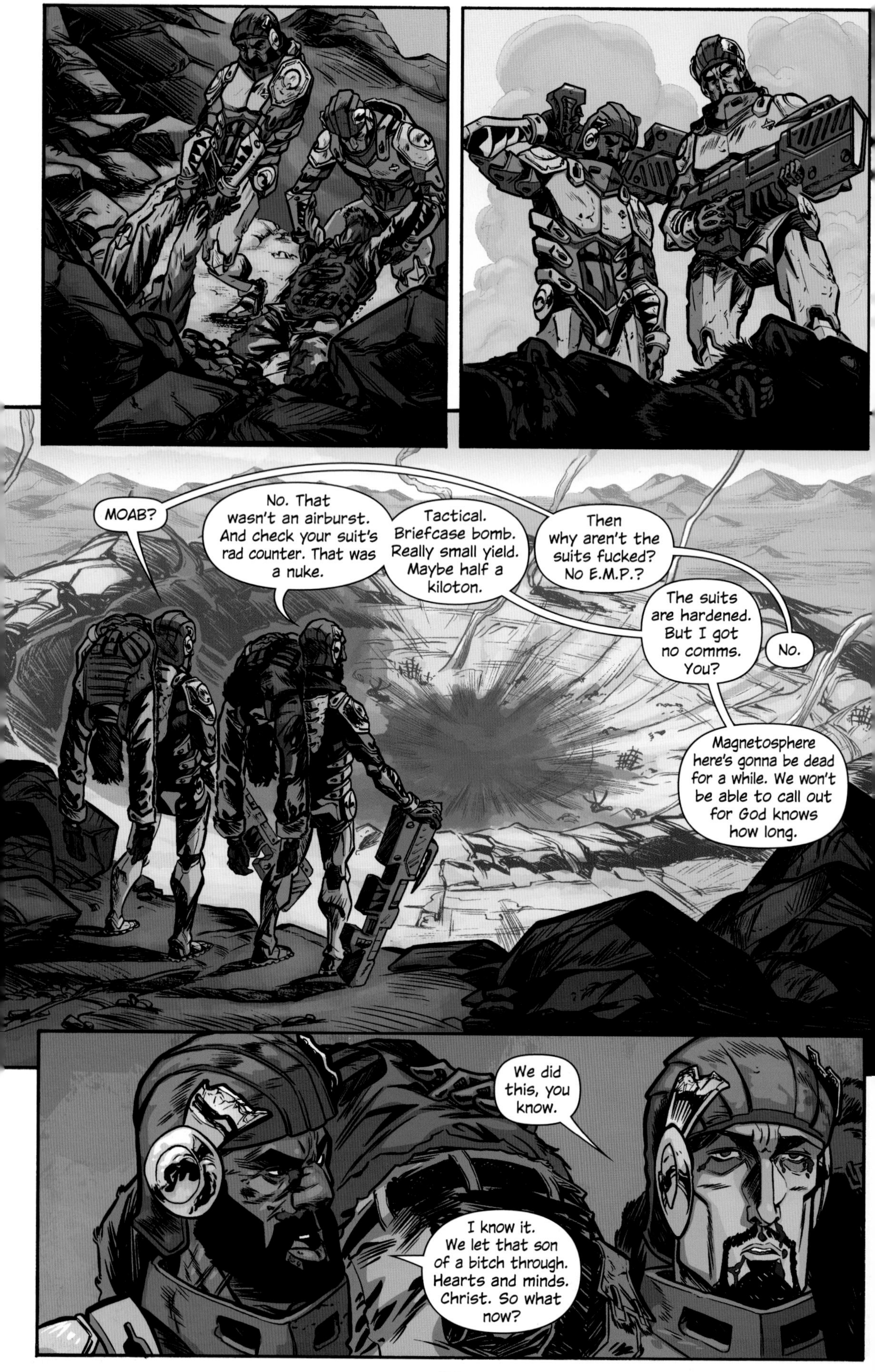
MOAB?
No. That wasn't an airburst. And check your suit's rad counter. That was a nuke.
Tactical. Briefcase bomb. Really small yield. Maybe half a kiloton.
Then why aren't the suits fucked? No E.M.P.?
The suits are hardened. But I got no comms. You?
No.
Magnetosphere here's gonna be dead for a while. We won't be able to call out for God knows how long.
We did this, you know.
I know it. We let that son of a bitch through. Hearts and minds. Christ. So what now?

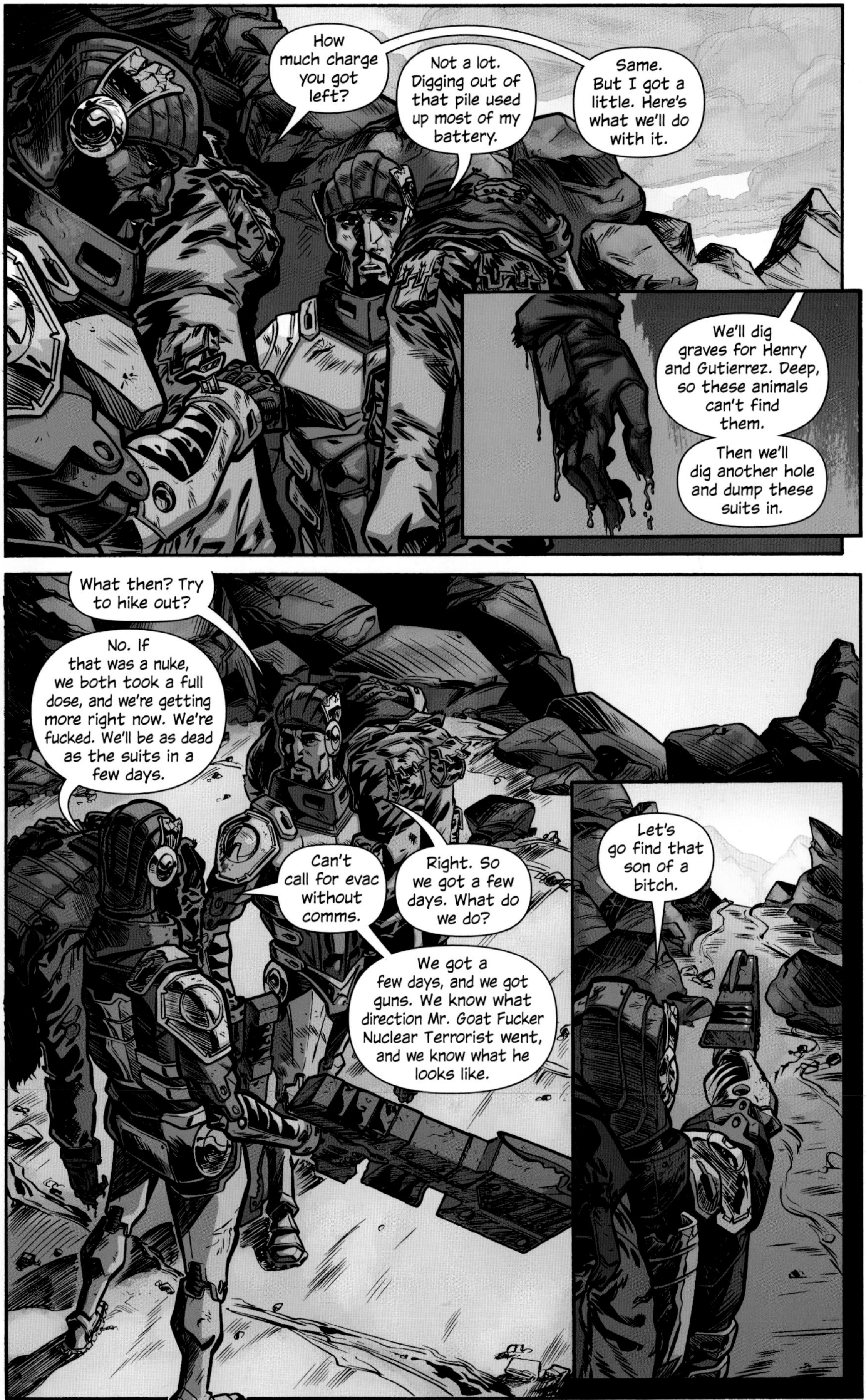
How much charge you got left?
Not a lot. Digging out of that pile used up most of my battery.
Same. But I got a little. Here's what we'll do with it.
We'll dig graves for Henry and Gutierrez. Deep, so these animals can't find them.
Then we'll dig another hole and dump these suits in.
What then? Try to hike out?
No. If that was a nuke, we both took a full dose, and we're getting more right now. We're fucked. We'll be as dead as the suits in a few days.
Can't call for evac without comms.
Right. So we got a few days. What do we do?
We got a few days, and we got guns. We know what direction Mr. Goat Fucker Nuclear Terrorist went, and we know what he looks like.
Let's go find that son of a bitch.

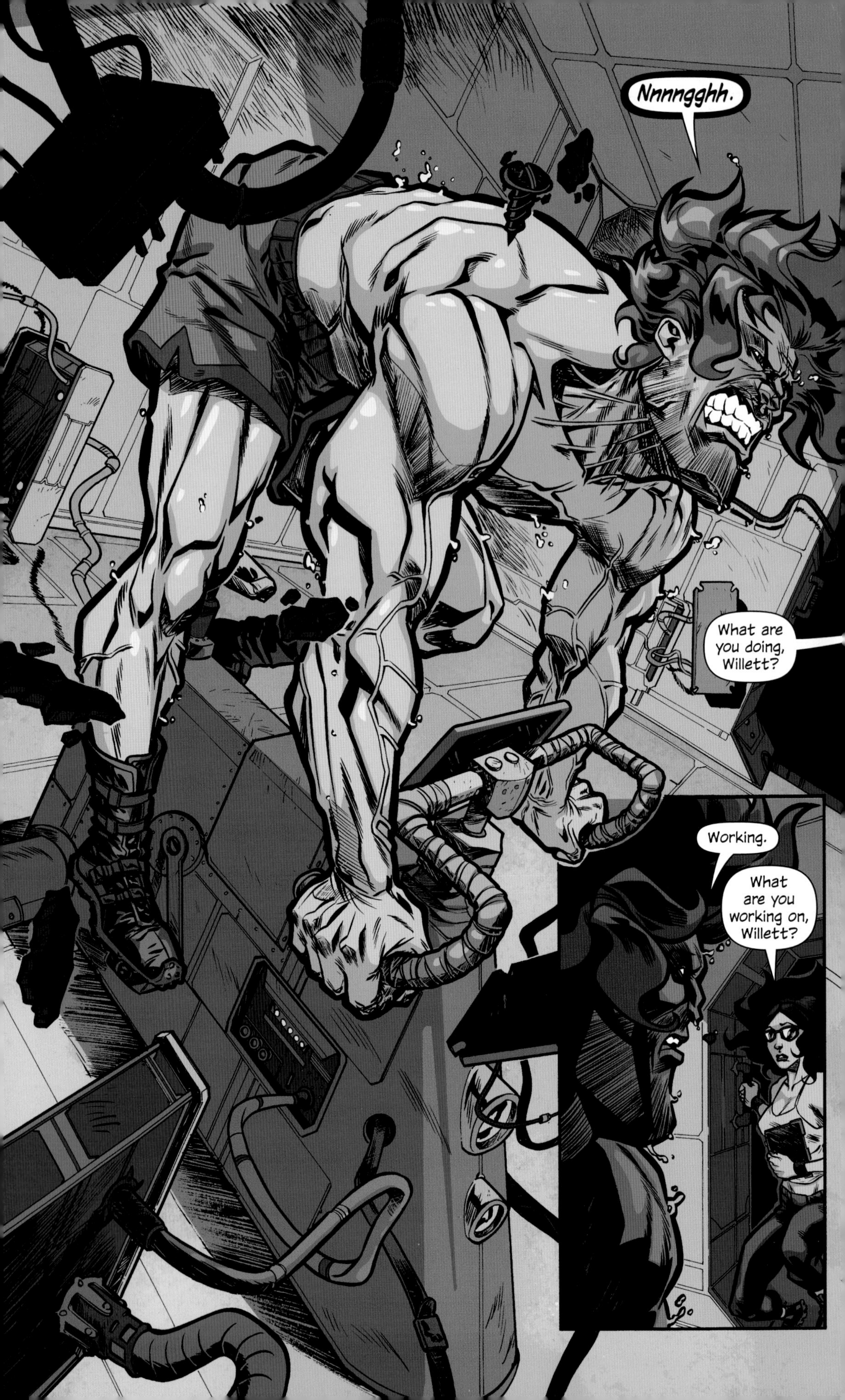
Nnnngghh.
What are you doing, Willett?
Working.
What are you working on, Willett?

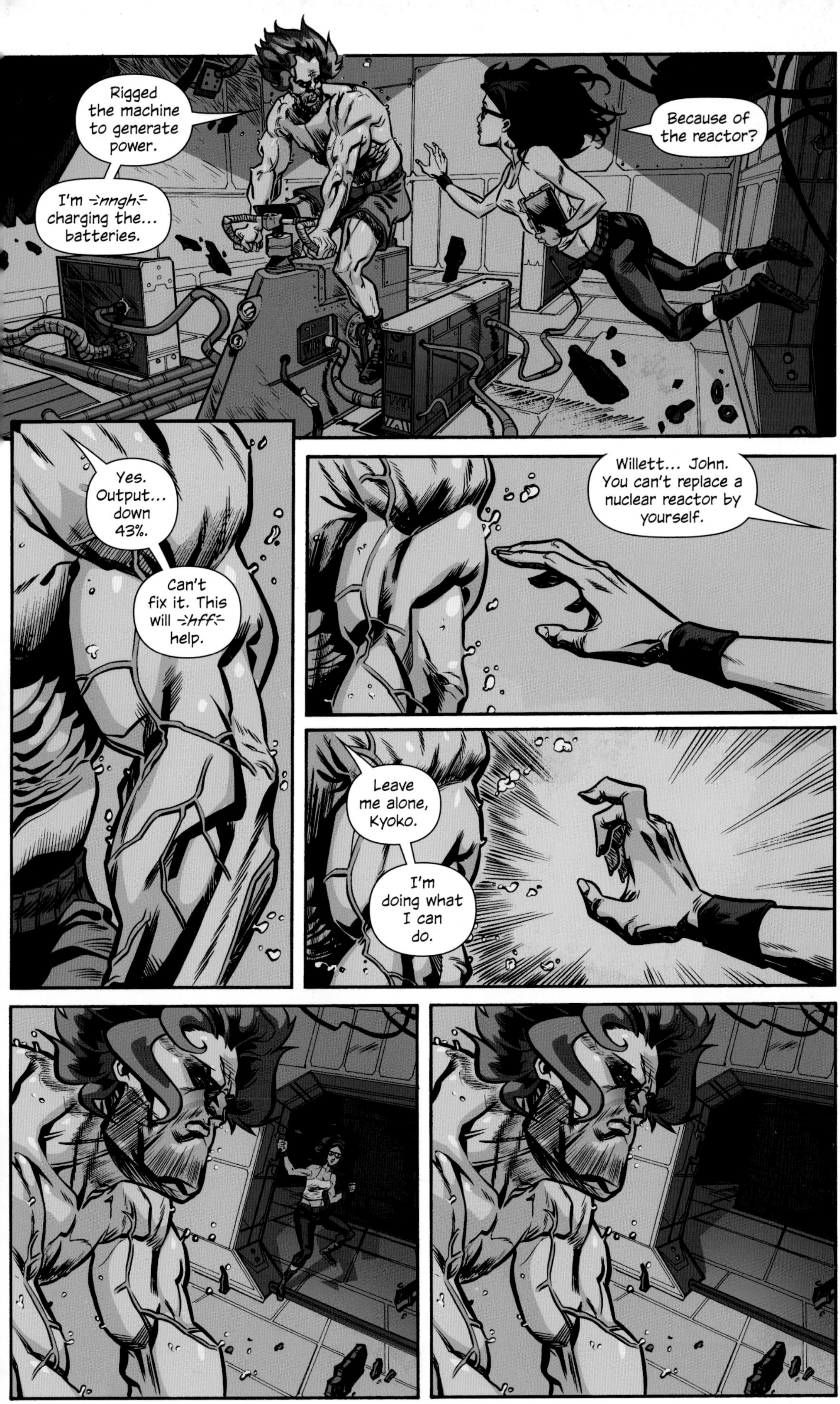
Rigged the machine to generate power.
I'm -nngh- charging the... batteries.
Because of the reactor?
Yes. Output... down 43%.
Can't fix it. This will -hff- help.
Willett... John. You can't replace a nuclear reactor by yourself.
Leave me alone, Kyoko.
I'm doing what I can do.

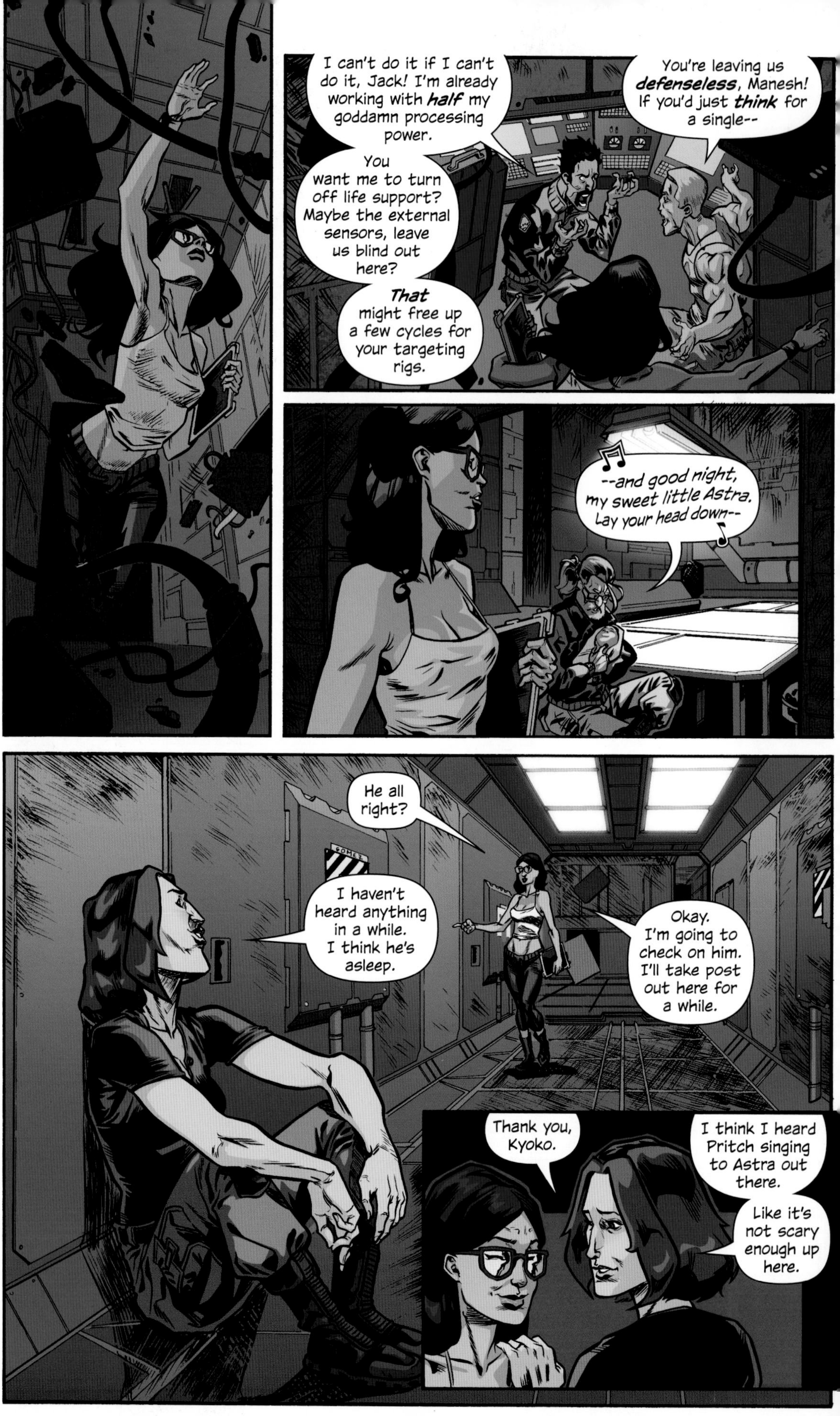
I can't do it if I can't do it, Jack! I'm already working with *half* my goddamn processing power.
You want me to turn off life support? Maybe the external sensors, leave us blind out here?
That might free up a few cycles for your targeting rigs.
You're leaving us *defenseless*, Manesh! If you'd just *think* for a single--
--and good night, my sweet little Astra. Lay your head down--
He all right?
I haven't heard anything in a while. I think he's asleep.
Okay. I'm going to check on him. I'll take post out here for a while.
GOMEZ
Thank you, Kyoko.
I think I heard Pritch singing to Astra out there.
Like it's not scary enough up here.

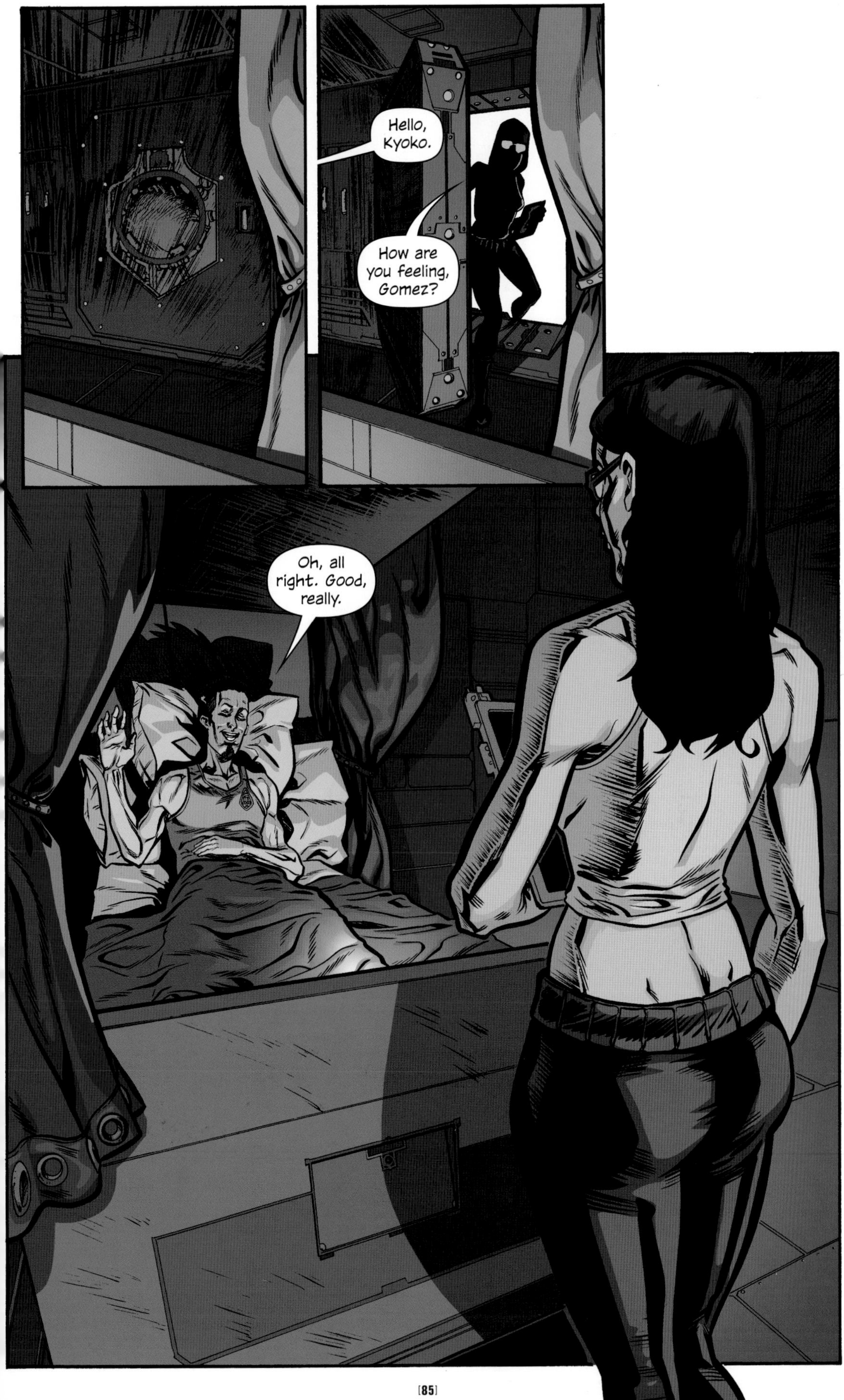
Hello, Kyoko.
How are you feeling, Gomez?
Oh, all right. Good, really.

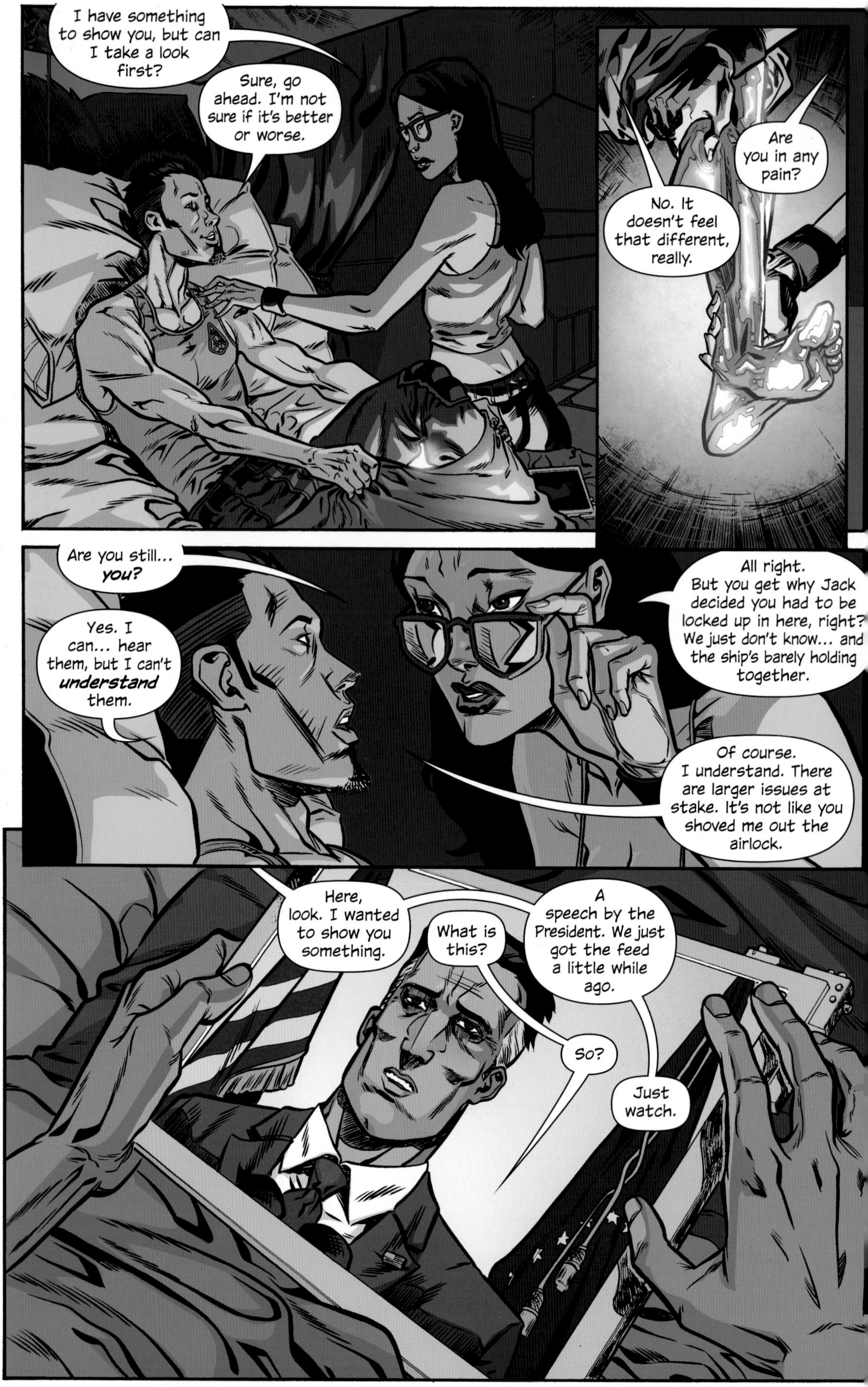

I have something to show you, but can I take a look first?
Sure, go ahead. I'm not sure if it's better or worse.
Are you in any pain?
No. It doesn't feel that different, really.
Are you still... *you?*
Yes. I can... hear them, but I can't ***understand*** them.
All right. But you get why Jack decided you had to be locked up in here, right? We just don't know... and the ship's barely holding together.
Of course. I understand. There are larger issues at stake. It's not like you shoved me out the airlock.
Here, look. I wanted to show you something.
What is this?
A speech by the President. We just got the feed a little while ago.
So?
Just watch.

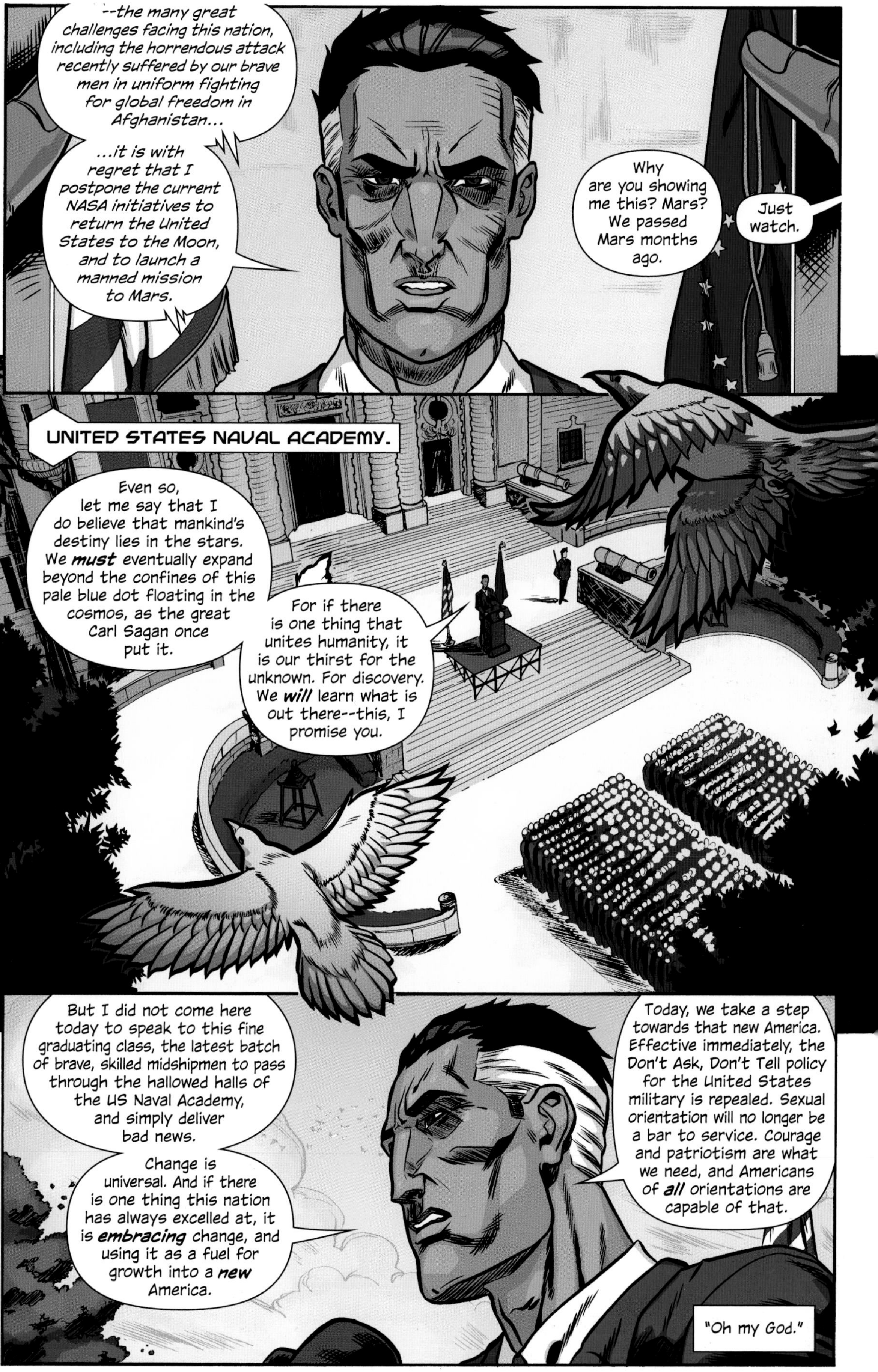
--the many great challenges facing this nation, including the horrendous attack recently suffered by our brave men in uniform fighting for global freedom in Afghanistan...
...it is with regret that I postpone the current NASA initiatives to return the United States to the Moon, and to launch a manned mission to Mars.
Why are you showing me this? Mars? We passed Mars months ago.
Just watch.
UNITED STATES NAVAL ACADEMY.
Even so, let me say that I do believe that mankind's destiny lies in the stars. We must eventually expand beyond the confines of this pale blue dot floating in the cosmos, as the great Carl Sagan once put it.
For if there is one thing that unites humanity, it is our thirst for the unknown. For discovery. We will learn what is out there--this, I promise you.
But I did not come here today to speak to this fine graduating class, the latest batch of brave, skilled midshipmen to pass through the hallowed halls of the US Naval Academy, and simply deliver bad news.
Change is universal. And if there is one thing this nation has always excelled at, it is embracing change, and using it as a fuel for growth into a new America.
Today, we take a step towards that new America. Effective immediately, the Don't Ask, Don't Tell policy for the United States military is repealed. Sexual orientation will no longer be a bar to service. Courage and patriotism are what we need, and Americans of all orientations are capable of that.
"Oh my God."

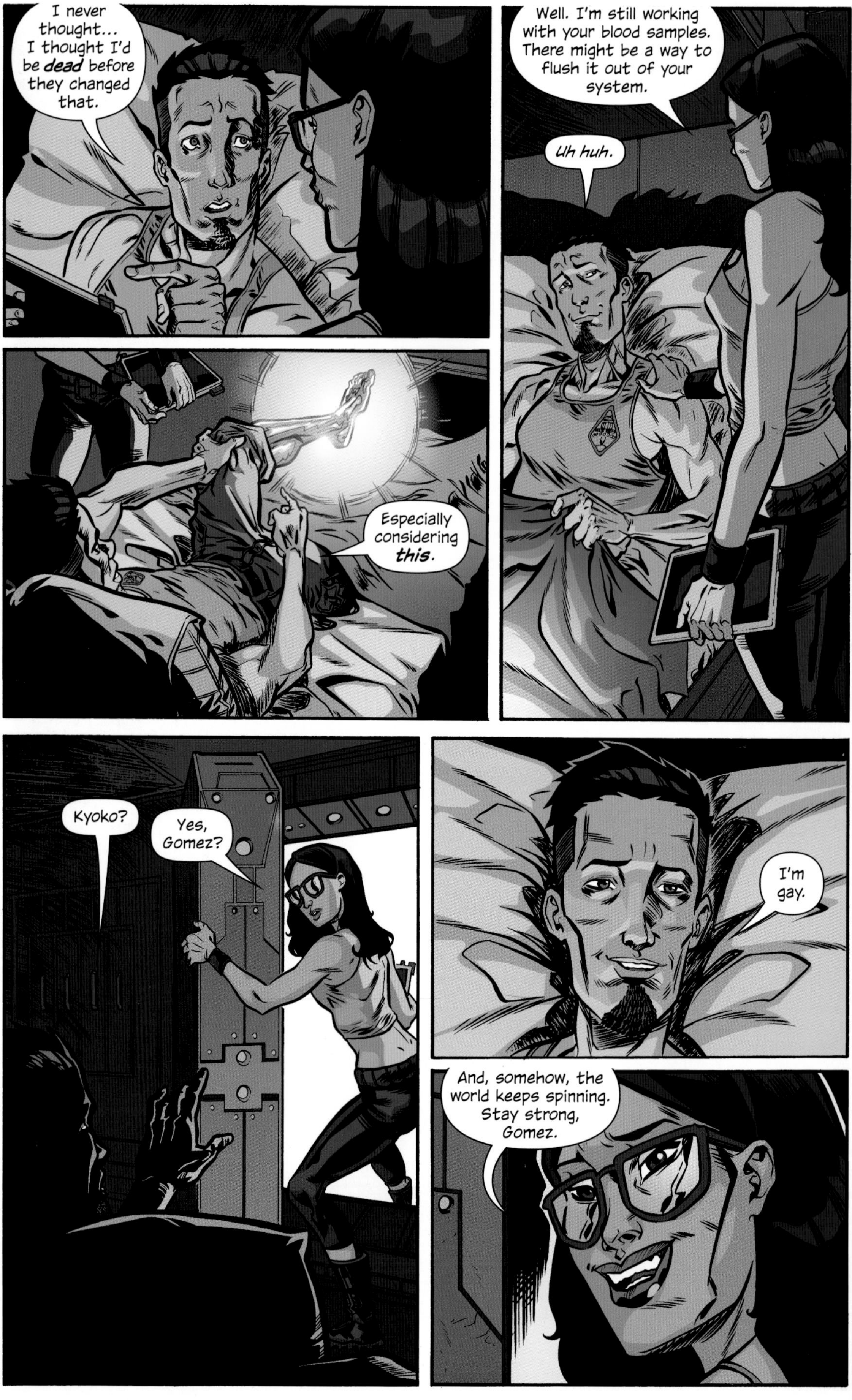
I never thought... I thought I'd be **dead** before they changed that.
Well. I'm still working with your blood samples. There might be a way to flush it out of your system.
Uh huh.
Especially considering ***this***.
Kyoko?
Yes, Gomez?
I'm gay.
And, somehow, the world keeps spinning. Stay strong, Gomez.

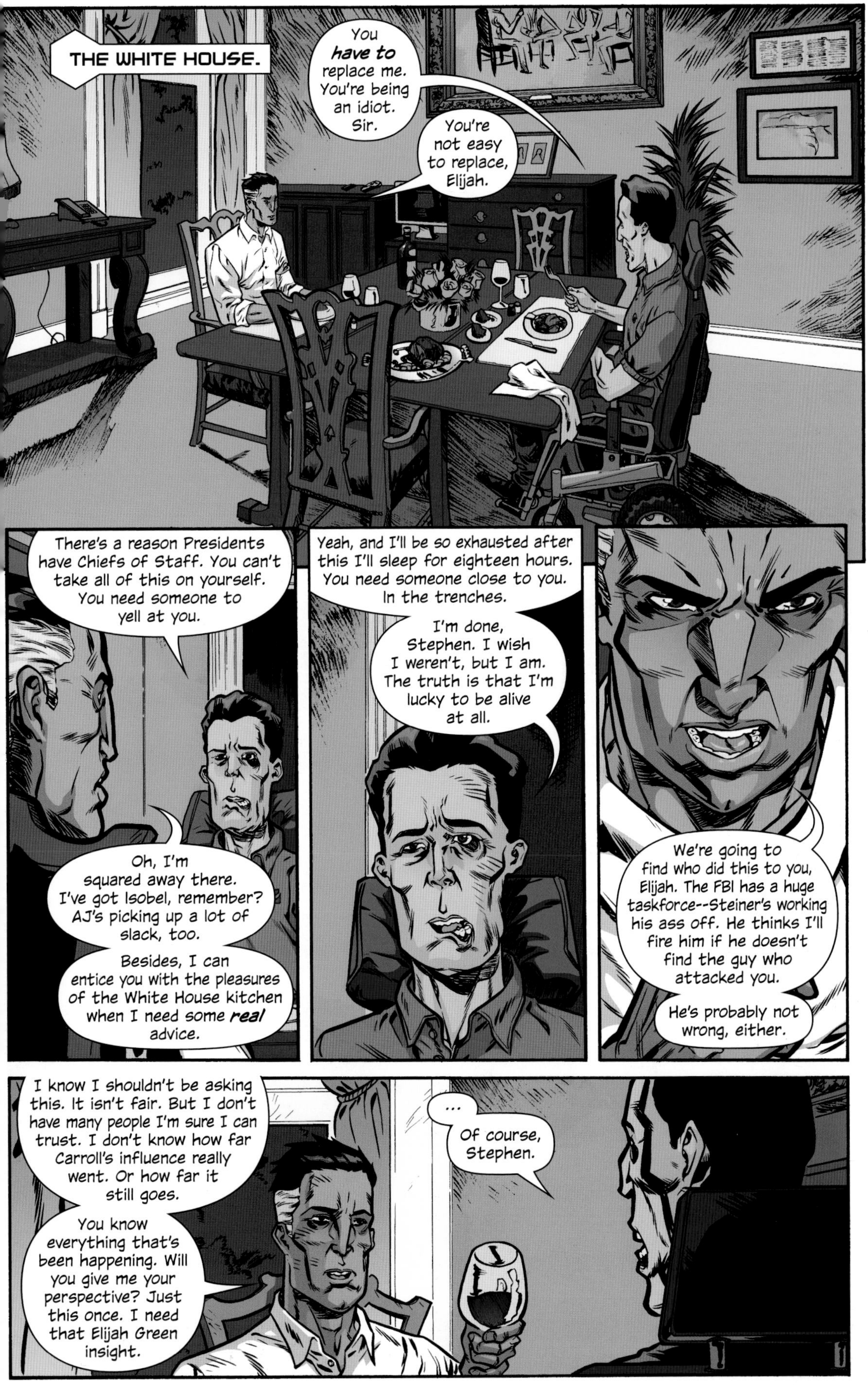
THE WHITE HOUSE.
You *have to* replace me. You're being an idiot. Sir.
You're not easy to replace, Elijah.
There's a reason Presidents have Chiefs of Staff. You can't take all of this on yourself. You need someone to yell at you.
Oh, I'm squared away there. I've got Isobel, remember? AJ's picking up a lot of slack, too.
Besides, I can entice you with the pleasures of the White House kitchen when I need some *real* advice.
Yeah, and I'll be so exhausted after this I'll sleep for eighteen hours. You need someone close to you. In the trenches.
I'm done, Stephen. I wish I weren't, but I am. The truth is that I'm lucky to be alive at all.
We're going to find who did this to you, Elijah. The FBI has a huge taskforce--Steiner's working his ass off. He thinks I'll fire him if he doesn't find the guy who attacked you.
He's probably not wrong, either.
I know I shouldn't be asking this. It isn't fair. But I don't have many people I'm sure I can trust. I don't know how far Carroll's influence really went. Or how far it still goes.
You know everything that's been happening. Will you give me your perspective? Just this once. I need that Elijah Green insight.
...
Of course, Stephen.

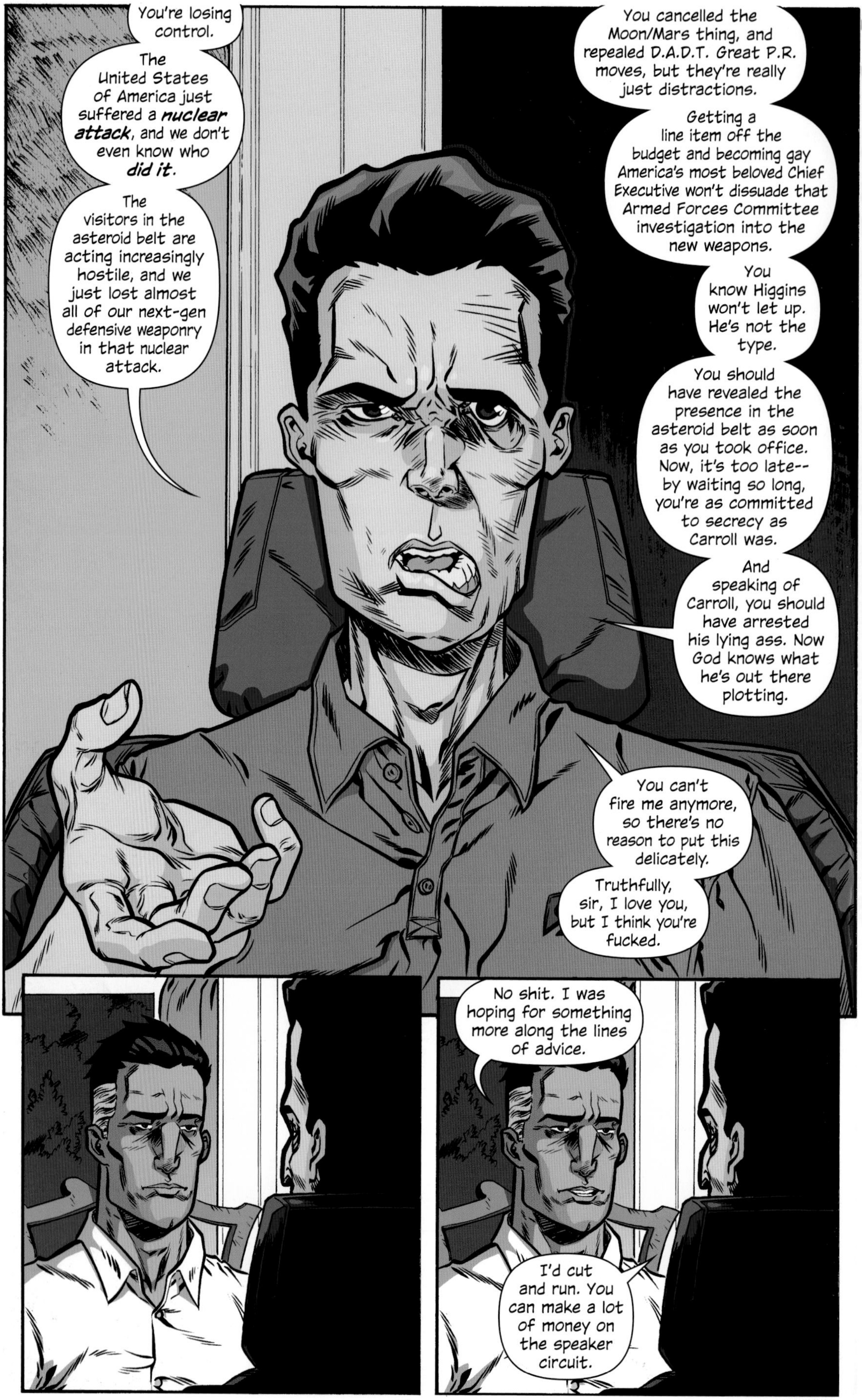

You're losing control.
The United States of America just suffered a ***nuclear attack***, and we don't even know who ***did it***.
The visitors in the asteroid belt are acting increasingly hostile, and we just lost almost all of our next-gen defensive weaponry in that nuclear attack.
You cancelled the Moon/Mars thing, and repealed D.A.D.T. Great P.R. moves, but they're really just distractions.
Getting a line item off the budget and becoming gay America's most beloved Chief Executive won't dissuade that Armed Forces Committee investigation into the new weapons.
You know Higgins won't let up. He's not the type.
You should have revealed the presence in the asteroid belt as soon as you took office. Now, it's too late-- by waiting so long, you're as committed to secrecy as Carroll was.
And speaking of Carroll, you should have arrested his lying ass. Now God knows what he's out there plotting.
You can't fire me anymore, so there's no reason to put this delicately.
Truthfully, sir, I love you, but I think you're fucked.
No shit. I was hoping for something more along the lines of advice.
I'd cut and run. You can make a lot of money on the speaker circuit.

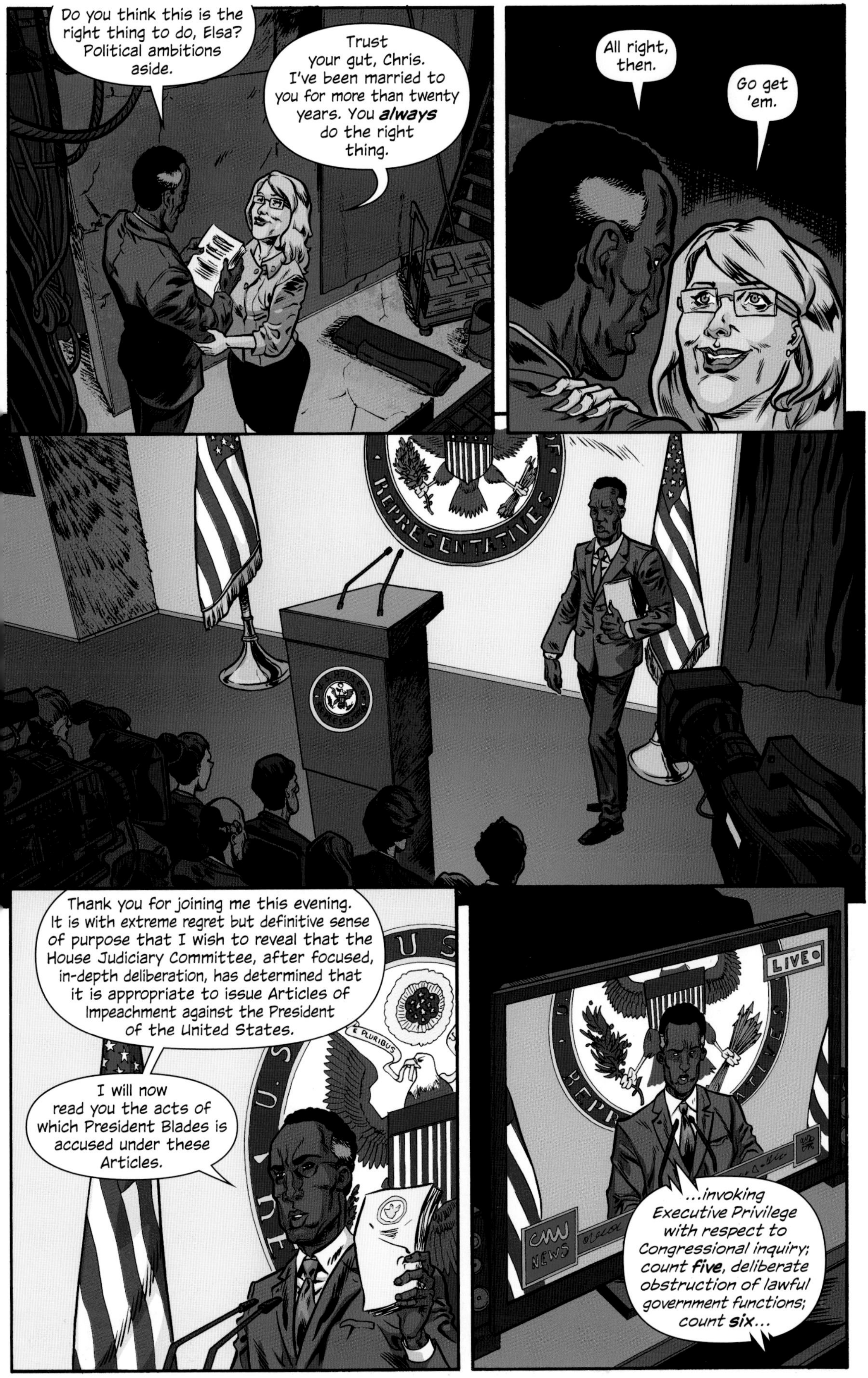
Do you think this is the right thing to do, Elsa? Political ambitions aside.
Trust your gut, Chris. I've been married to you for more than twenty years. You ***always*** do the right thing.
All right, then.
Go get 'em.
LIVE
Thank you for joining me this evening. It is with extreme regret but definitive sense of purpose that I wish to reveal that the House Judiciary Committee, after focused, in-depth deliberation, has determined that it is appropriate to issue Articles of Impeachment against the President of the United States.
I will now read you the acts of which President Blades is accused under these Articles.
CNN NEWS
...invoking Executive Privilege with respect to Congressional inquiry; count ***five****, deliberate obstruction of lawful government functions; count* ***six****...*

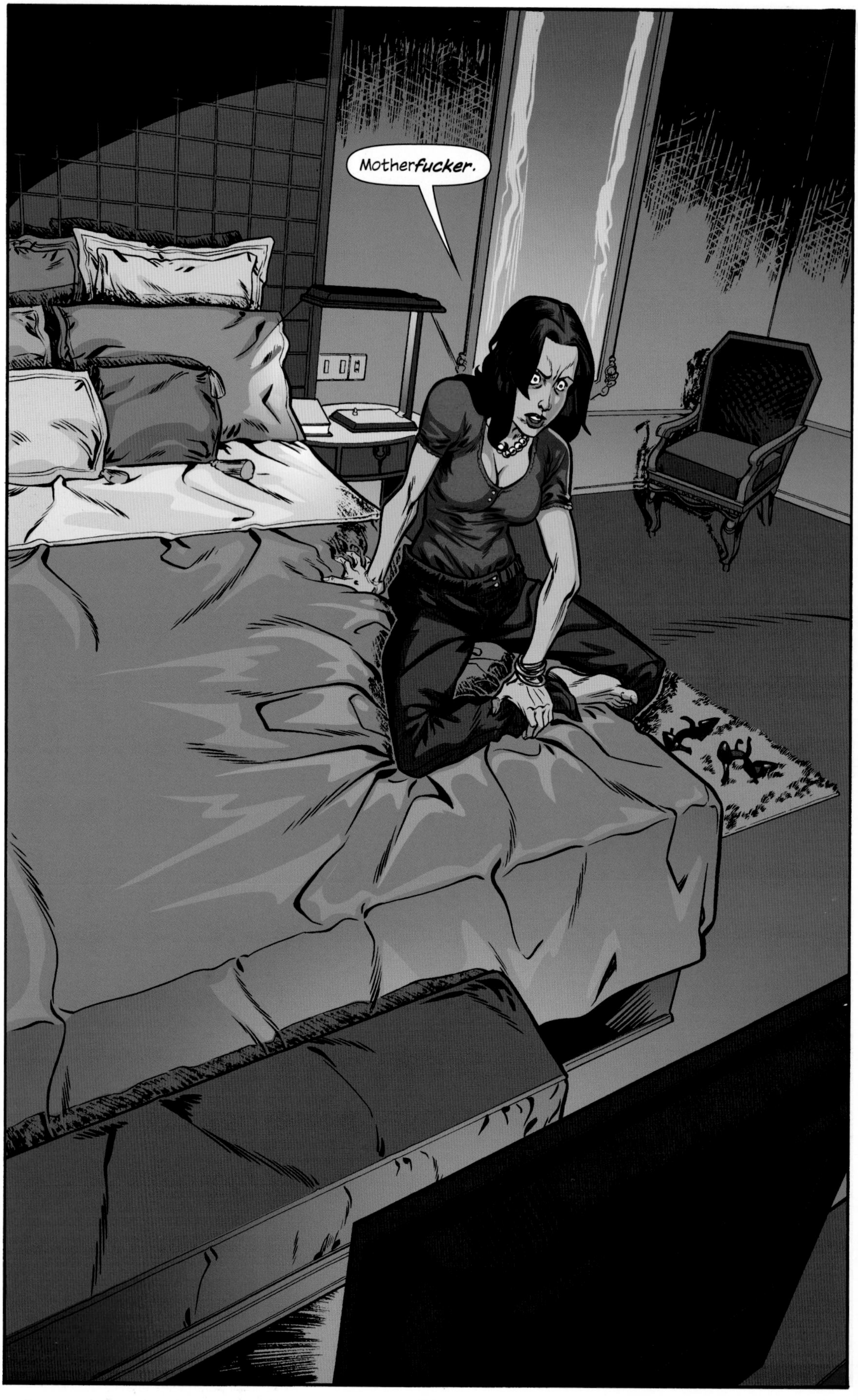
Mother**fucker**.

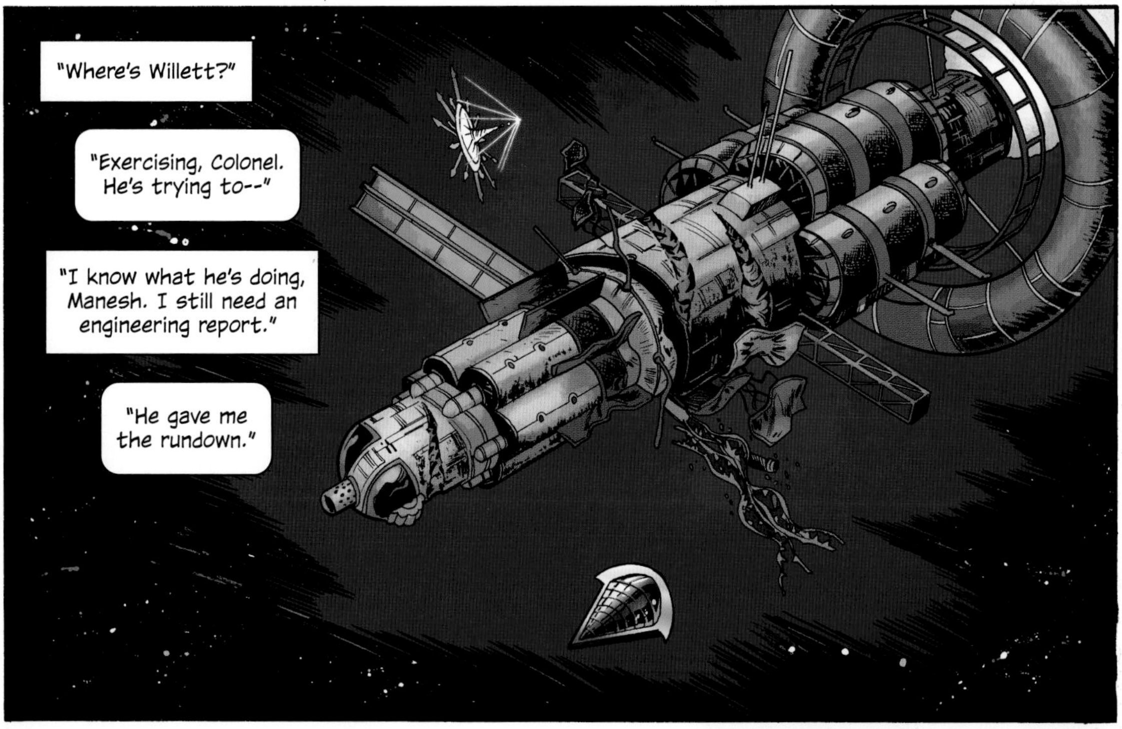

"Where's Willett?"
"Exercising, Colonel. He's trying to--"
"I know what he's doing, Manesh. I still need an engineering report."
"He gave me the rundown."

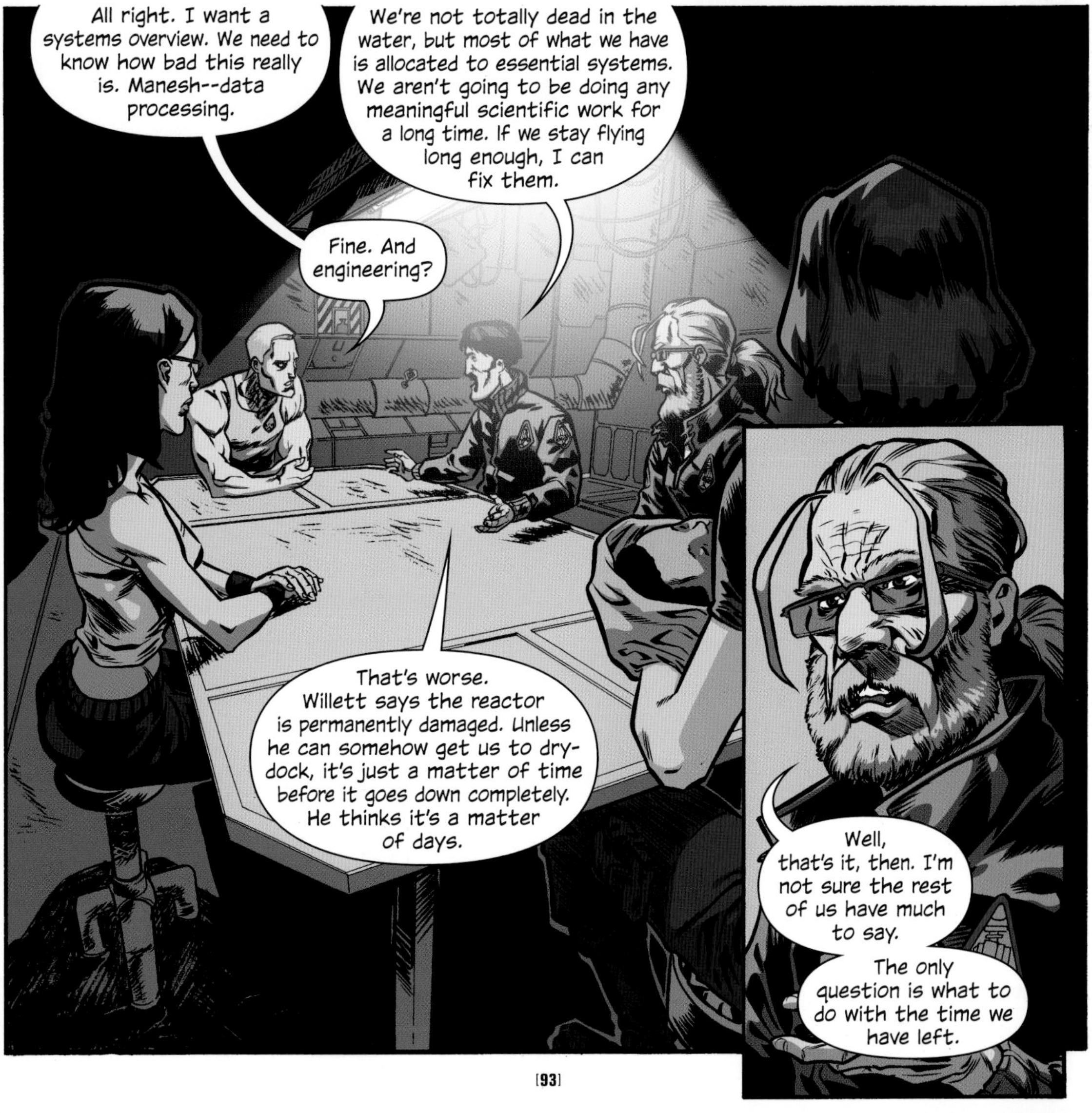

All right. I want a systems overview. We need to know how bad this really is. Manesh--data processing.
We're not totally dead in the water, but most of what we have is allocated to essential systems. We aren't going to be doing any meaningful scientific work for a long time. If we stay flying long enough, I can fix them.
Fine. And engineering?
That's worse. Willett says the reactor is permanently damaged. Unless he can somehow get us to dry-dock, it's just a matter of time before it goes down completely. He thinks it's a matter of days.
Well, that's it, then. I'm not sure the rest of us have much to say.
The only question is what to do with the time we have left.

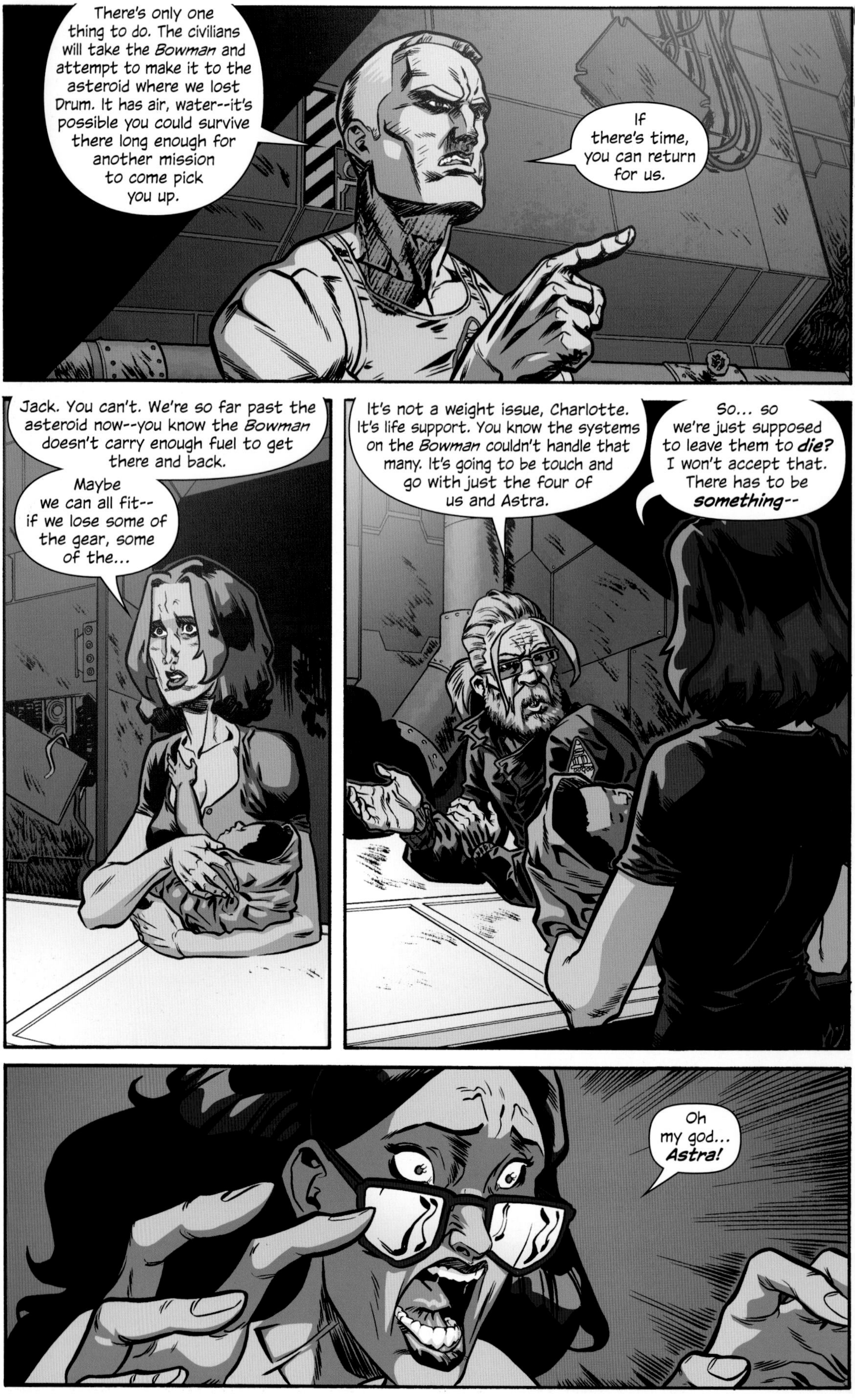
There's only one thing to do. The civilians will take the *Bowman* and attempt to make it to the asteroid where we lost Drum. It has air, water--it's possible you could survive there long enough for another mission to come pick you up.
If there's time, you can return for us.
Jack. You can't. We're so far past the asteroid now--you know the *Bowman* doesn't carry enough fuel to get there and back.
Maybe we can all fit--if we lose some of the gear, some of the...
It's not a weight issue, Charlotte. It's life support. You know the systems on the *Bowman* couldn't handle that many. It's going to be touch and go with just the four of us and Astra.
So... so we're just supposed to leave them to ***die?*** I won't accept that. There has to be ***something***--
Oh my god... ***Astra!***

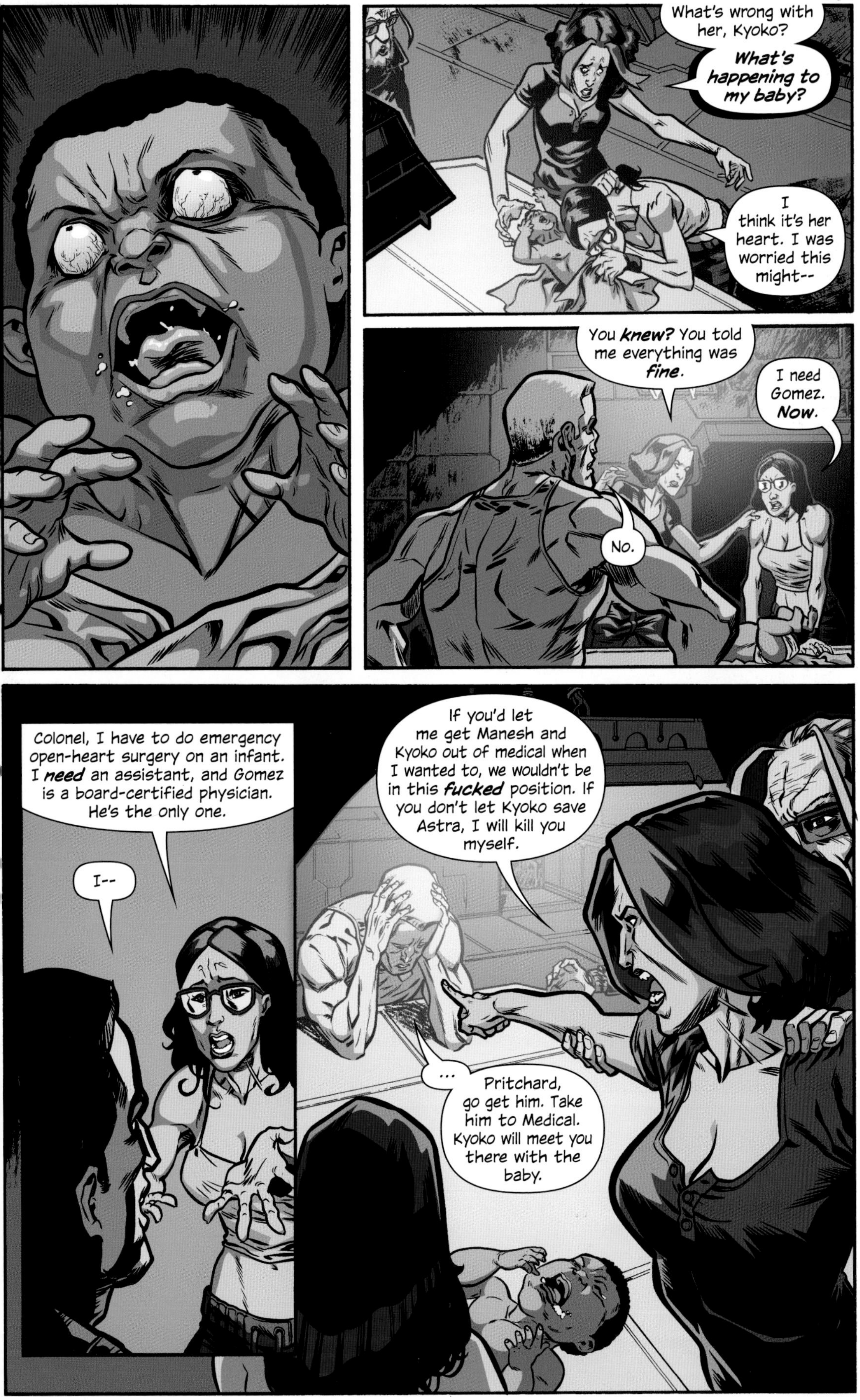
What's wrong with her, Kyoko?
What's happening to my baby?
I think it's her heart. I was worried this might--
You knew? You told me everything was fine.
I need Gomez. Now.
No.
Colonel, I have to do emergency open-heart surgery on an infant. I need an assistant, and Gomez is a board-certified physician. He's the only one.
I--
If you'd let me get Manesh and Kyoko out of medical when I wanted to, we wouldn't be in this fucked position. If you don't let Kyoko save Astra, I will kill you myself.
...
Pritchard, go get him. Take him to Medical. Kyoko will meet you there with the baby.

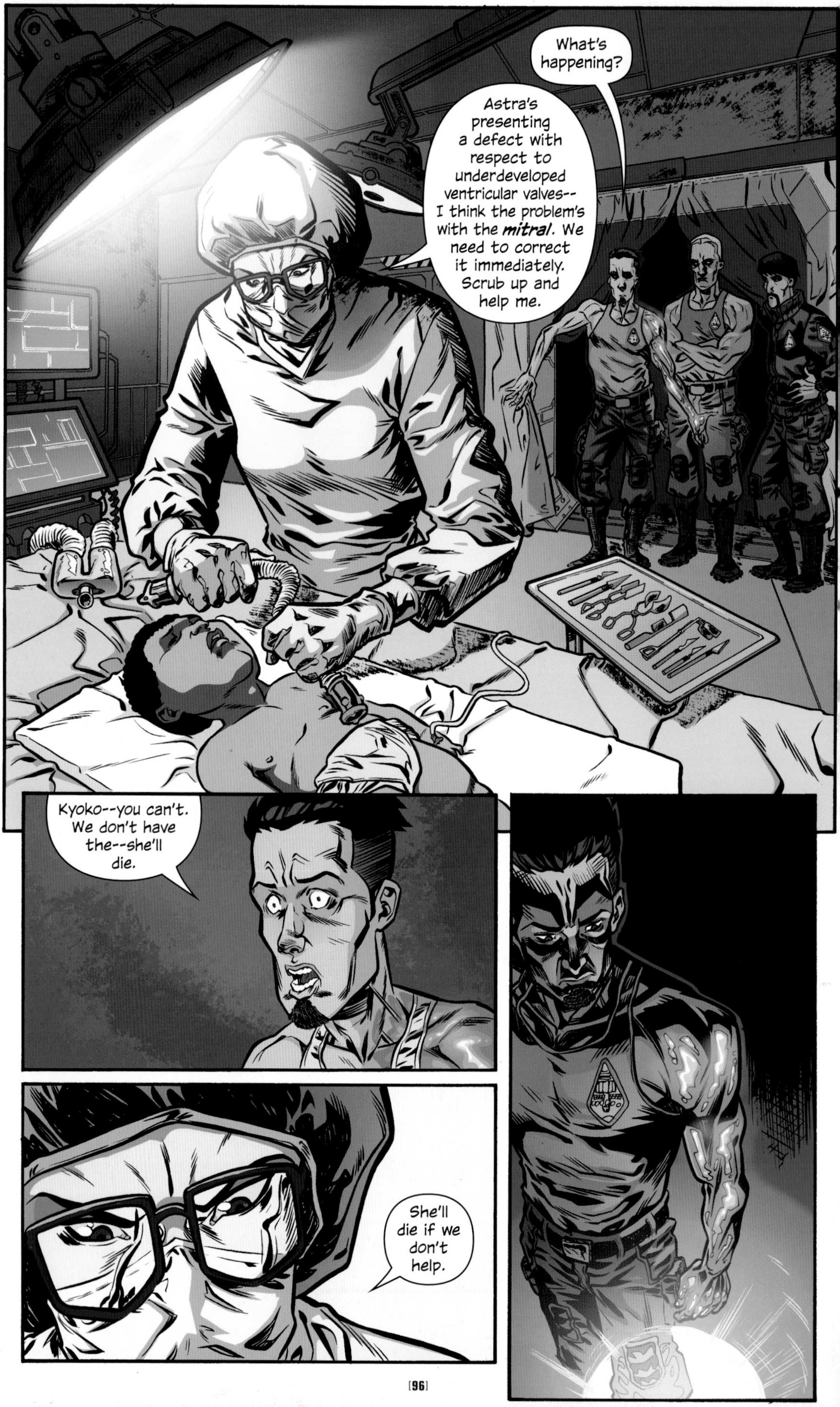
What's happening?
Astra's presenting a defect with respect to underdeveloped ventricular valves--I think the problem's with the *mitral*. We need to correct it immediately. Scrub up and help me.
Kyoko--you can't. We don't have the--she'll die.
She'll die if we don't help.

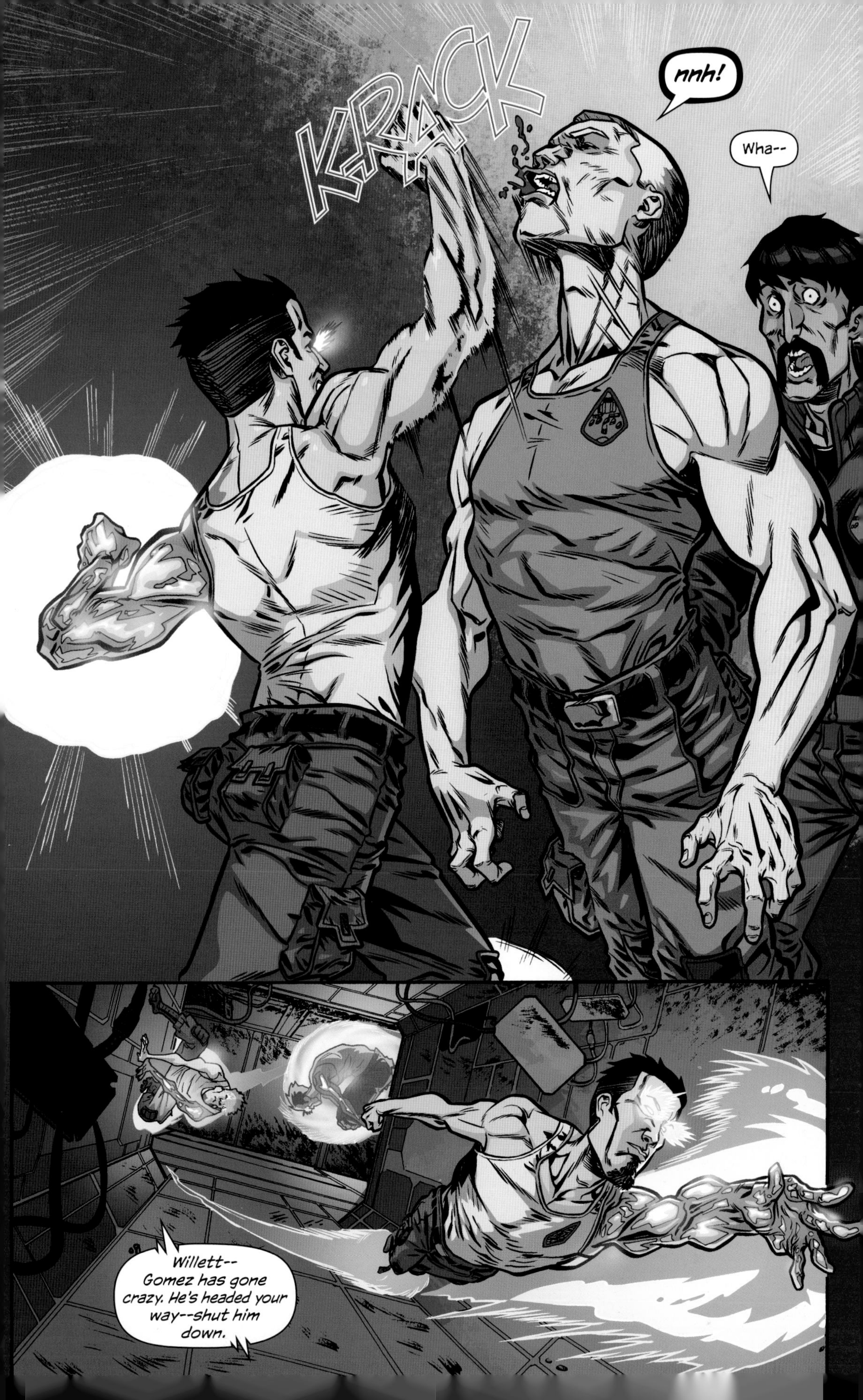
KRACK
nnh!
Wha--
Willett-- Gomez has gone crazy. He's headed your way--shut him down.

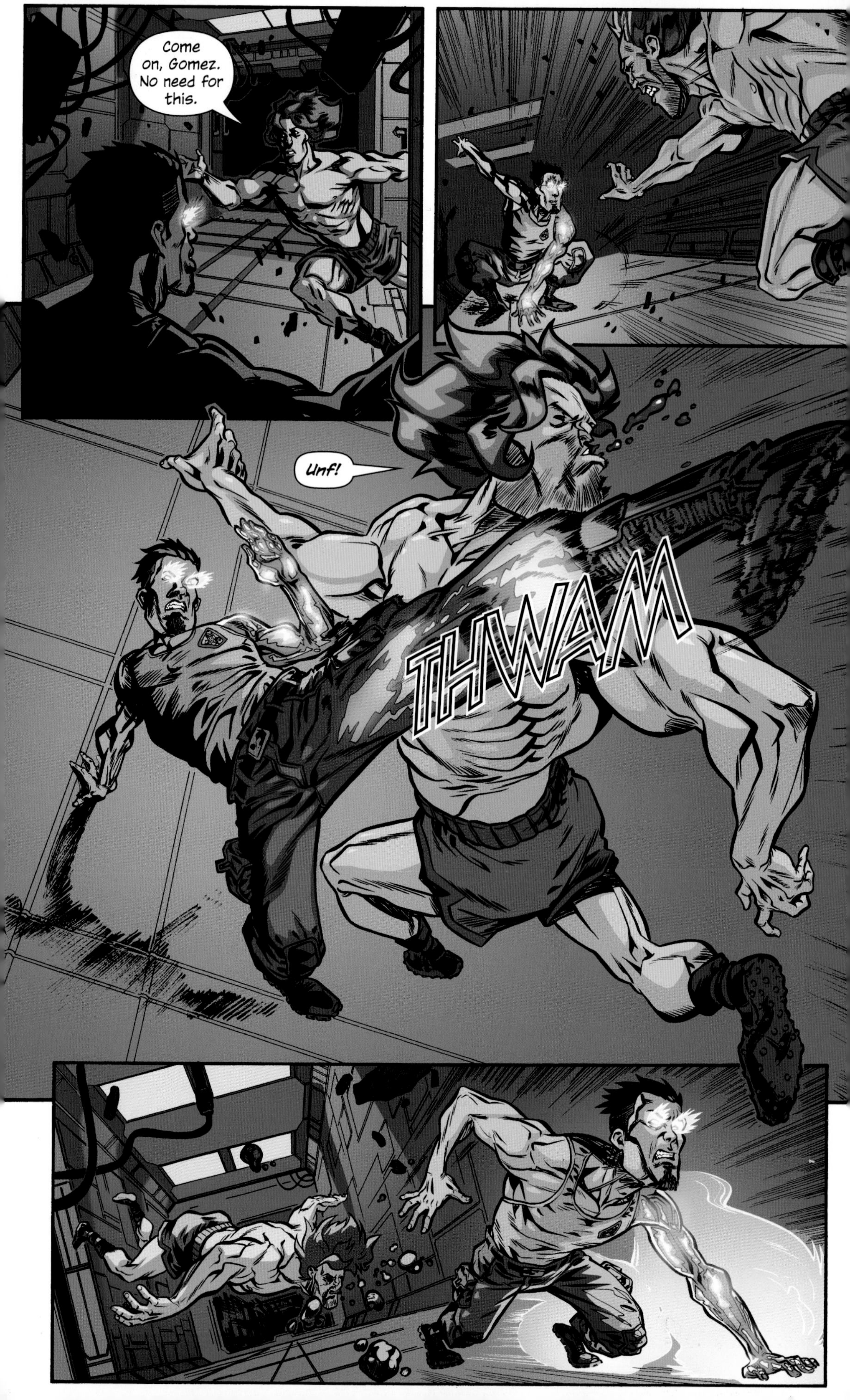

Come on, Gomez. No need for this.
Unf!
THWAM

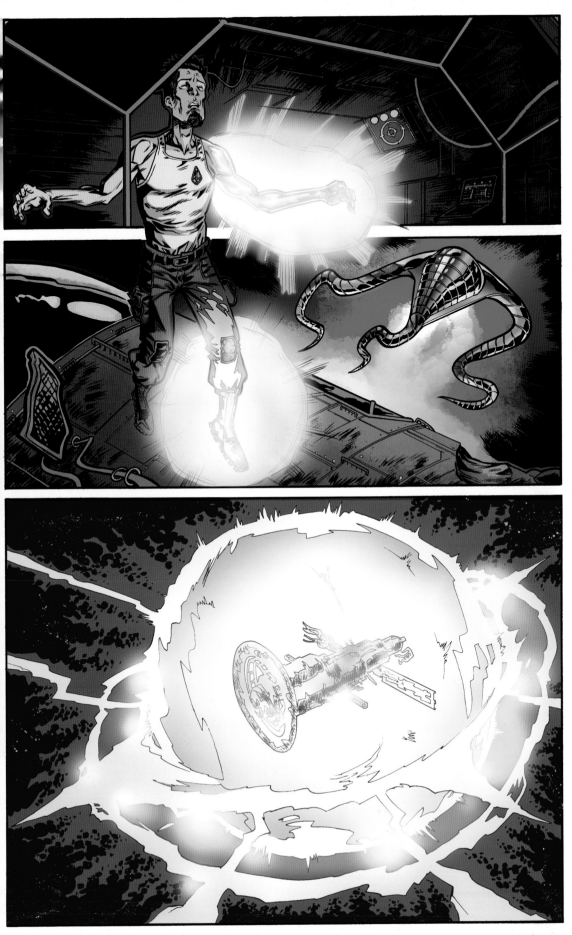

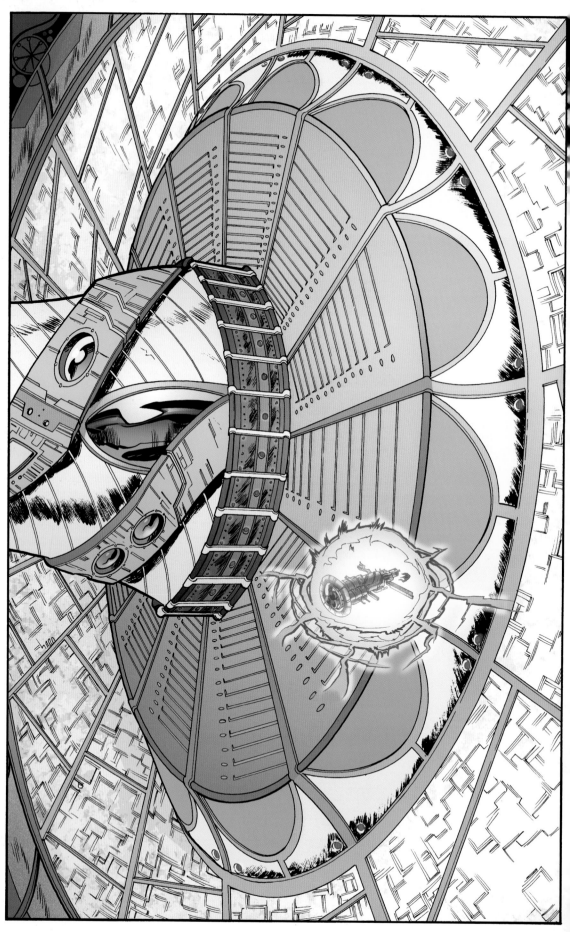

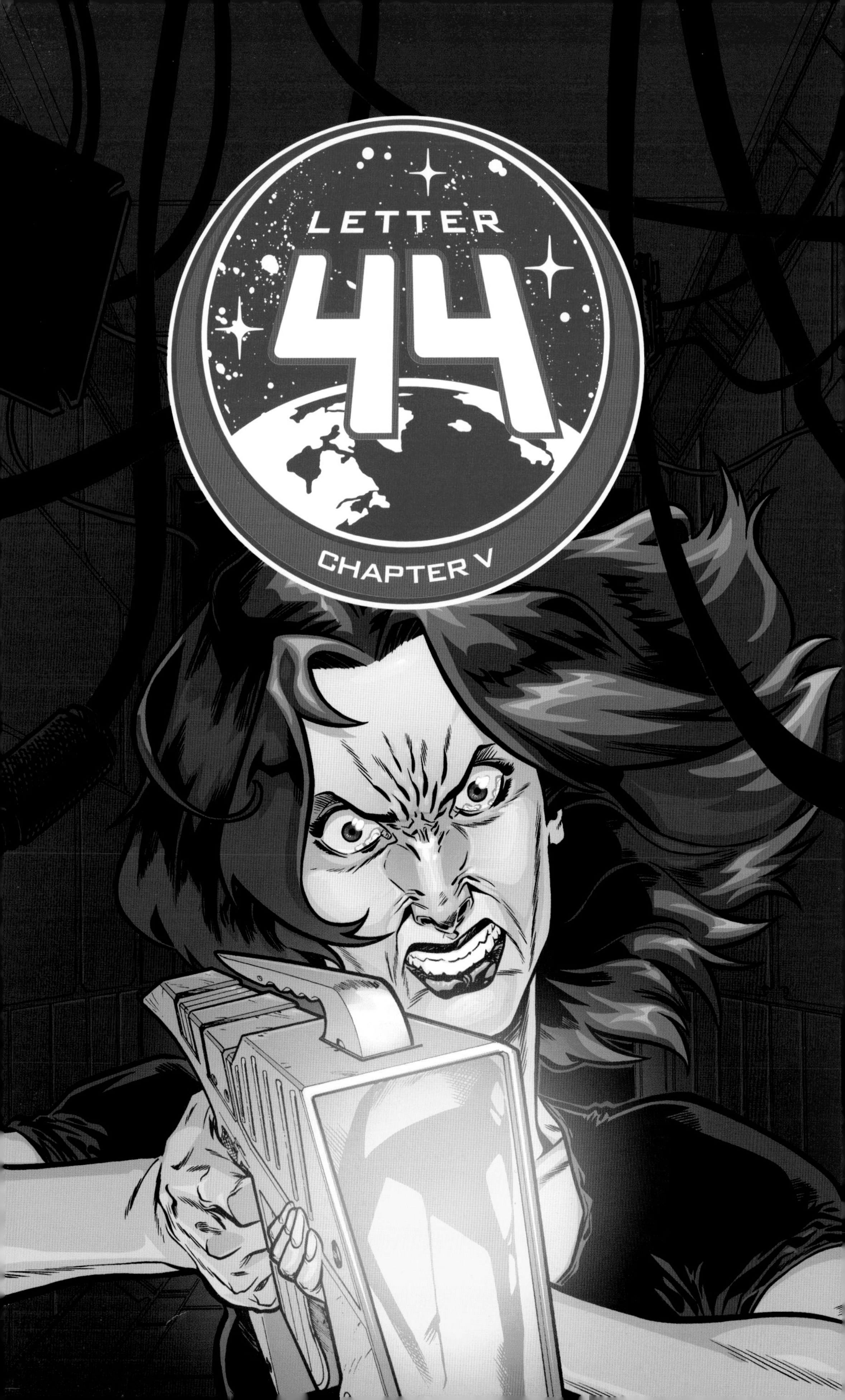
LETTER
44
CHAPTER V

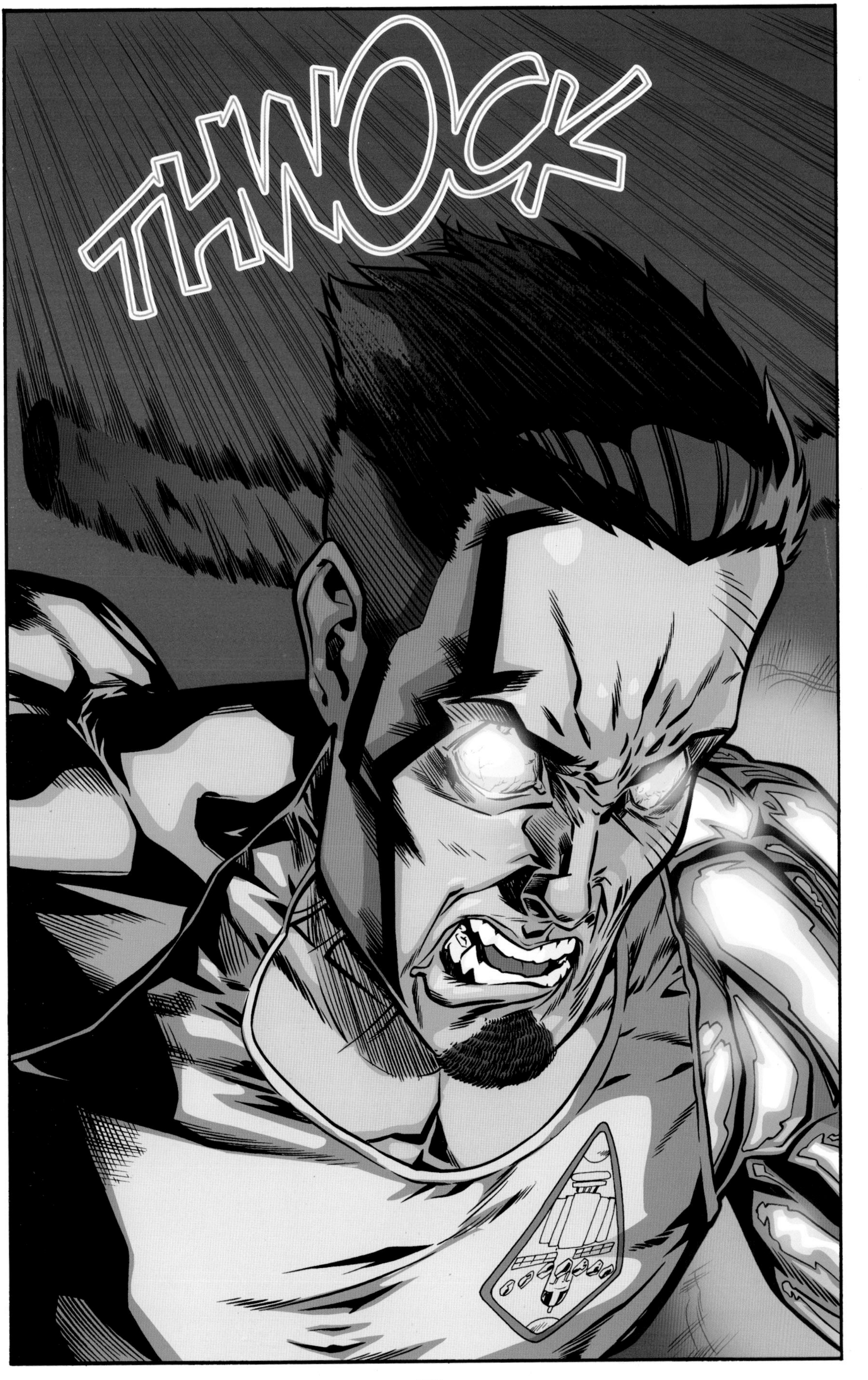
THWOCK

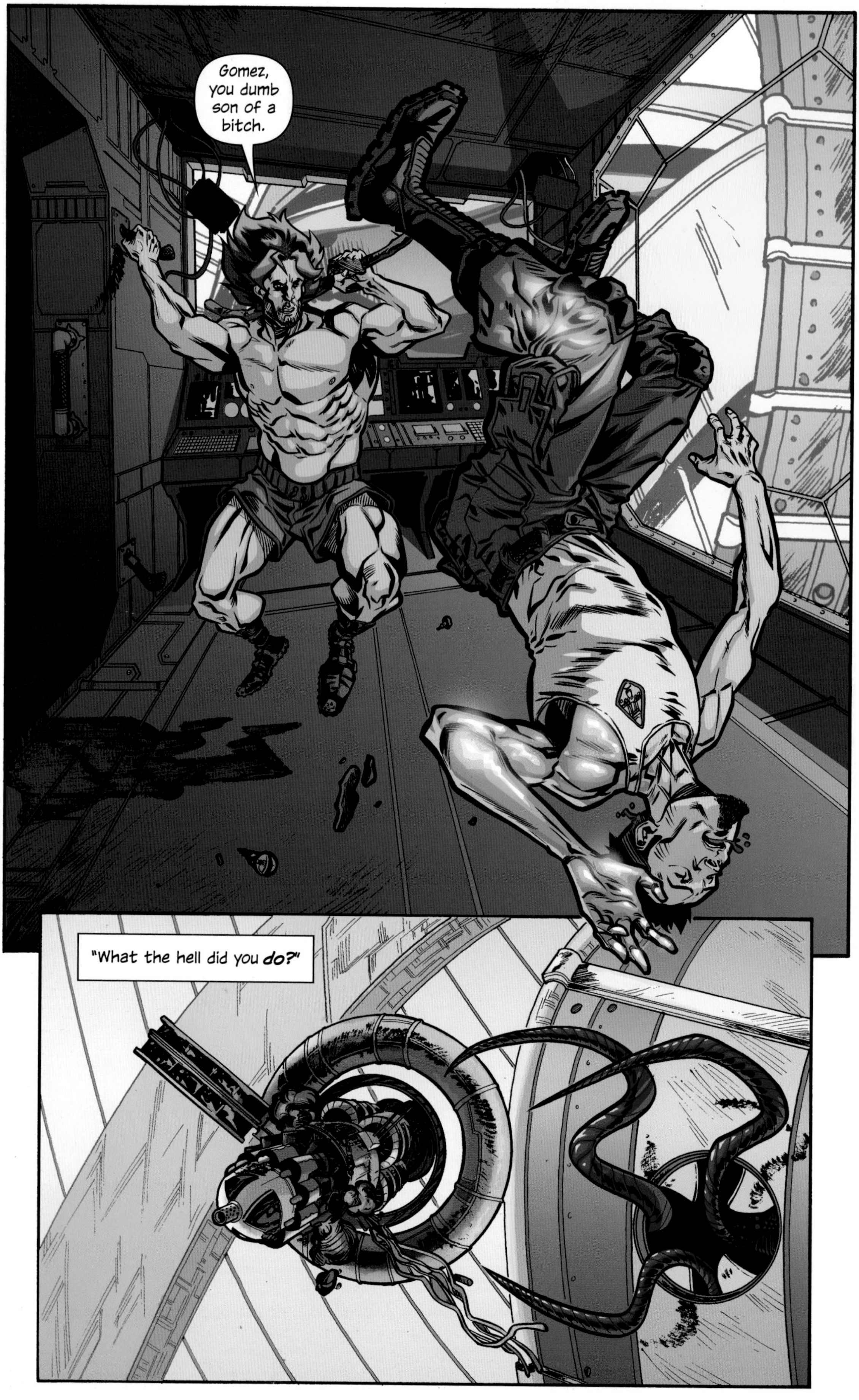
Gomez, you dumb son of a bitch.
"What the hell did you ***do?***"

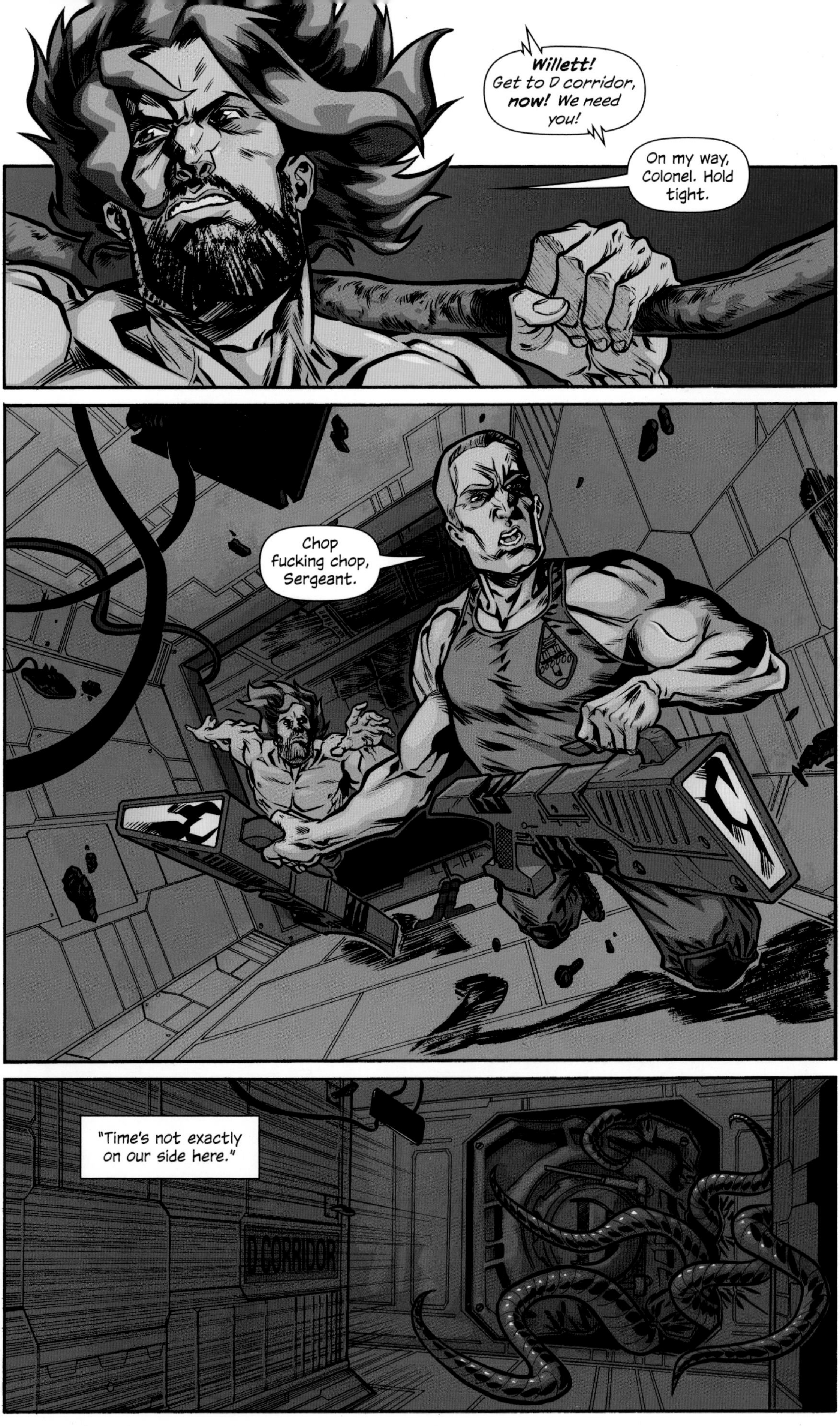

Willett! Get to D corridor, now! We need you!
On my way, Colonel. Hold tight.
Chop fucking chop, Sergeant.
"Time's not exactly on our side here."
D CORRIDOR

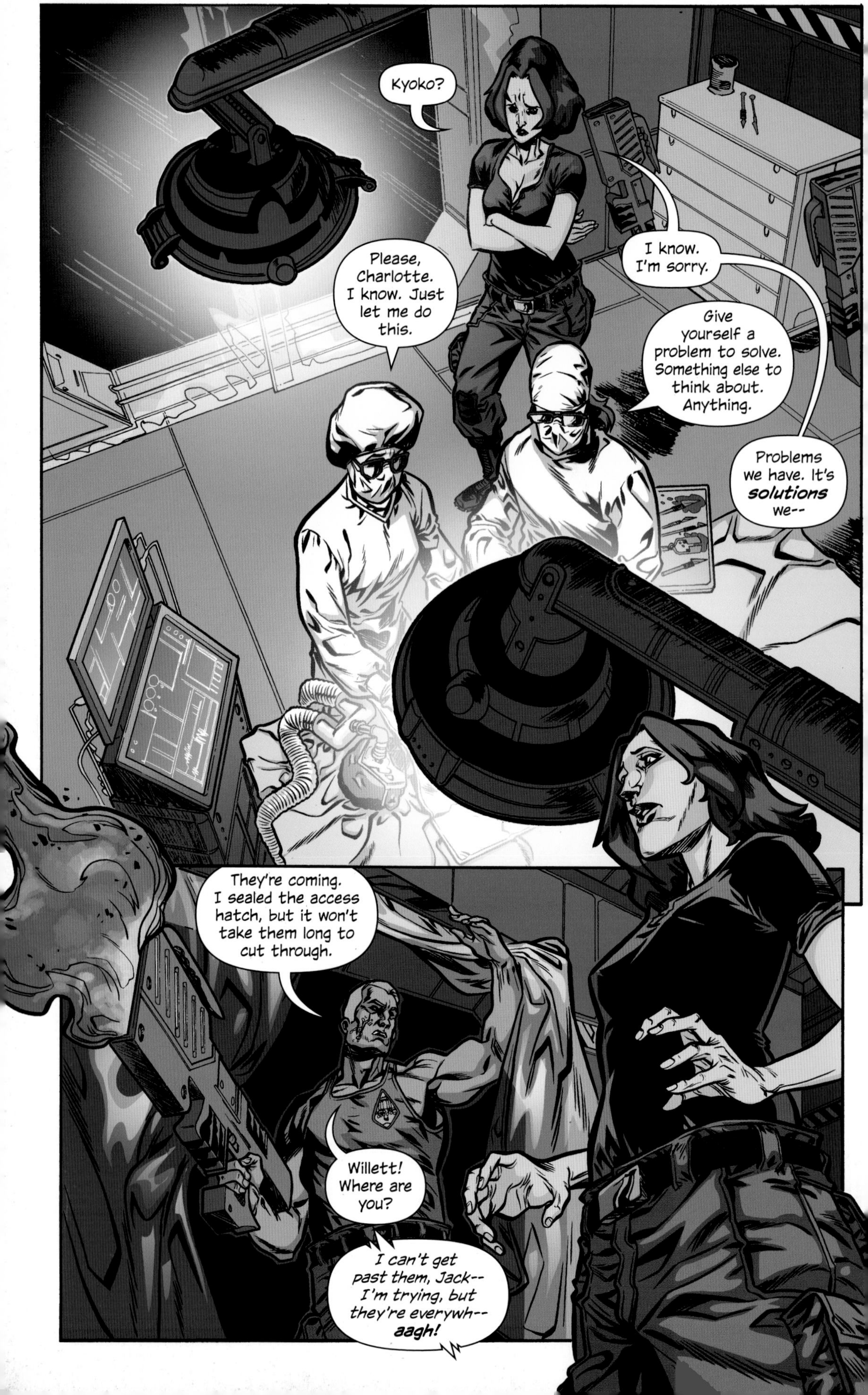
Kyoko?
Please, Charlotte. I know. Just let me do this.
I know. I'm sorry.
Give yourself a problem to solve. Something else to think about. Anything.
Problems we have. It's **solutions** we--
They're coming. I sealed the access hatch, but it won't take them long to cut through.
Willett! Where are you?
I can't get past them, Jack-- I'm trying, but they're everywh-- ***aagh!***

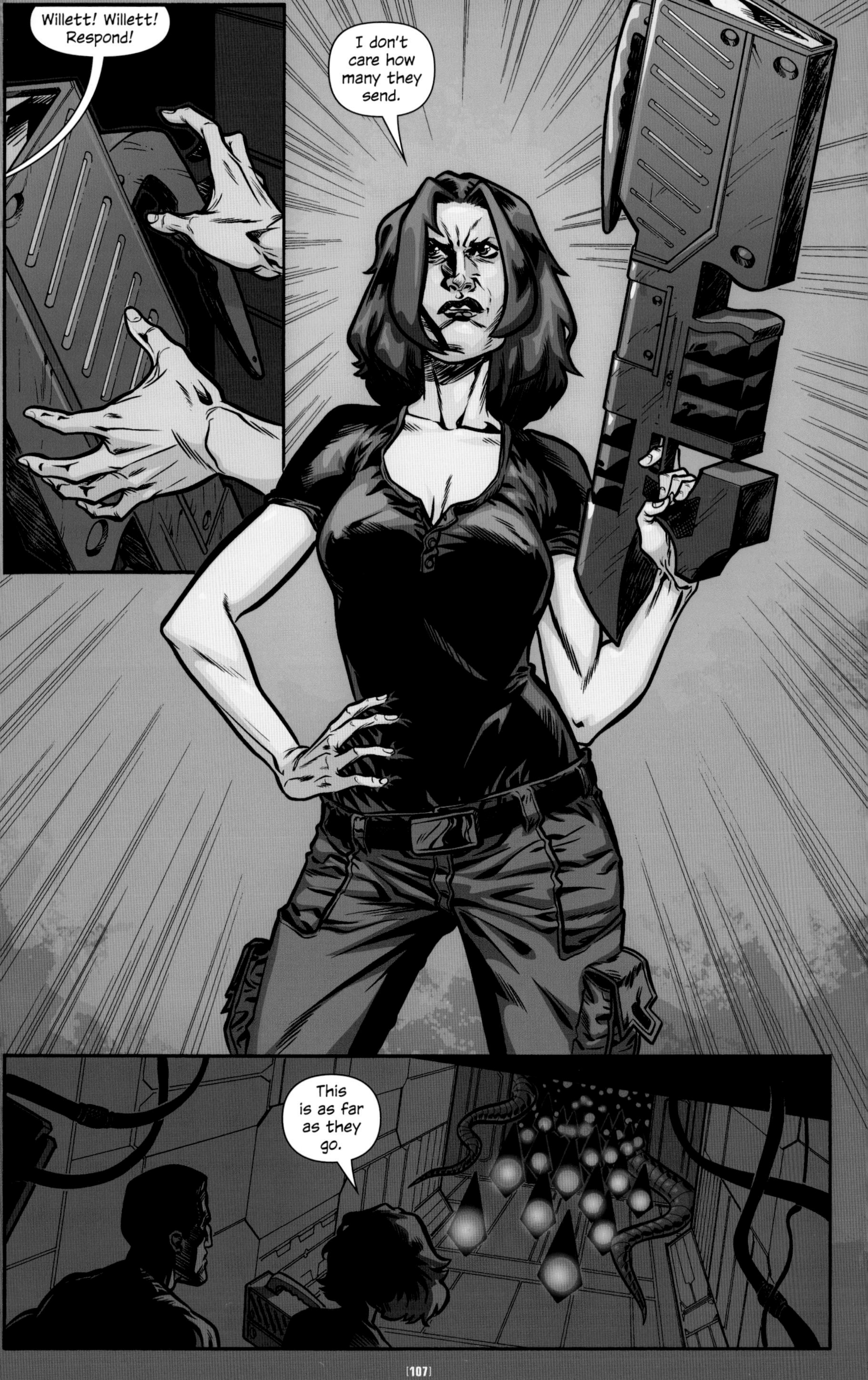
Willett! Willett! Respond!
I don't care how many they send.
This is as far as they go.

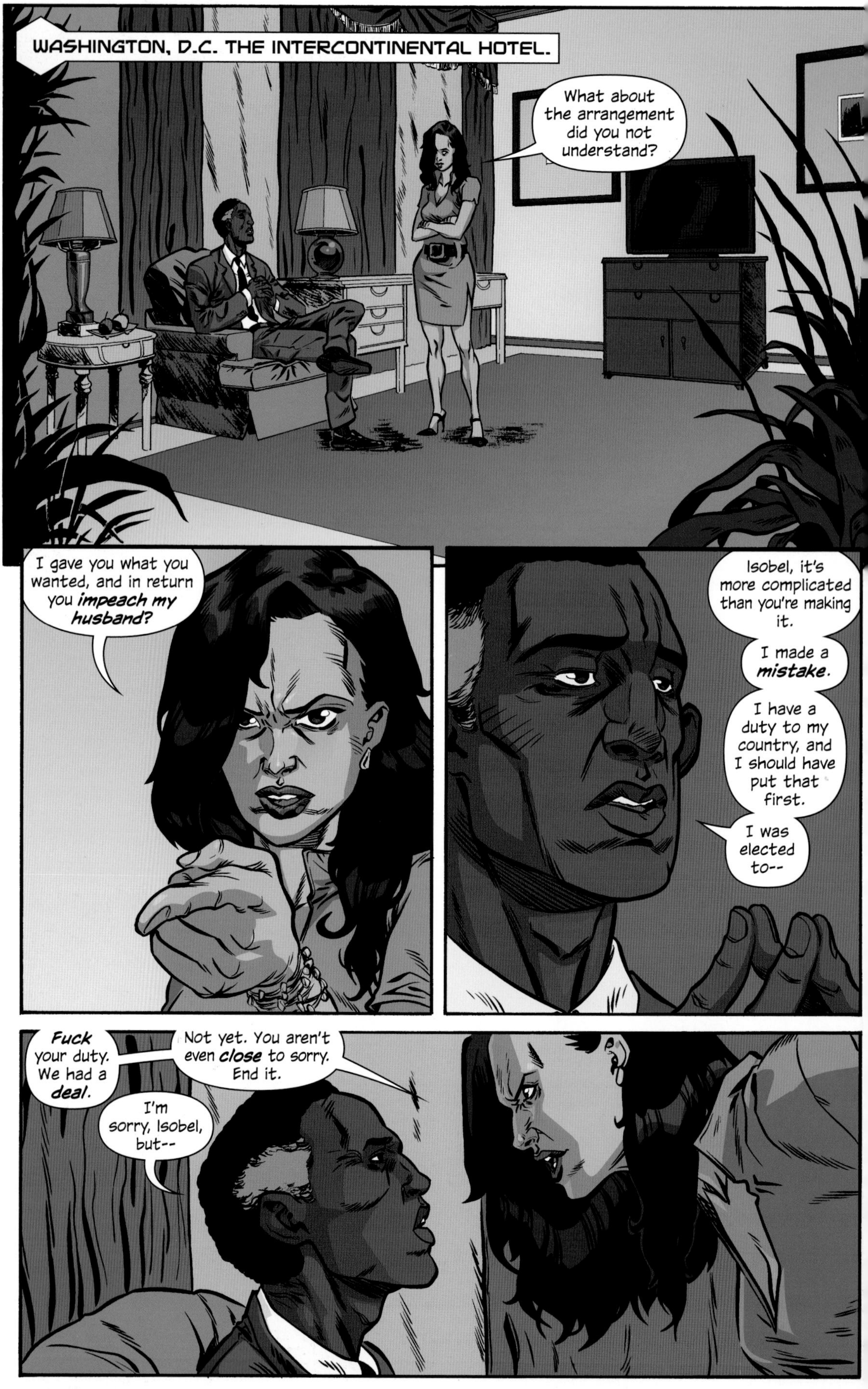
WASHINGTON, D.C. THE INTERCONTINENTAL HOTEL.
What about the arrangement did you not understand?
I gave you what you wanted, and in return you *impeach my husband?*
Isobel, it's more complicated than you're making it.
I made a *mistake*.
I have a duty to my country, and I should have put that first.
I was elected to--
Fuck your duty. We had a *deal*.
I'm sorry, Isobel, but--
Not yet. You aren't even *close* to sorry. End it.

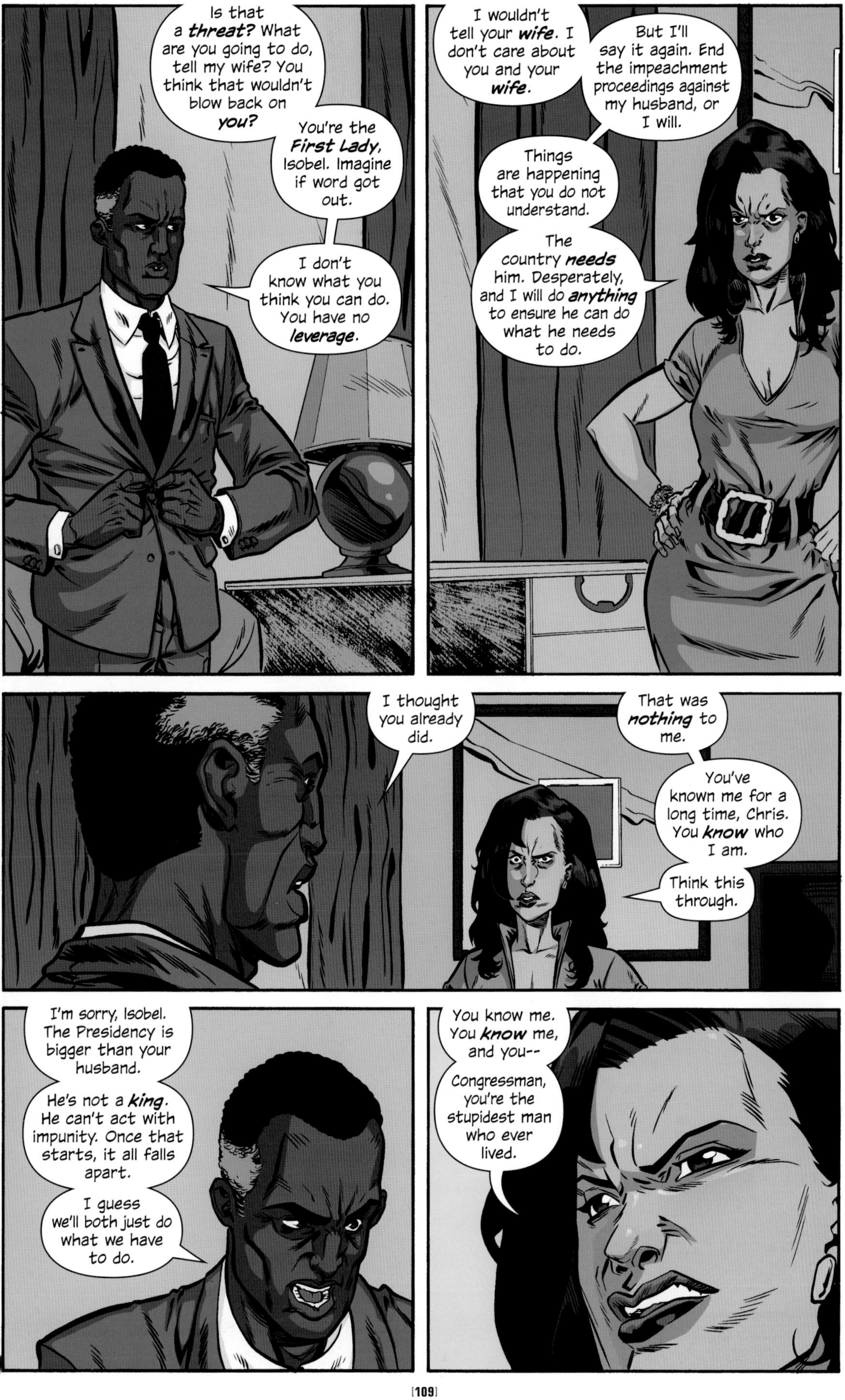

Is that a *threat?* What are you going to do, tell my wife? You think that wouldn't blow back on *you?*
You're the *First Lady*, Isobel. Imagine if word got out.
I don't know what you think you can do. You have no *leverage*.
I wouldn't tell your *wife*. I don't care about you and your *wife*.
But I'll say it again. End the impeachment proceedings against my husband, or I will.
Things are happening that you do not understand.
The country *needs* him. Desperately, and I will do *anything* to ensure he can do what he needs to do.
I thought you already did.
That was *nothing* to me.
You've known me for a long time, Chris. You *know* who I am.
Think this through.
I'm sorry, Isobel. The Presidency is bigger than your husband.
He's not a *king*. He can't act with impunity. Once that starts, it all falls apart.
I guess we'll both just do what we have to do.
You know me. You *know* me, and you--
Congressman, you're the stupidest man who ever lived.

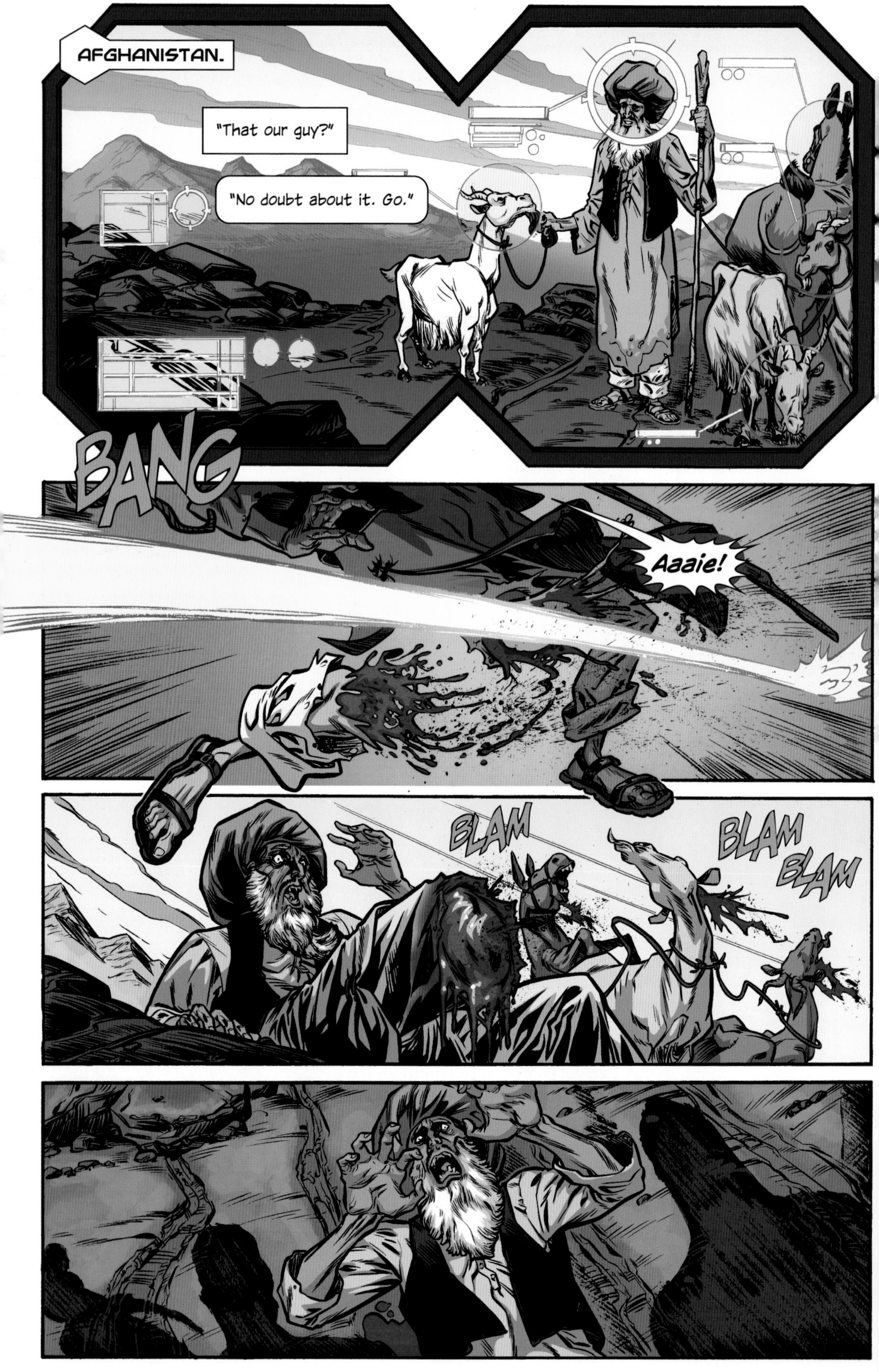

AFGHANISTAN.
"That our guy?"
"No doubt about it. Go."
BANG
Aaaie!
BLAM
BLAM
BLAM

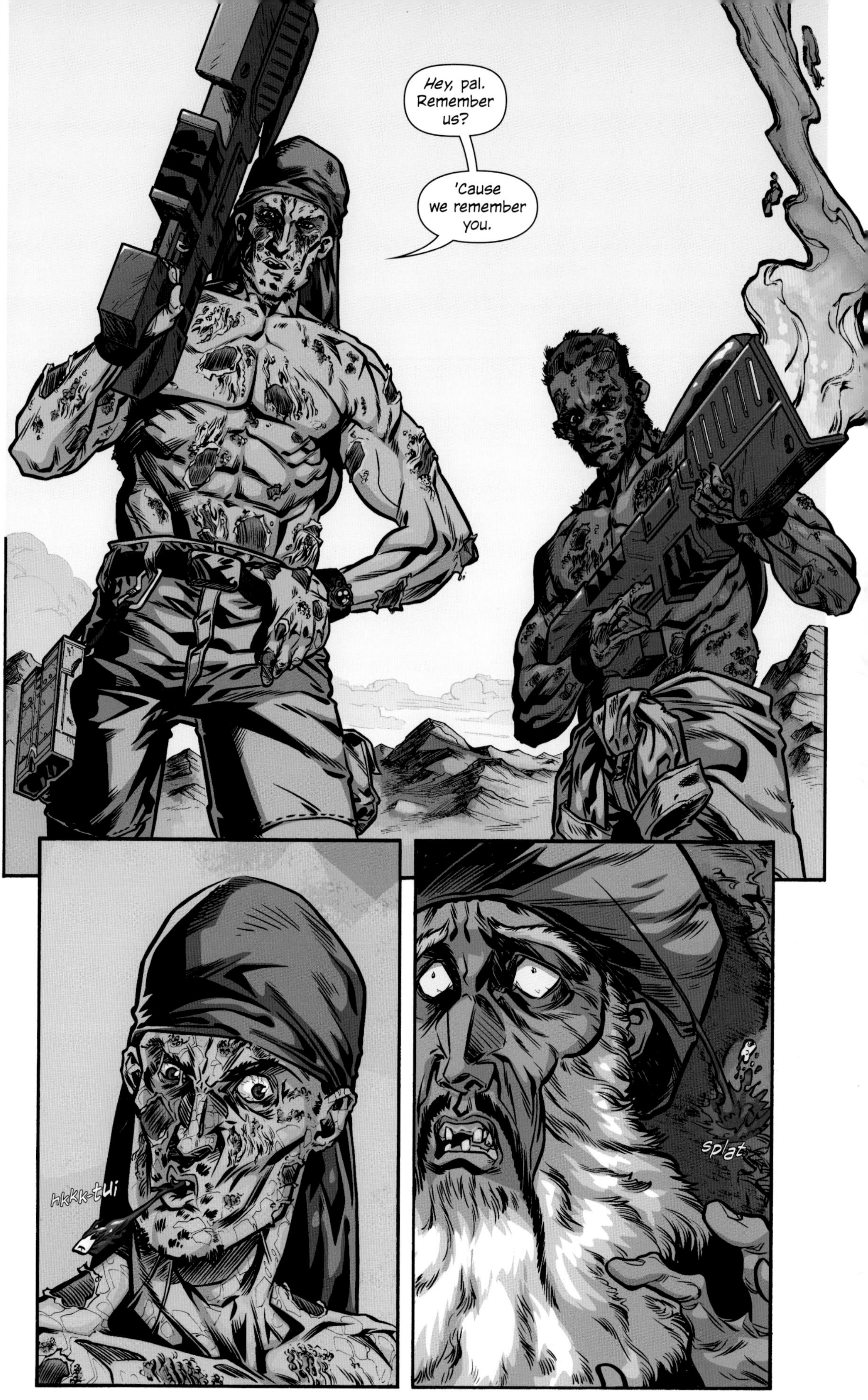

Hey, pal. Remember us?
'Cause we remember you.
hkkk-tui
splat

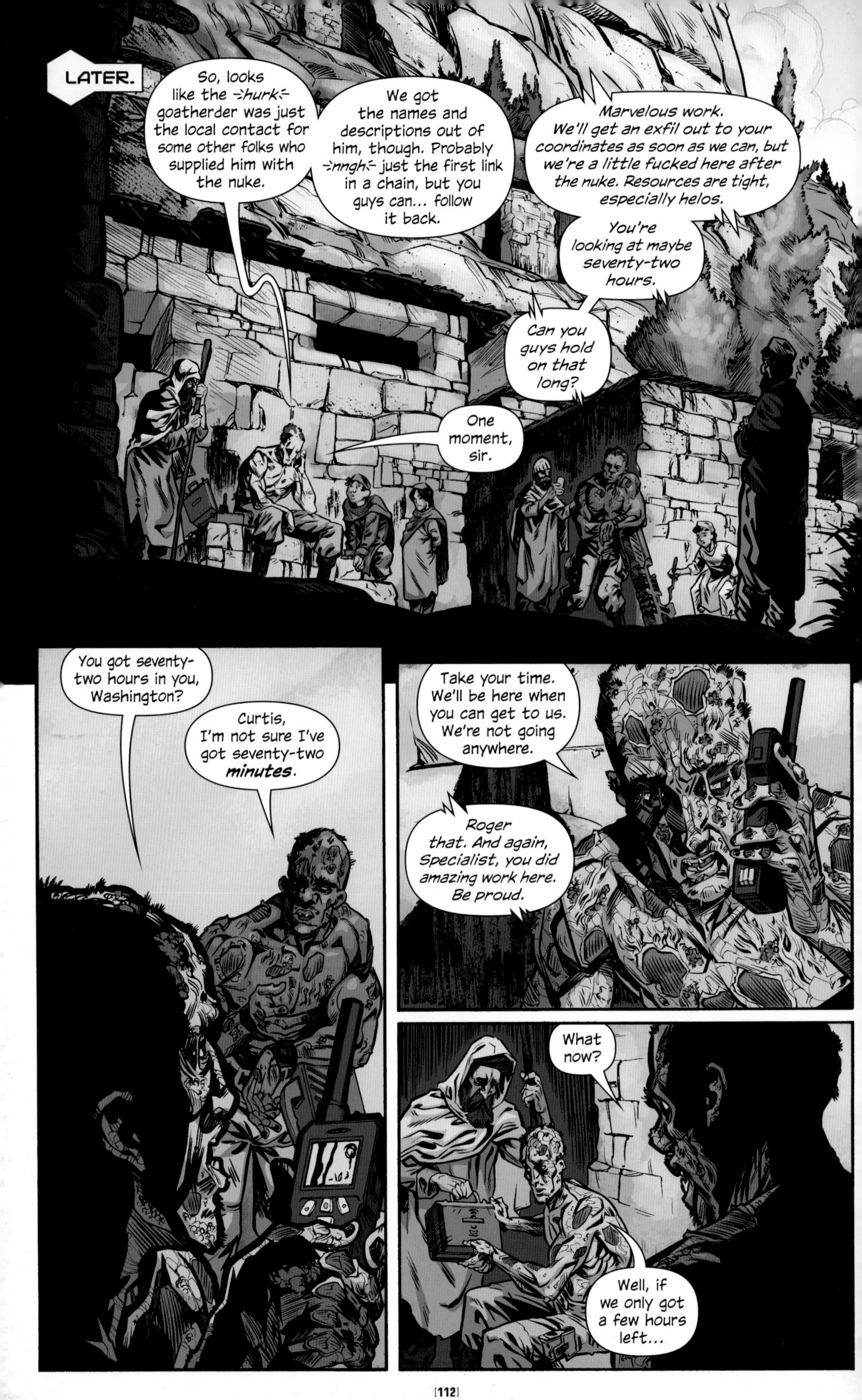
LATER.
So, looks like the -hurk- goatherder was just the local contact for some other folks who supplied him with the nuke.
We got the names and descriptions out of him, though. Probably -nngh- just the first link in a chain, but you guys can... follow it back.
Marvelous work. We'll get an exfil out to your coordinates as soon as we can, but we're a little fucked here after the nuke. Resources are tight, especially helos.
You're looking at maybe seventy-two hours.
Can you guys hold on that long?
One moment, sir.
You got seventy-two hours in you, Washington?
Curtis, I'm not sure I've got seventy-two minutes.
Take your time. We'll be here when you can get to us. We're not going anywhere.
Roger that. And again, Specialist, you did amazing work here. Be proud.
What now?
Well, if we only got a few hours left...

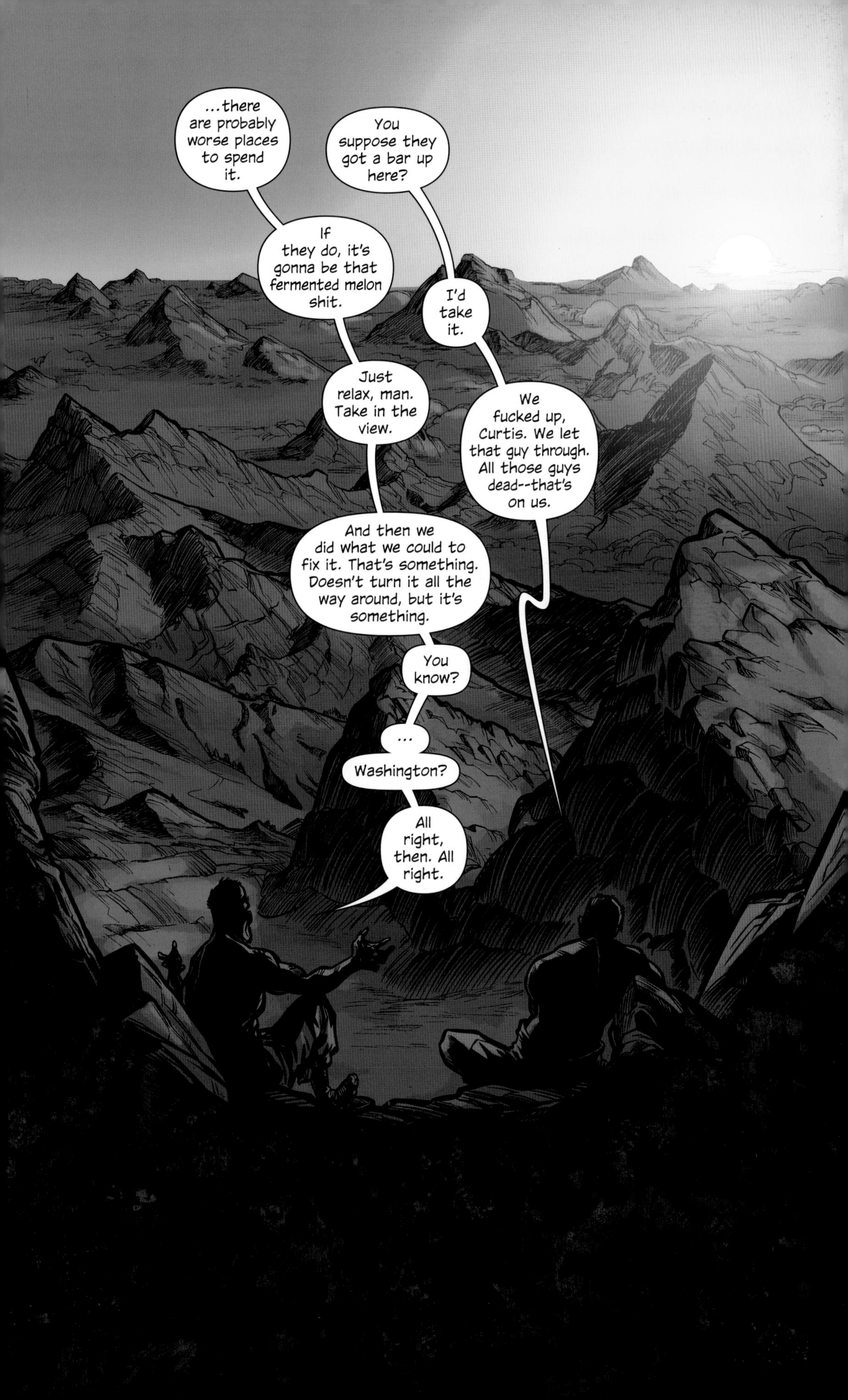
...there are probably worse places to spend it.
You suppose they got a bar up here?
If they do, it's gonna be that fermented melon shit.
I'd take it.
Just relax, man. Take in the view.
We fucked up, Curtis. We let that guy through. All those guys dead--that's on us.
And then we did what we could to fix it. That's something. Doesn't turn it all the way around, but it's something.
You know?
...
Washington?
All right, then. All right.

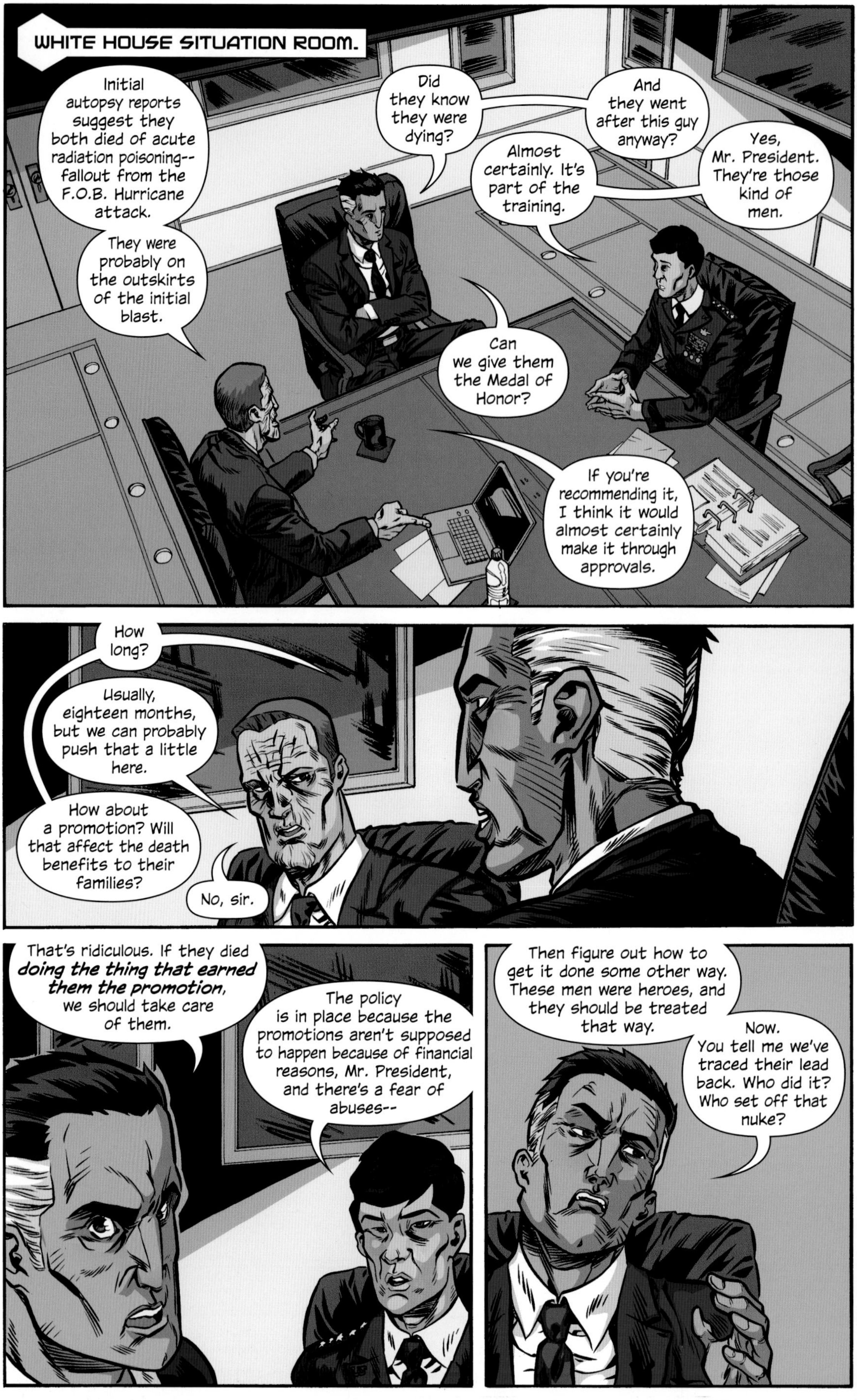
WHITE HOUSE SITUATION ROOM.
Initial autopsy reports suggest they both died of acute radiation poisoning--fallout from the F.O.B. Hurricane attack.
They were probably on the outskirts of the initial blast.
Did they know they were dying?
Almost certainly. It's part of the training.
And they went after this guy anyway?
Yes, Mr. President. They're those kind of men.
Can we give them the Medal of Honor?
If you're recommending it, I think it would almost certainly make it through approvals.
How long?
Usually, eighteen months, but we can probably push that a little here.
How about a promotion? Will that affect the death benefits to their families?
No, sir.
That's ridiculous. If they died *doing the thing that earned them the promotion*, we should take care of them.
The policy is in place because the promotions aren't supposed to happen because of financial reasons, Mr. President, and there's a fear of abuses--
Then figure out how to get it done some other way. These men were heroes, and they should be treated that way.
Now. You tell me we've traced their lead back. Who did it? Who set off that nuke?

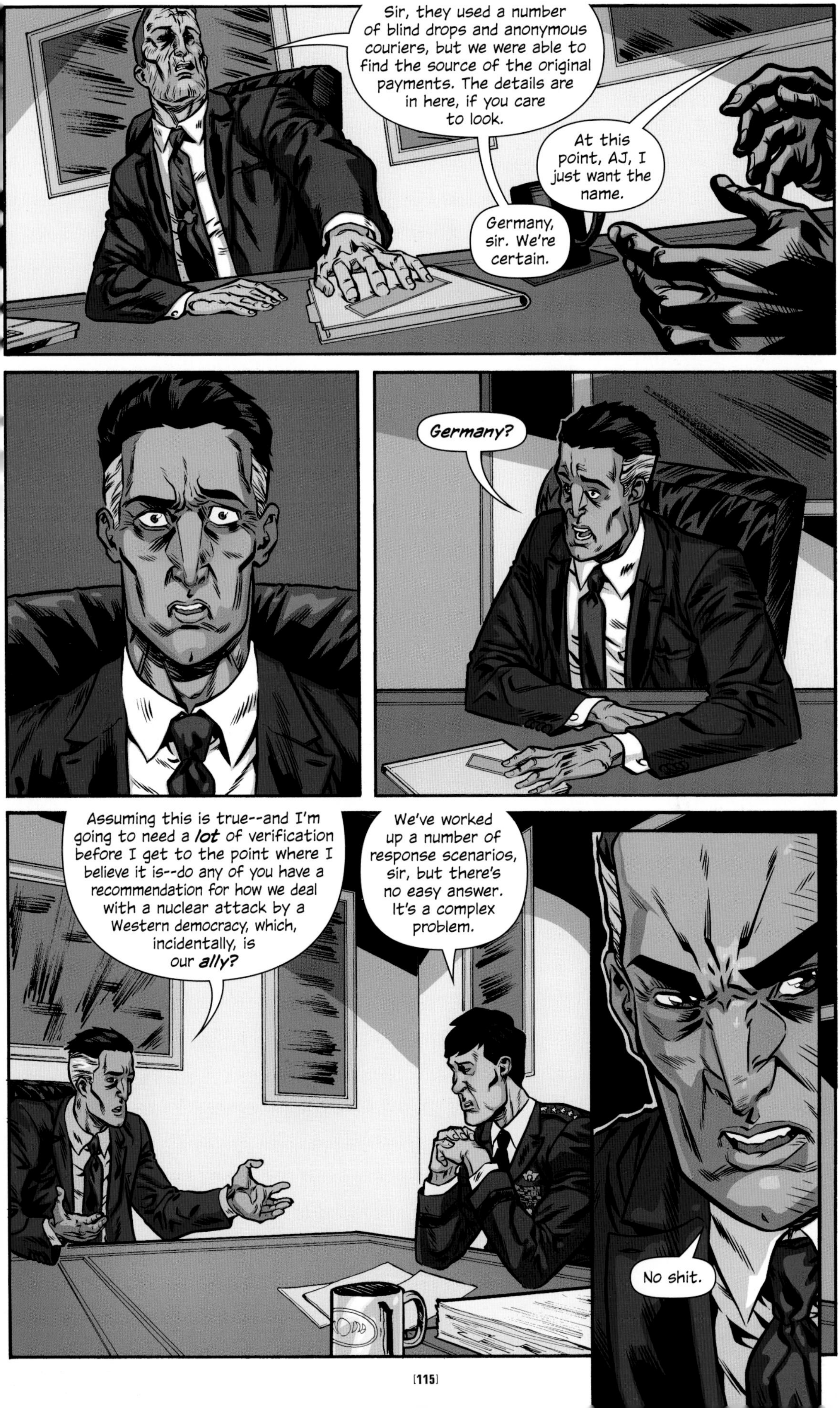
Sir, they used a number of blind drops and anonymous couriers, but we were able to find the source of the original payments. The details are in here, if you care to look.
At this point, AJ, I just want the name.
Germany, sir. We're certain.
Germany?
Assuming this is true--and I'm going to need a *lot* of verification before I get to the point where I believe it is--do any of you have a recommendation for how we deal with a nuclear attack by a Western democracy, which, incidentally, is our *ally?*
We've worked up a number of response scenarios, sir, but there's no easy answer. It's a complex problem.
No shit.

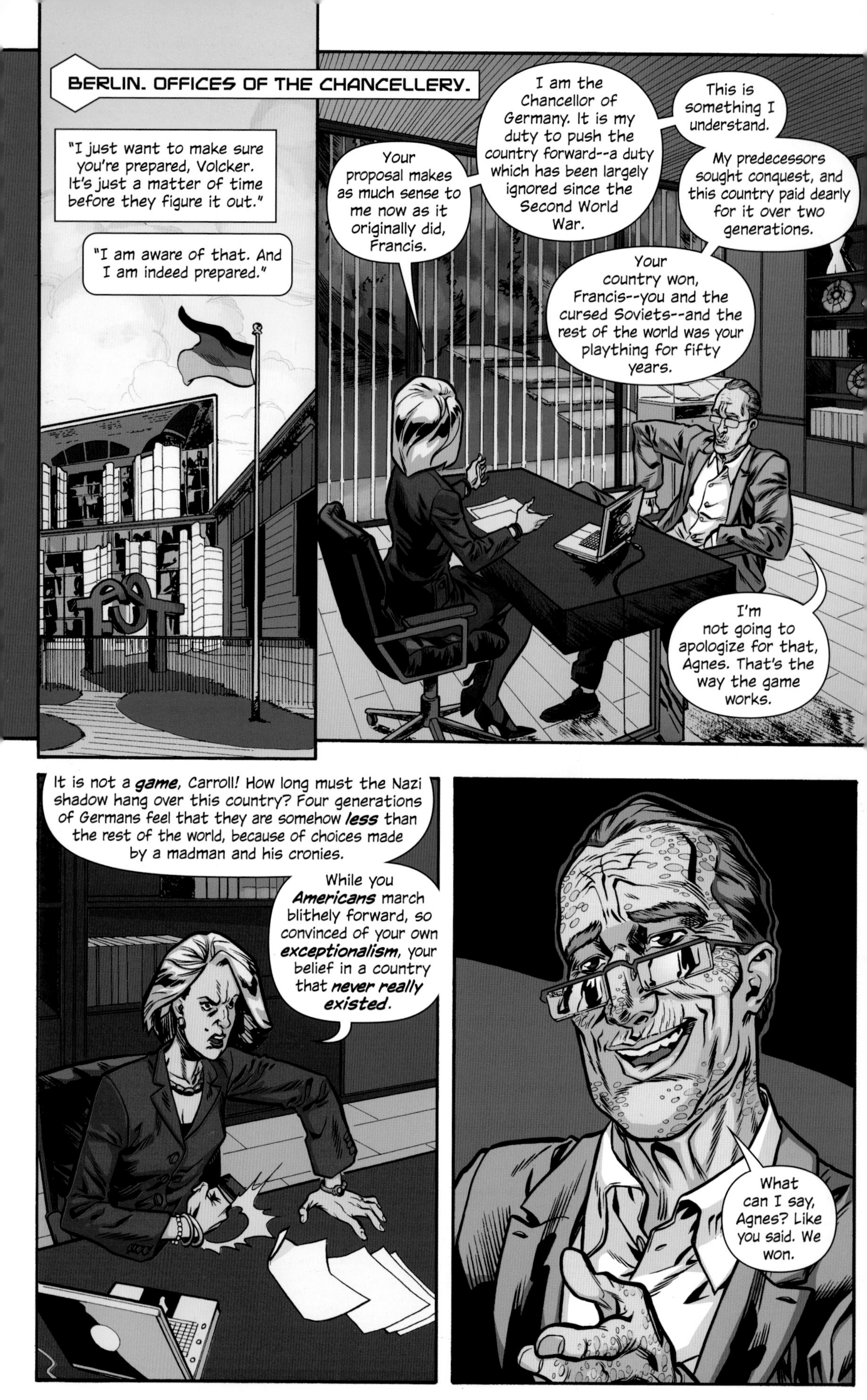
BERLIN. OFFICES OF THE CHANCELLERY.
"I just want to make sure you're prepared, Volcker. It's just a matter of time before they figure it out."
"I am aware of that. And I am indeed prepared."
Your proposal makes as much sense to me now as it originally did, Francis.
I am the Chancellor of Germany. It is my duty to push the country forward--a duty which has been largely ignored since the Second World War.
This is something I understand.
My predecessors sought conquest, and this country paid dearly for it over two generations.
Your country won, Francis--you and the cursed Soviets--and the rest of the world was your plaything for fifty years.
I'm not going to apologize for that, Agnes. That's the way the game works.
It is not a *game*, Carroll! How long must the Nazi shadow hang over this country? Four generations of Germans feel that they are somehow *less* than the rest of the world, because of choices made by a madman and his cronies.
While you *Americans* march blithely forward, so convinced of your own *exceptionalism*, your belief in a country that *never really existed*.
What can I say, Agnes? Like you said. We won.

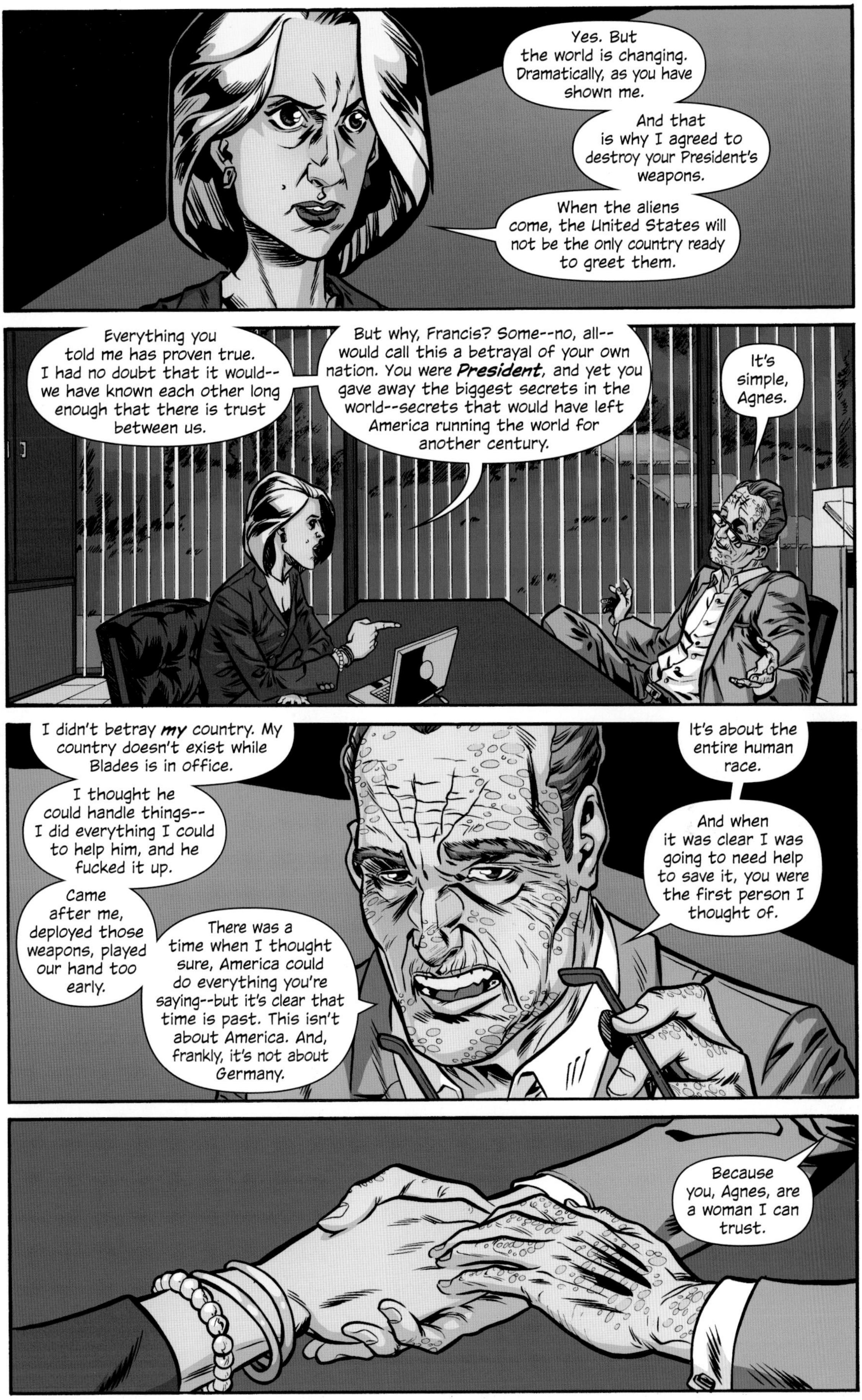
Yes. But the world is changing. Dramatically, as you have shown me.
And that is why I agreed to destroy your President's weapons.
When the aliens come, the United States will not be the only country ready to greet them.
Everything you told me has proven true. I had no doubt that it would--we have known each other long enough that there is trust between us.
But why, Francis? Some--no, all--would call this a betrayal of your own nation. You were *President*, and yet you gave away the biggest secrets in the world--secrets that would have left America running the world for another century.
It's simple, Agnes.
I didn't betray *my* country. My country doesn't exist while Blades is in office.
I thought he could handle things--I did everything I could to help him, and he fucked it up.
Came after me, deployed those weapons, played our hand too early.
There was a time when I thought sure, America could do everything you're saying--but it's clear that time is past. This isn't about America. And, frankly, it's not about Germany.
It's about the entire human race.
And when it was clear I was going to need help to save it, you were the first person I thought of.
Because you, Agnes, are a woman I can trust.

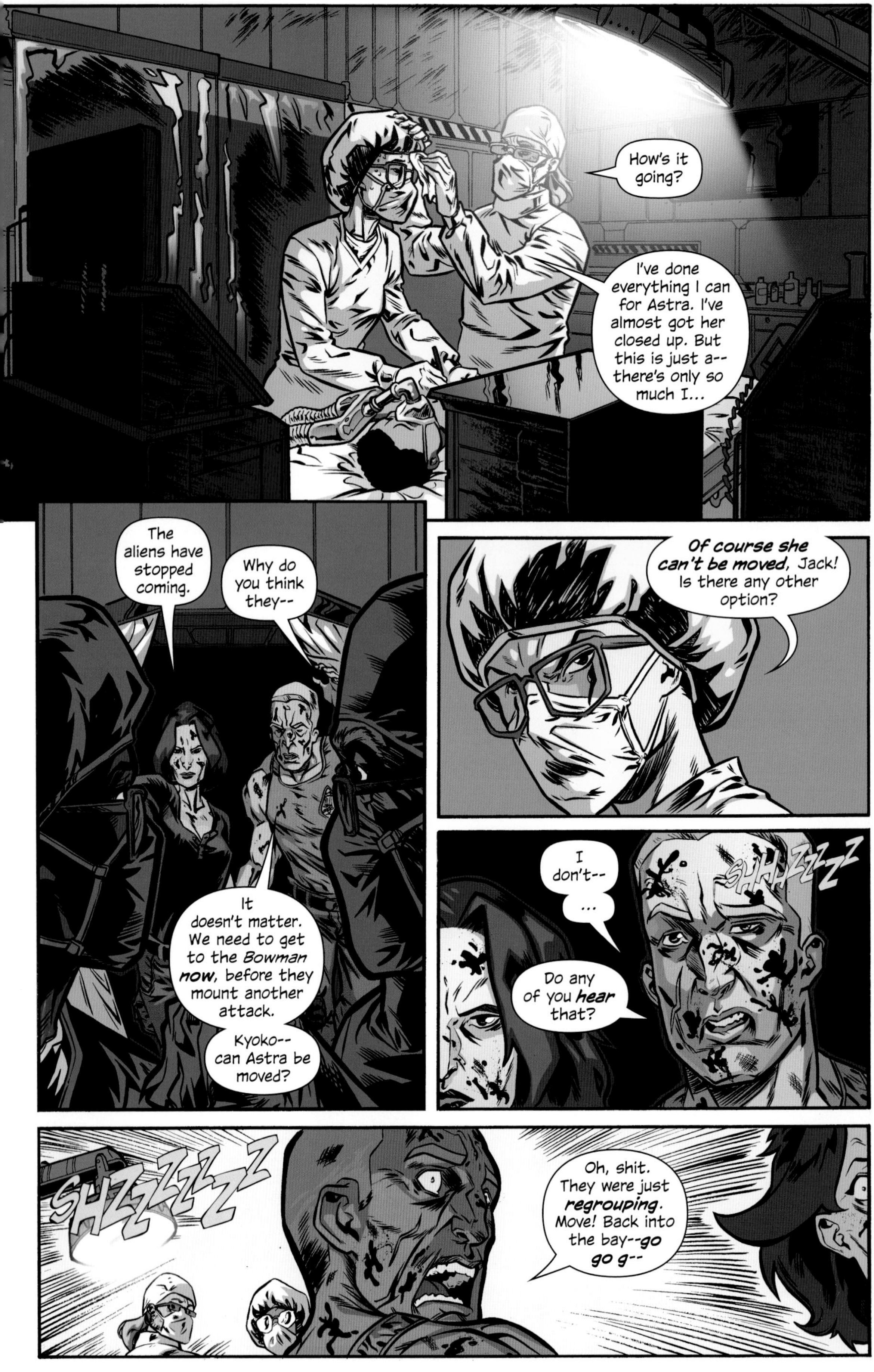
How's it going?
I've done everything I can for Astra. I've almost got her closed up. But this is just a-- there's only so much I...
The aliens have stopped coming.
Why do you think they--
It doesn't matter. We need to get to the *Bowman* ***now***, before they mount another attack.
Kyoko-- can Astra be moved?
Of course she can't be moved, Jack! Is there any other option?
I don't--
...
SHHZZZZ
Do any of you ***hear*** that?
SHZZZZZZZ
Oh, shit. They were just ***regrouping***. Move! Back into the bay--***go go g--***

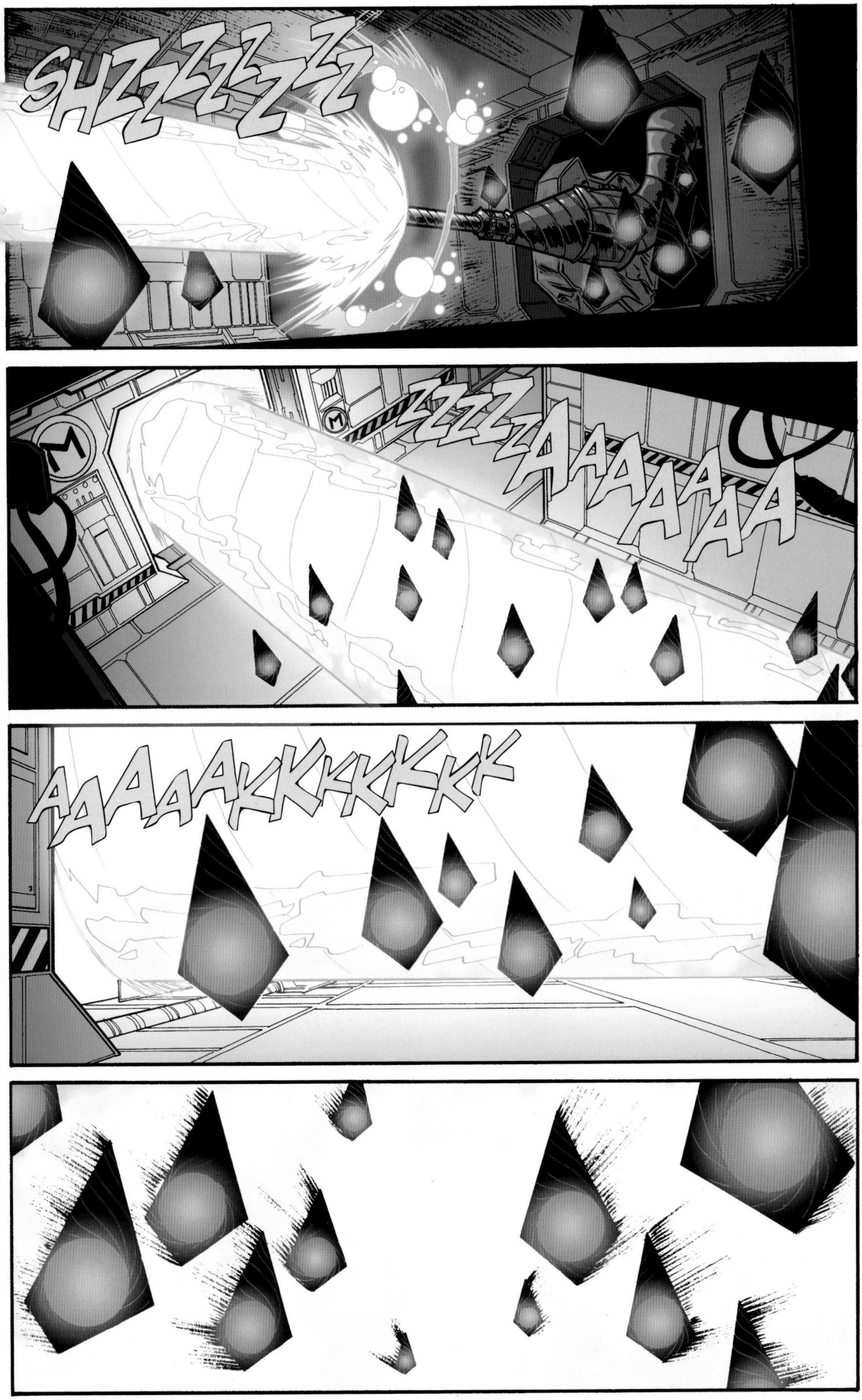
SHZZZZZZZ
ZZZZZAAAAAAAAA
AAAAAKKKKKKK

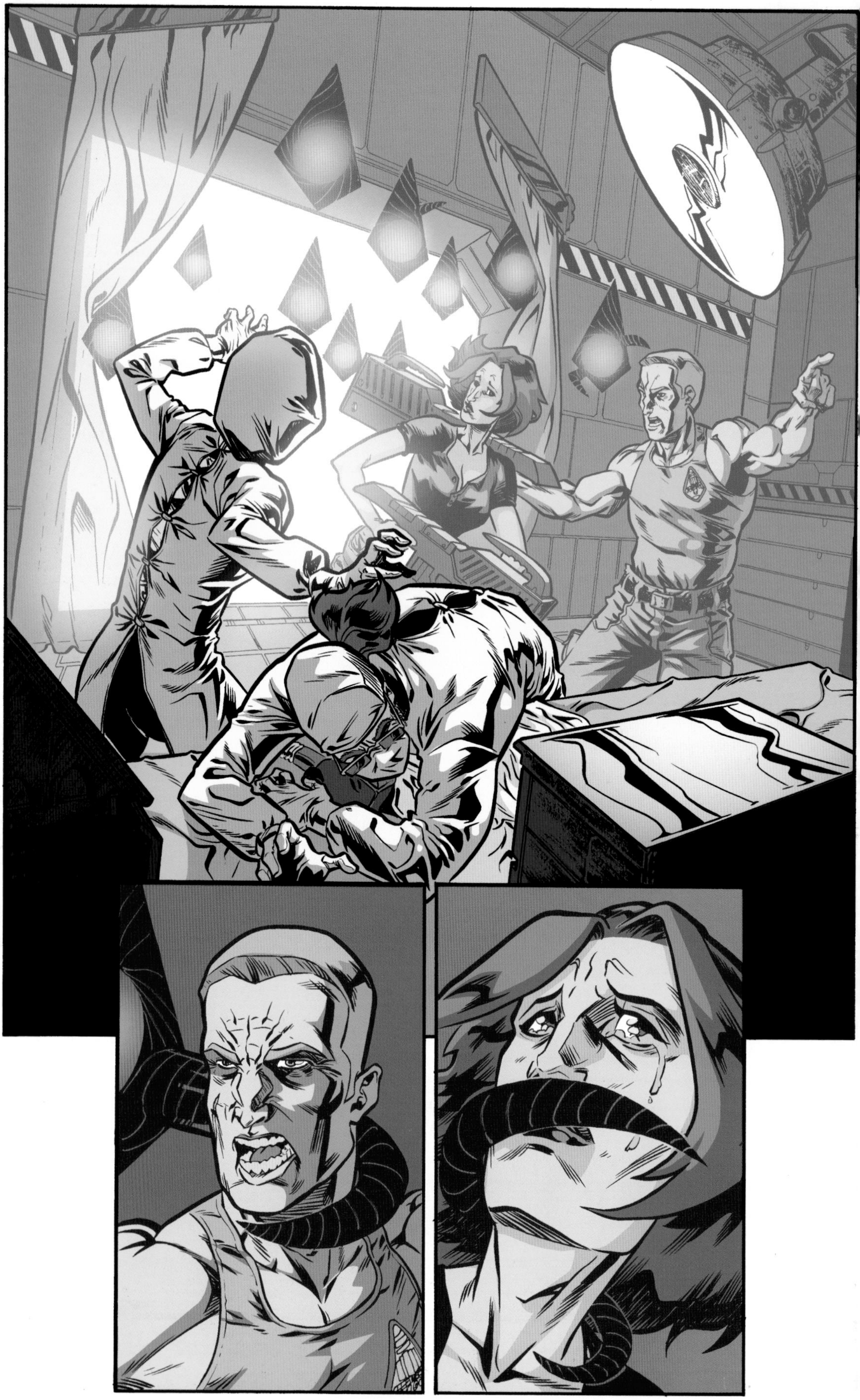

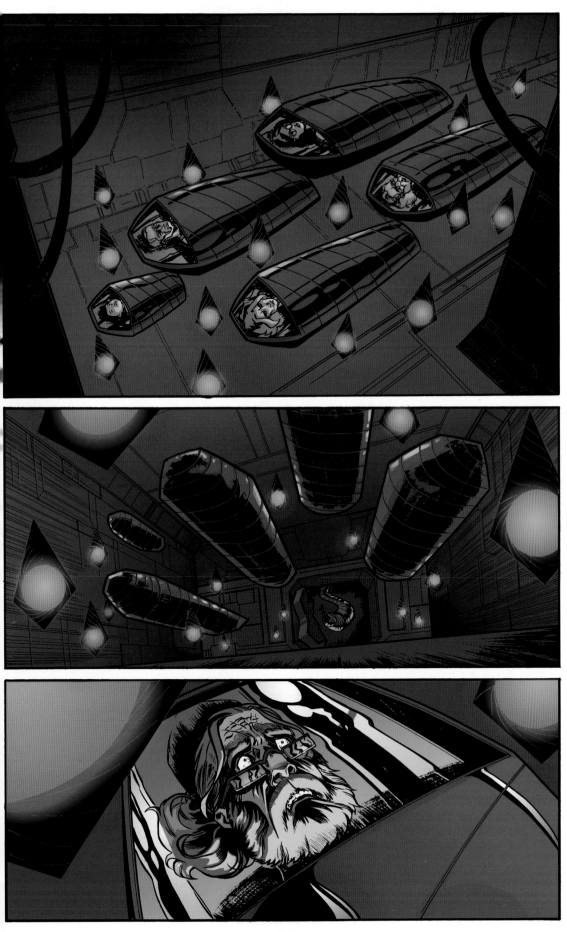

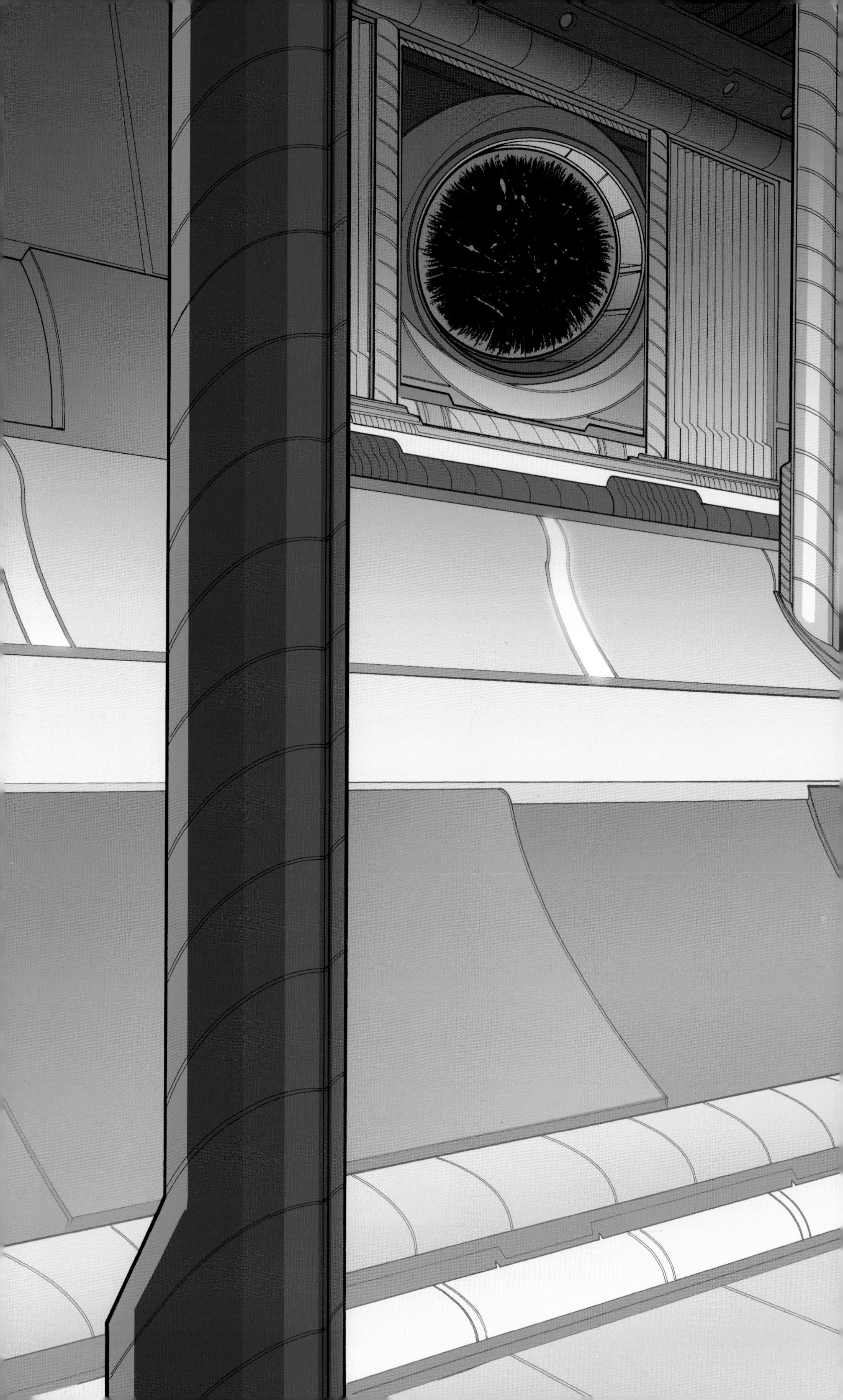

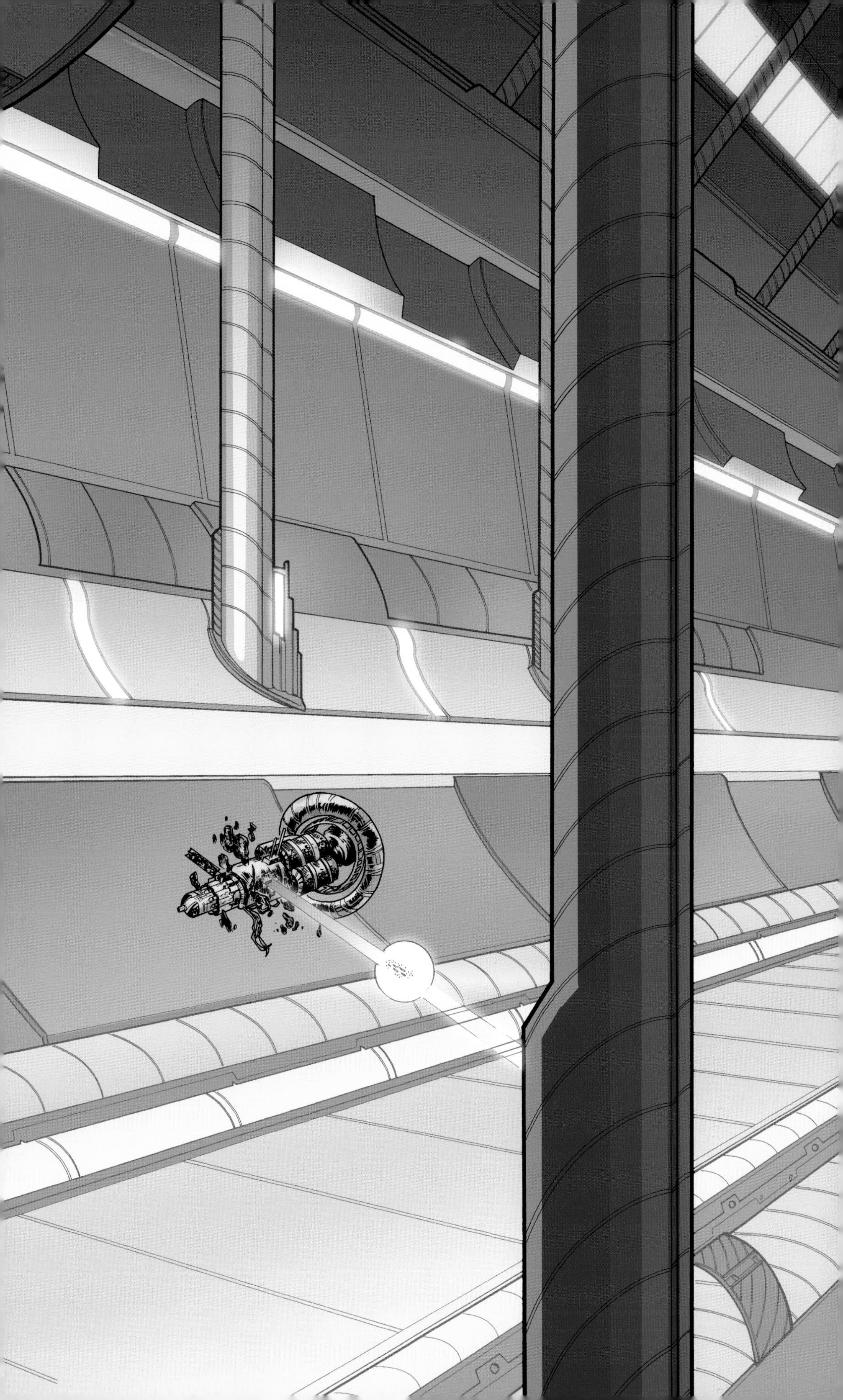

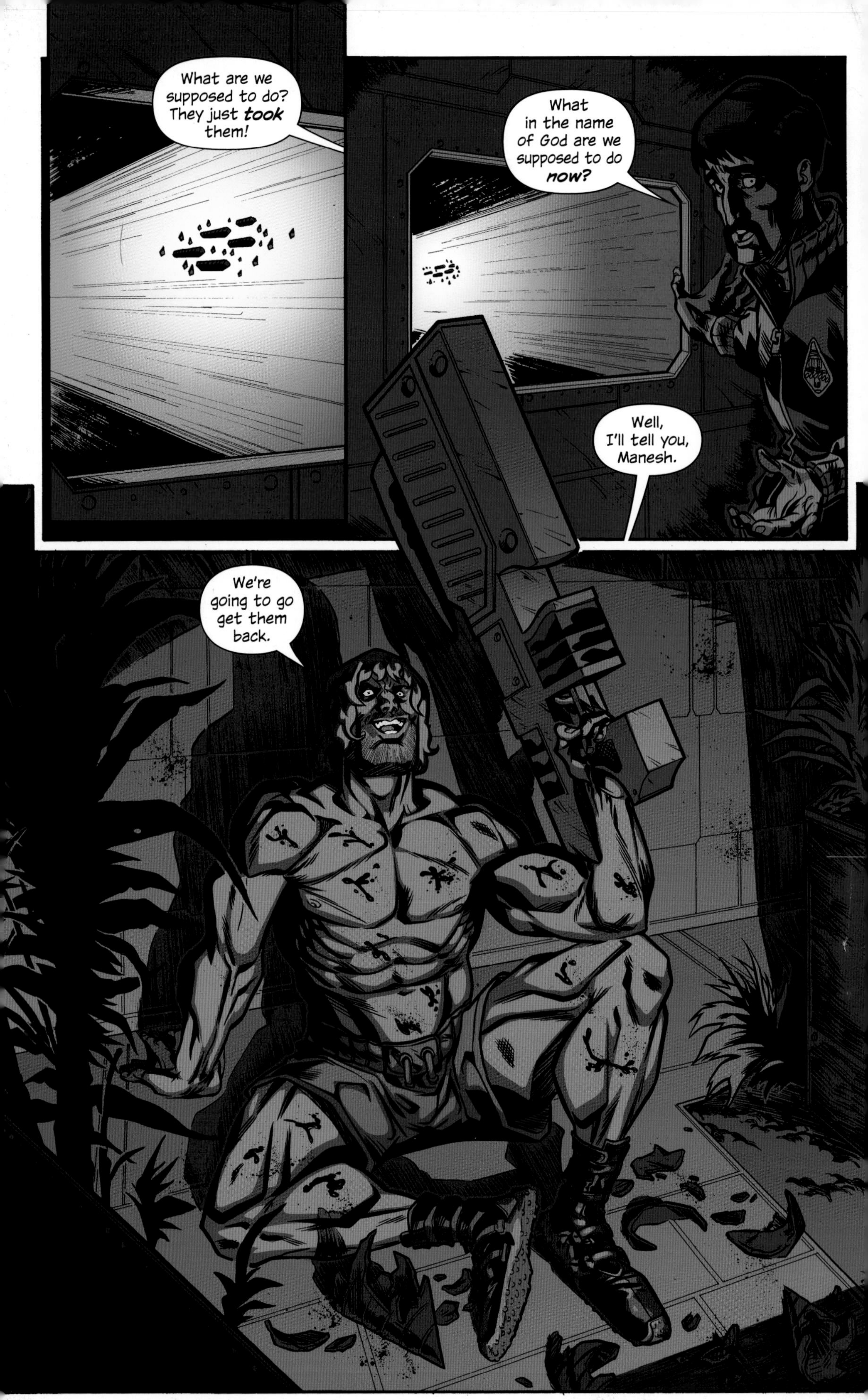
What are we supposed to do? They just *took* them!
What in the name of God are we supposed to do *now?*
Well, I'll tell you, Manesh.
We're going to go get them back.

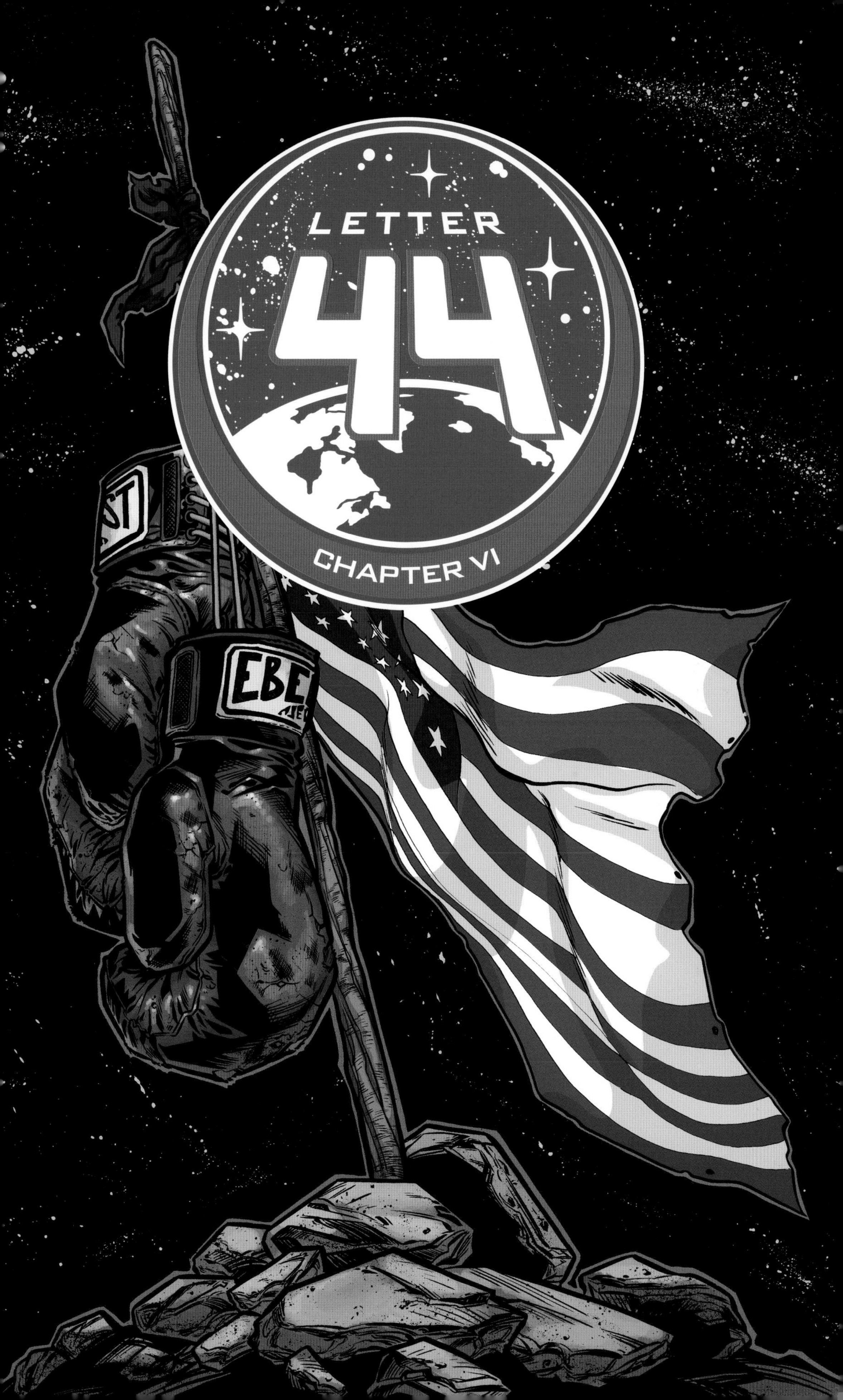
LETTER
44
CHAPTER VI
EBE

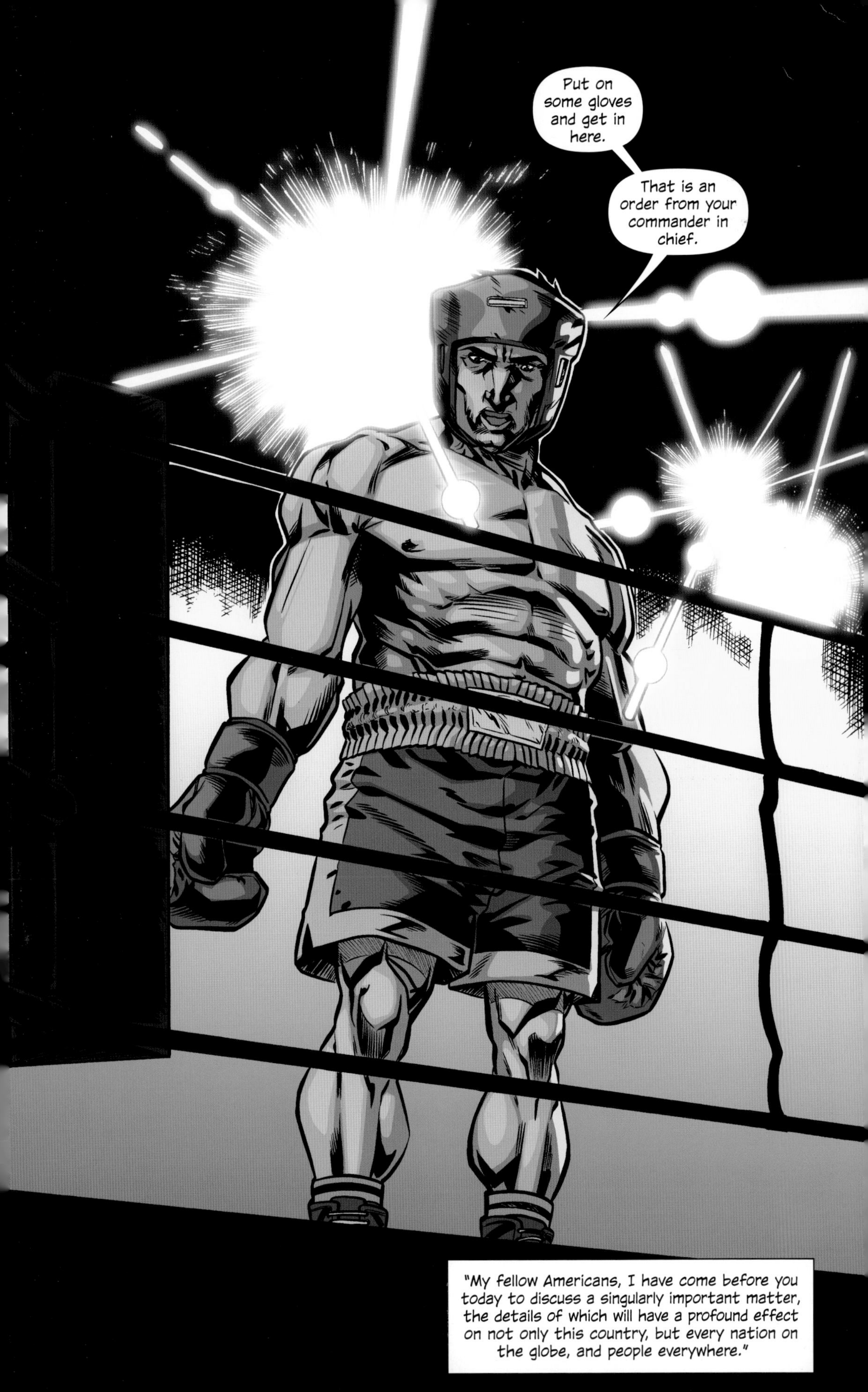
Put on some gloves and get in here.
That is an order from your commander in chief.
"My fellow Americans, I have come before you today to discuss a singularly important matter, the details of which will have a profound effect on not only this country, but every nation on the globe, and people everywhere."

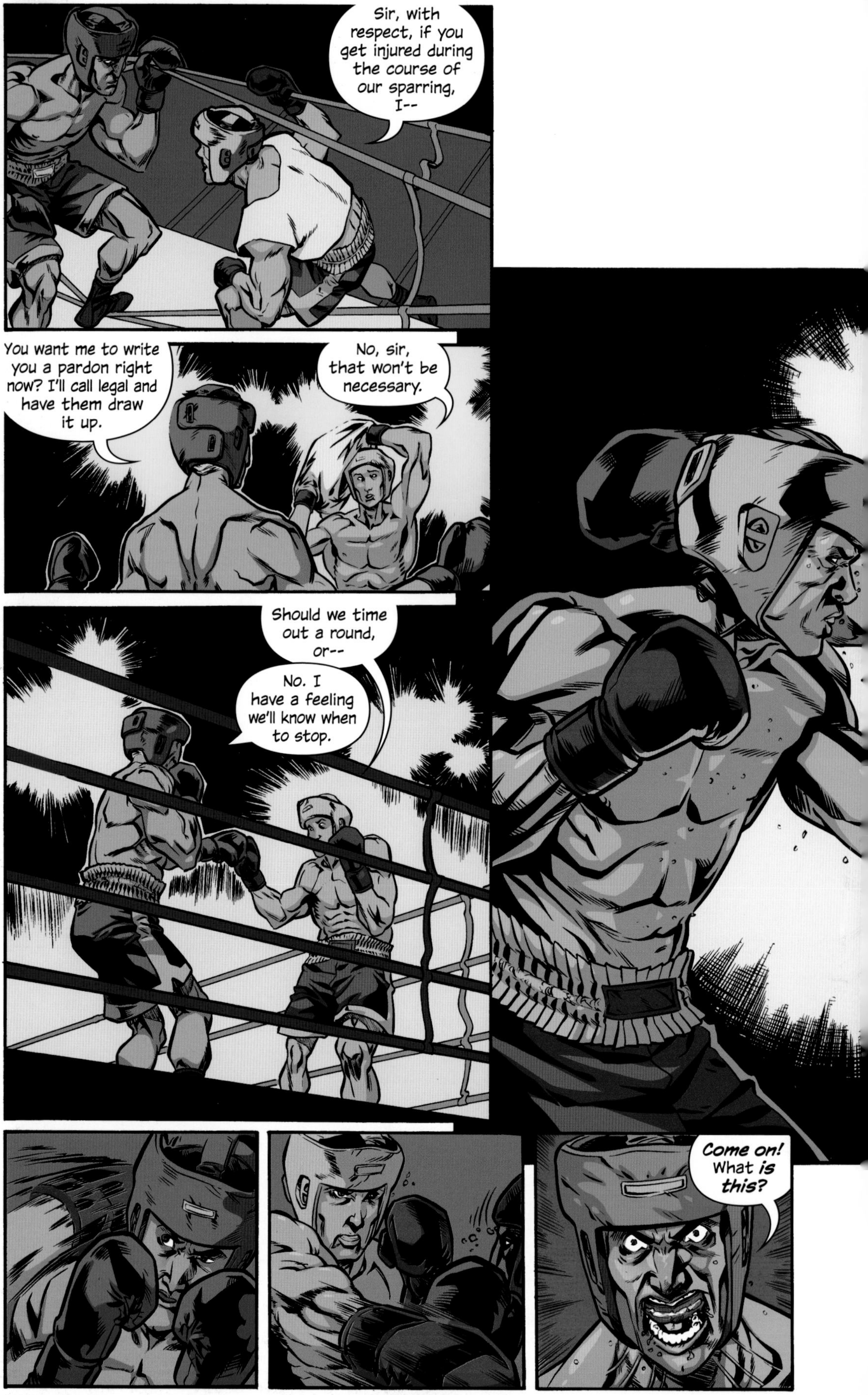
Sir, with respect, if you get injured during the course of our sparring, I--
You want me to write you a pardon right now? I'll call legal and have them draw it up.
No, sir, that won't be necessary.
Should we time out a round, or--
No. I have a feeling we'll know when to stop.
Come on! What *is* *this?*

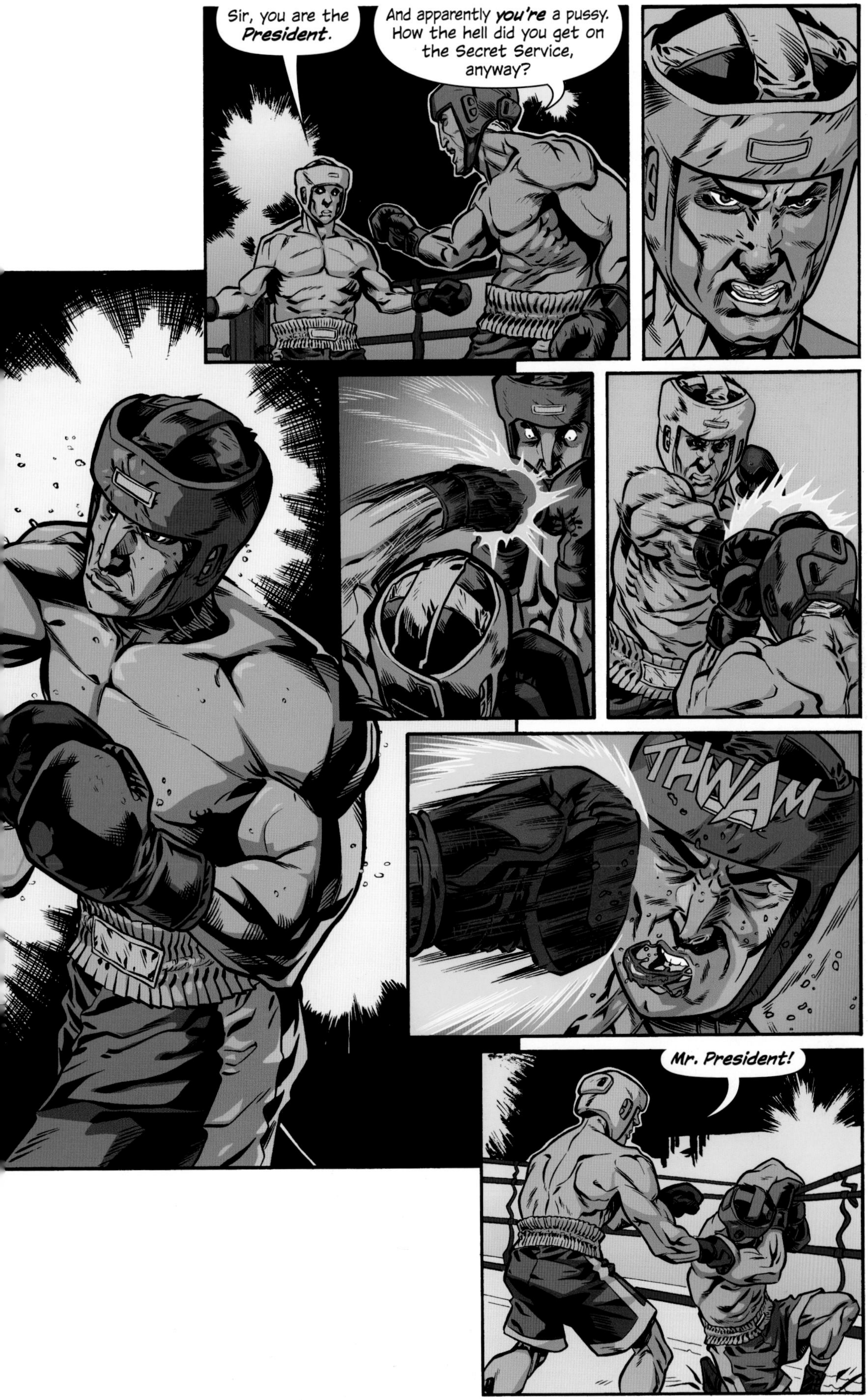
Sir, you are the *President*.
And apparently *you're* a pussy. How the hell did you get on the Secret Service, anyway?
THWAM
Mr. President!

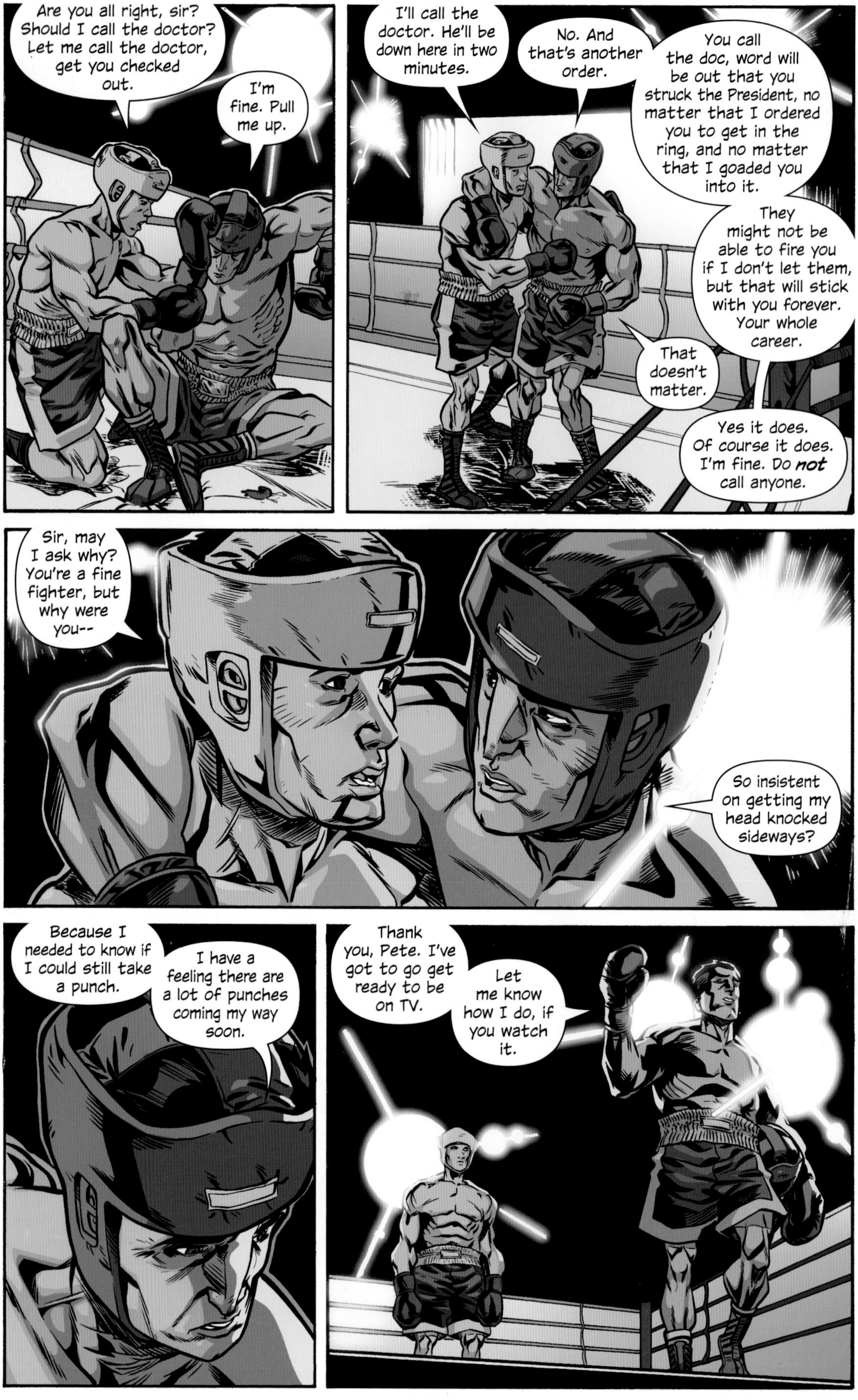

Are you all right, sir? Should I call the doctor? Let me call the doctor, get you checked out.
I'm fine. Pull me up.
I'll call the doctor. He'll be down here in two minutes.
No. And that's another order.
You call the doc, word will be out that you struck the President, no matter that I ordered you to get in the ring, and no matter that I goaded you into it.
They might not be able to fire you if I don't let them, but that will stick with you forever. Your whole career.
That doesn't matter.
Yes it does. Of course it does. I'm fine. Do *not* call anyone.
Sir, may I ask why? You're a fine fighter, but why were you--
So insistent on getting my head knocked sideways?
Because I needed to know if I could still take a punch.
I have a feeling there are a lot of punches coming my way soon.
Thank you, Pete. I've got to go get ready to be on TV.
Let me know how I do, if you watch it.

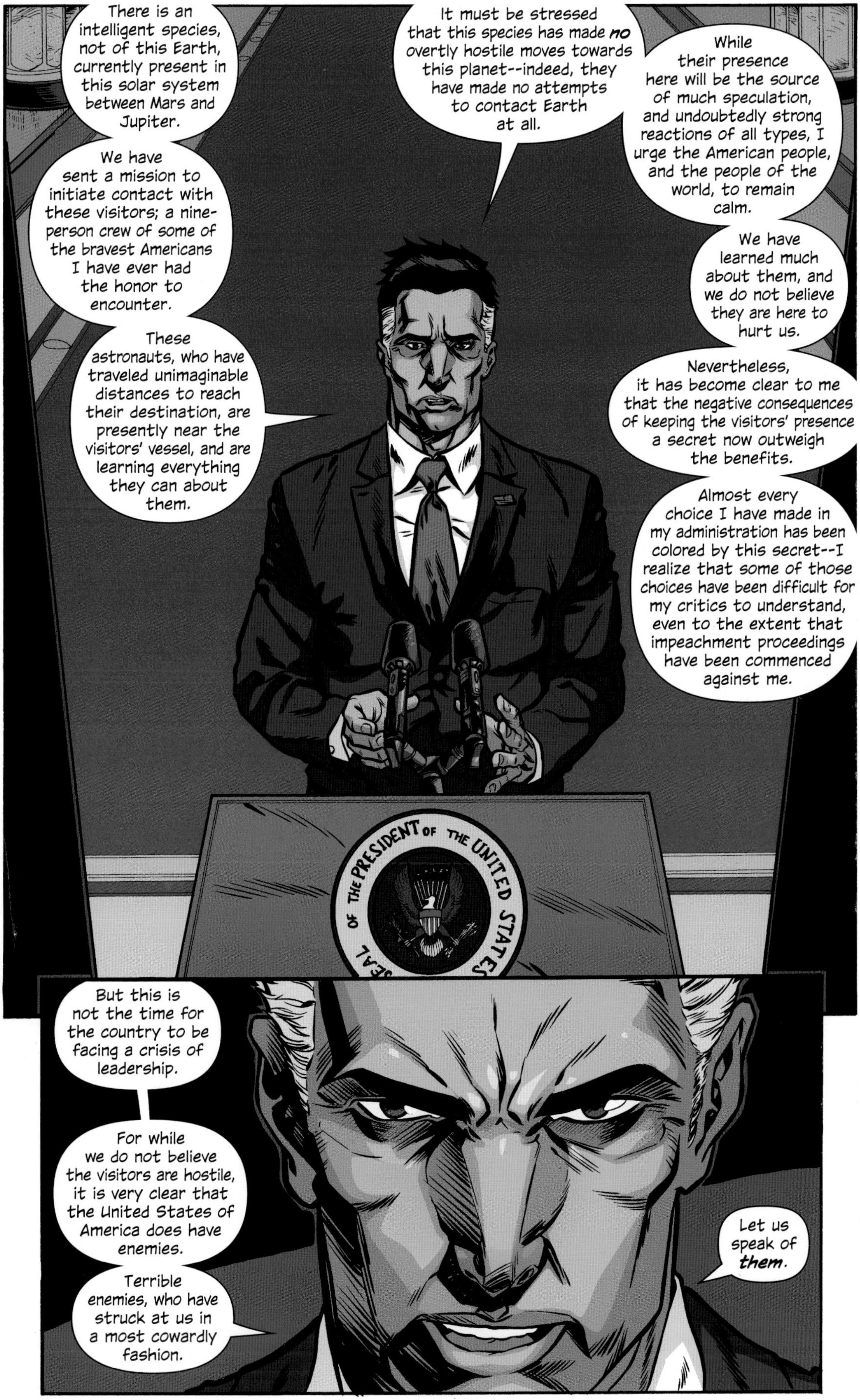
There is an intelligent species, not of this Earth, currently present in this solar system between Mars and Jupiter.
We have sent a mission to initiate contact with these visitors; a nine-person crew of some of the bravest Americans I have ever had the honor to encounter.
These astronauts, who have traveled unimaginable distances to reach their destination, are presently near the visitors' vessel, and are learning everything they can about them.
It must be stressed that this species has made *no* overtly hostile moves towards this planet--indeed, they have made no attempts to contact Earth at all.
While their presence here will be the source of much speculation, and undoubtedly strong reactions of all types, I urge the American people, and the people of the world, to remain calm.
We have learned much about them, and we do not believe they are here to hurt us.
Nevertheless, it has become clear to me that the negative consequences of keeping the visitors' presence a secret now outweigh the benefits.
Almost every choice I have made in my administration has been colored by this secret--I realize that some of those choices have been difficult for my critics to understand, even to the extent that impeachment proceedings have been commenced against me.
SEAL OF THE PRESIDENT OF THE UNITED STATES
But this is not the time for the country to be facing a crisis of leadership.
For while we do not believe the visitors are hostile, it is very clear that the United States of America does have enemies.
Terrible enemies, who have struck at us in a most cowardly fashion.
Let us speak of *them*.

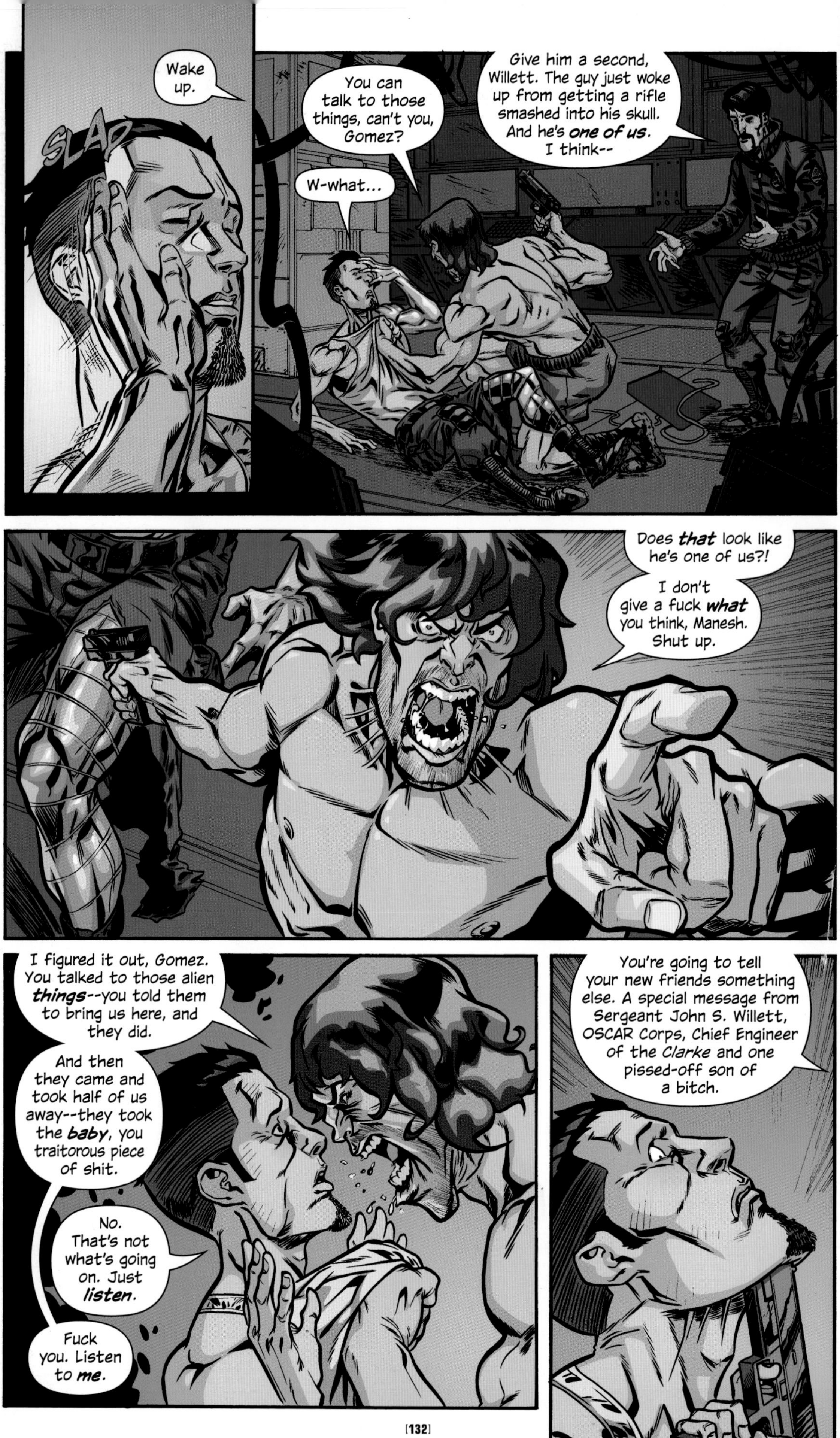
Wake up.
SLAP
You can talk to those things, can't you, Gomez?
W-what...
Give him a second, Willett. The guy just woke up from getting a rifle smashed into his skull. And he's ***one of us***. I think--
Does ***that*** look like he's one of us?!
I don't give a fuck ***what*** you think, Manesh. Shut up.
I figured it out, Gomez. You talked to those alien ***things***--you told them to bring us here, and they did.
And then they came and took half of us away--they took the ***baby***, you traitorous piece of shit.
No. That's not what's going on. Just ***listen***.
Fuck you. Listen to ***me***.
You're going to tell your new friends something else. A special message from Sergeant John S. Willett, OSCAR Corps, Chief Engineer of the *Clarke* and one pissed-off son of a bitch.

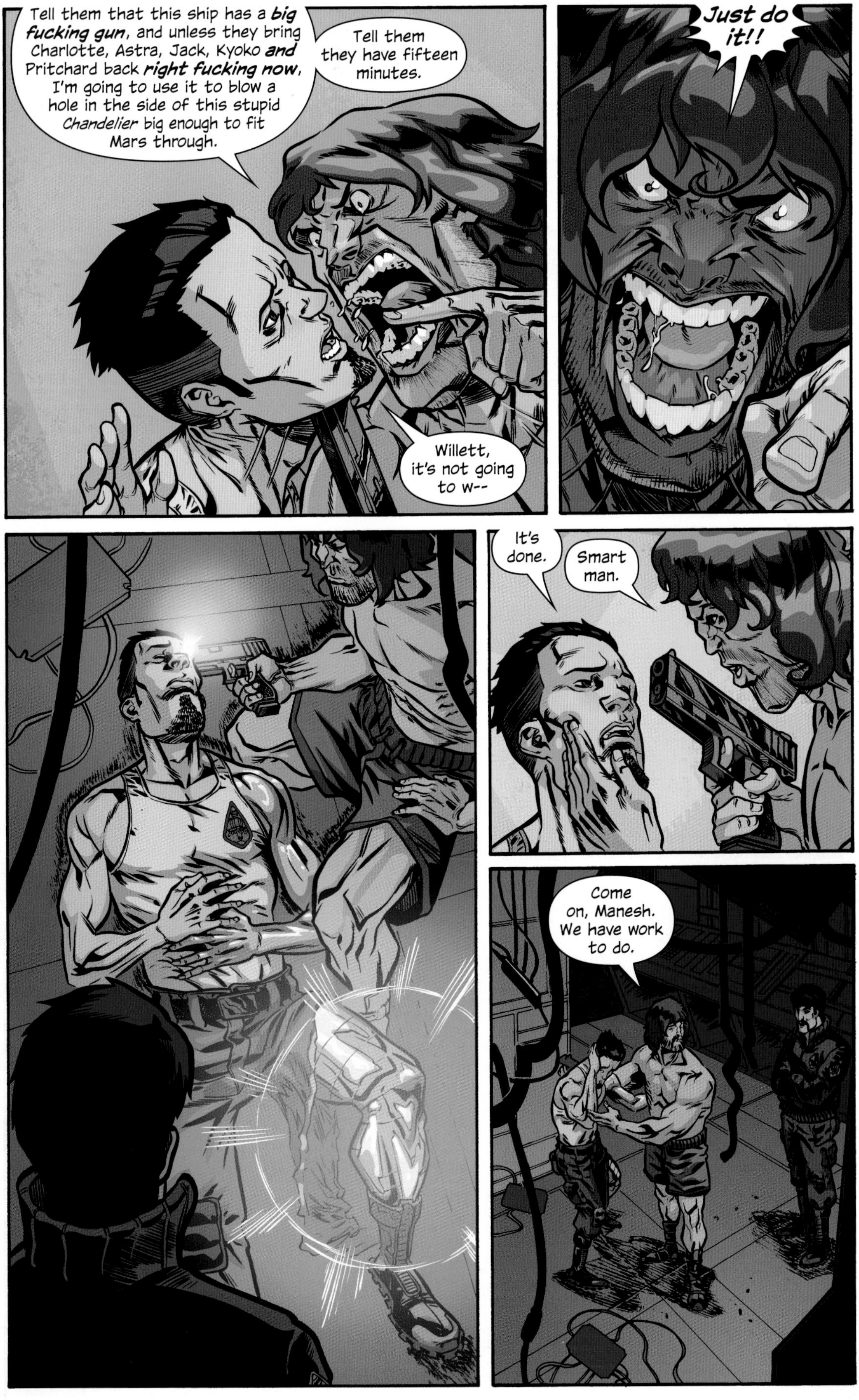
Tell them that this ship has a **big fucking gun**, and unless they bring Charlotte, Astra, Jack, Kyoko **and** Pritchard back **right fucking now**, I'm going to use it to blow a hole in the side of this stupid *Chandelier* big enough to fit Mars through.
Tell them they have fifteen minutes.
Willett, it's not going to w--
Just do it!!
It's done.
Smart man.
Come on, Manesh. We have work to do.

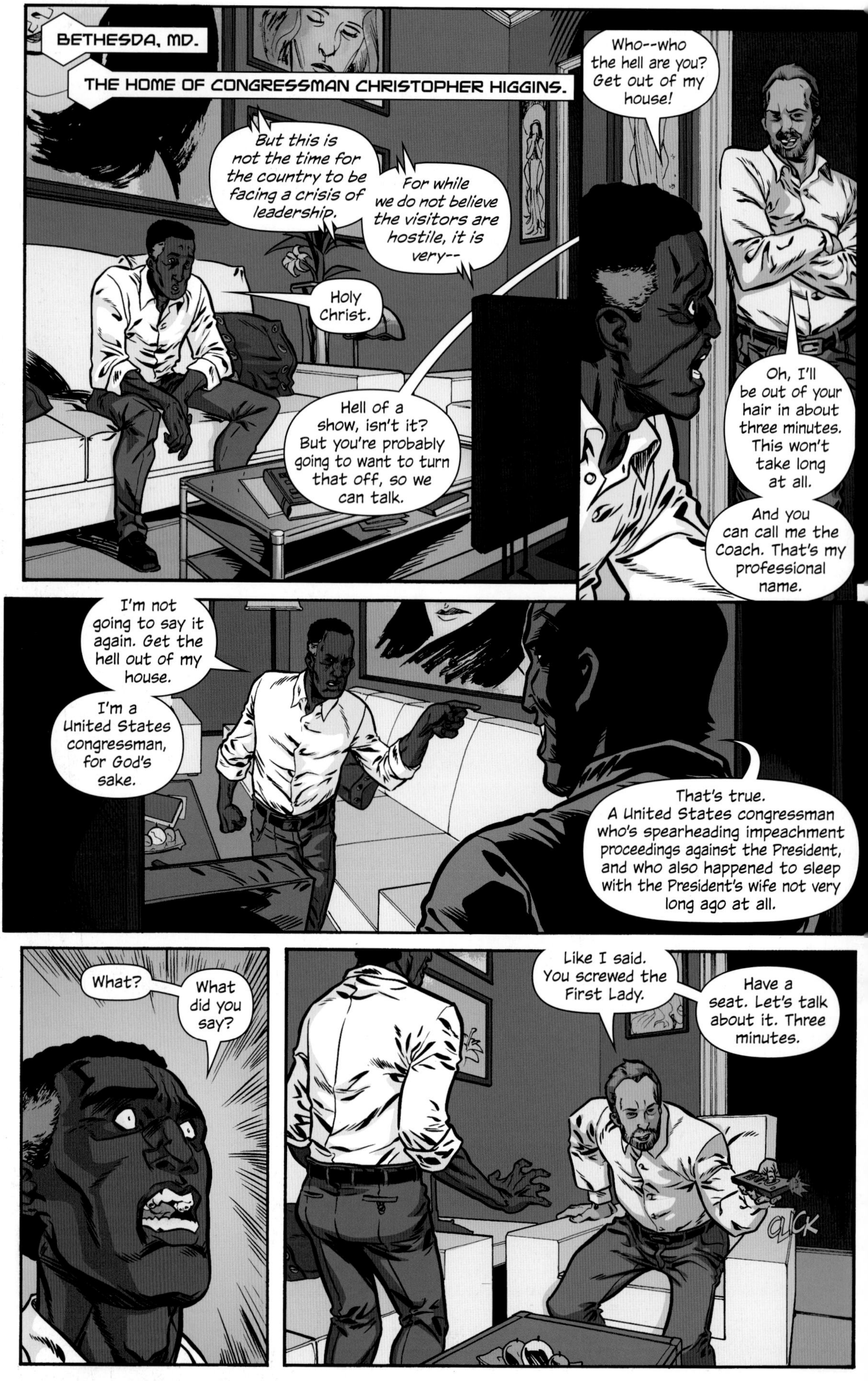

BETHESDA, MD.
THE HOME OF CONGRESSMAN CHRISTOPHER HIGGINS.
But this is not the time for the country to be facing a crisis of leadership.
For while we do not believe the visitors are hostile, it is very--
Holy Christ.
Hell of a show, isn't it? But you're probably going to want to turn that off, so we can talk.
Who--who the hell are you? Get out of my house!
Oh, I'll be out of your hair in about three minutes. This won't take long at all.
And you can call me the Coach. That's my professional name.
I'm not going to say it again. Get the hell out of my house.
I'm a United States congressman, for God's sake.
That's true. A United States congressman who's spearheading impeachment proceedings against the President, and who also happened to sleep with the President's wife not very long ago at all.
What?
What did you say?
Like I said. You screwed the First Lady.
Have a seat. Let's talk about it. Three minutes.
CLICK

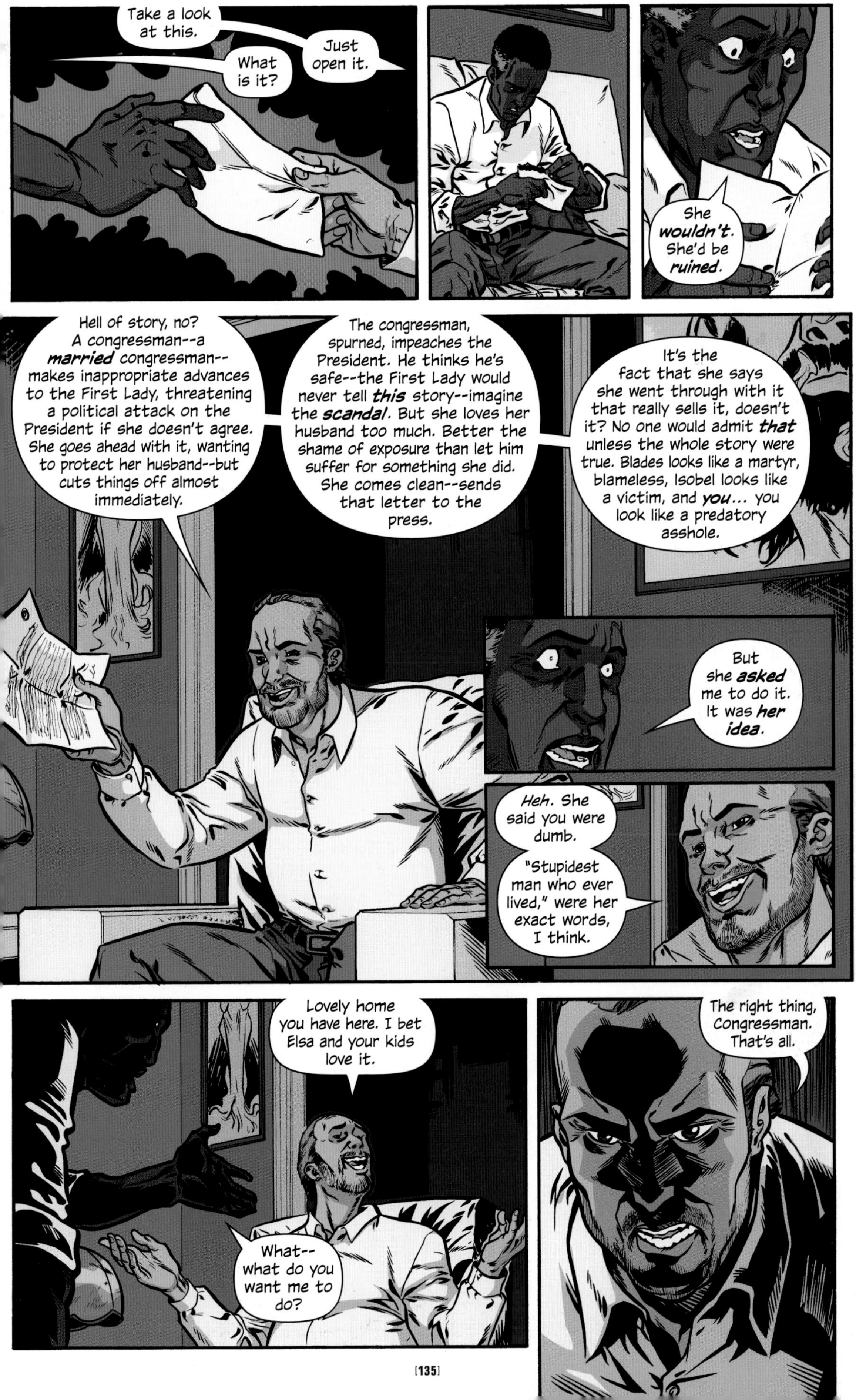
Take a look at this.
What is it?
Just open it.
She ***wouldn't***. She'd be ***ruined***.
Hell of story, no? A congressman--a ***married*** congressman--makes inappropriate advances to the First Lady, threatening a political attack on the President if she doesn't agree. She goes ahead with it, wanting to protect her husband--but cuts things off almost immediately.
The congressman, spurned, impeaches the President. He thinks he's safe--the First Lady would never tell ***this*** story--imagine the ***scandal***. But she loves her husband too much. Better the shame of exposure than let him suffer for something she did. She comes clean--sends that letter to the press.
It's the fact that she says she went through with it that really sells it, doesn't it? No one would admit ***that*** unless the whole story were true. Blades looks like a martyr, blameless, Isobel looks like a victim, and ***you***... you look like a predatory asshole.
But she ***asked*** me to do it. It was ***her idea***.
Heh. She said you were dumb.
"Stupidest man who ever lived," were her exact words, I think.
Lovely home you have here. I bet Elsa and your kids love it.
What--what do you want me to do?
The right thing, Congressman. That's all.

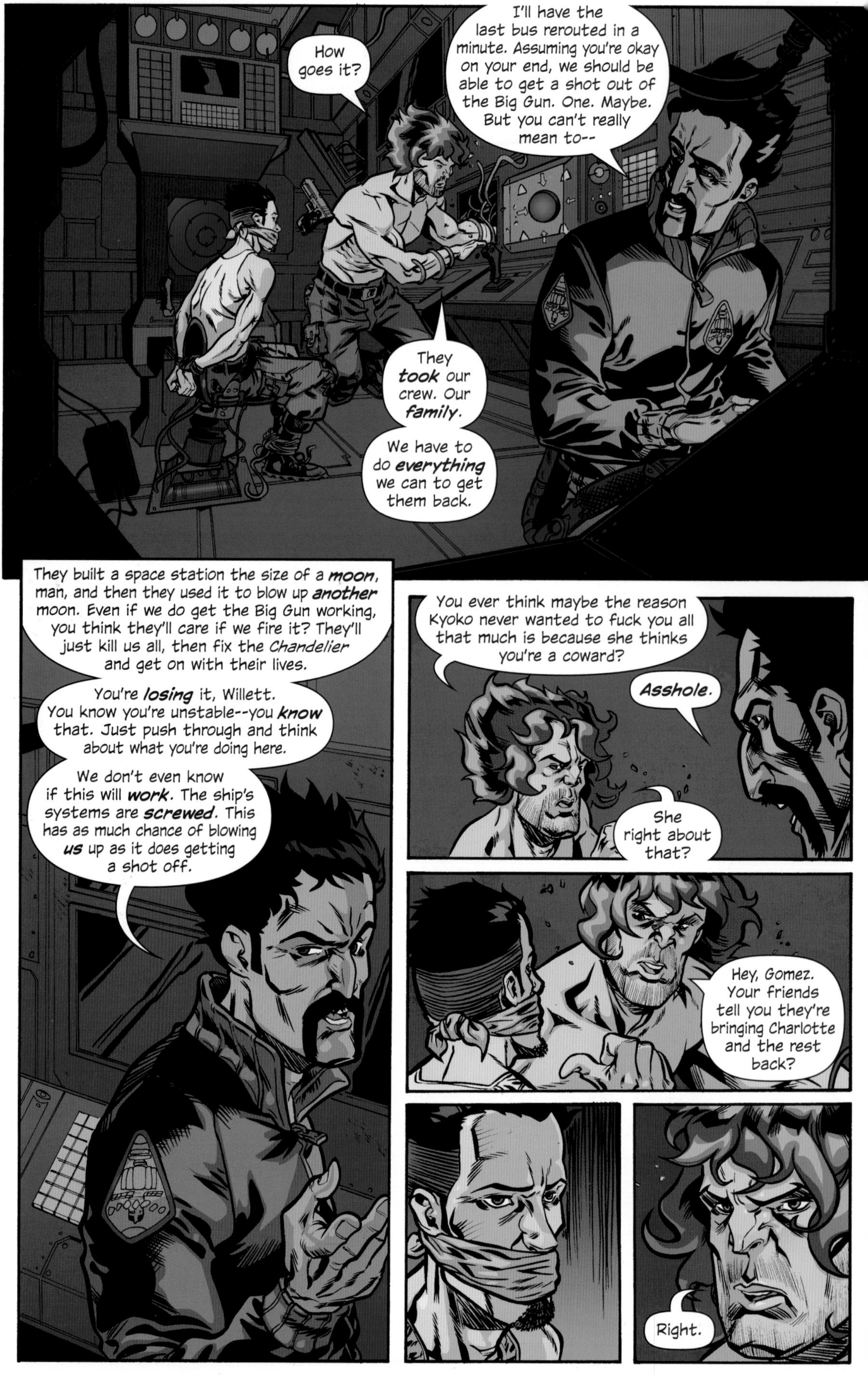
How goes it?
I'll have the last bus rerouted in a minute. Assuming you're okay on your end, we should be able to get a shot out of the Big Gun. One. Maybe. But you can't really mean to--
They *took* our crew. Our *family*.
We have to do *everything* we can to get them back.
They built a space station the size of a *moon*, man, and then they used it to blow up *another* moon. Even if we do get the Big Gun working, you think they'll care if we fire it? They'll just kill us all, then fix the *Chandelier* and get on with their lives.
You're *losing* it, Willett. You know you're unstable--you *know* that. Just push through and think about what you're doing here.
We don't even know if this will *work*. The ship's systems are *screwed*. This has as much chance of blowing *us* up as it does getting a shot off.
You ever think maybe the reason Kyoko never wanted to fuck you all that much is because she thinks you're a coward?
Asshole.
She right about that?
Hey, Gomez. Your friends tell you they're bringing Charlotte and the rest back?
Right.

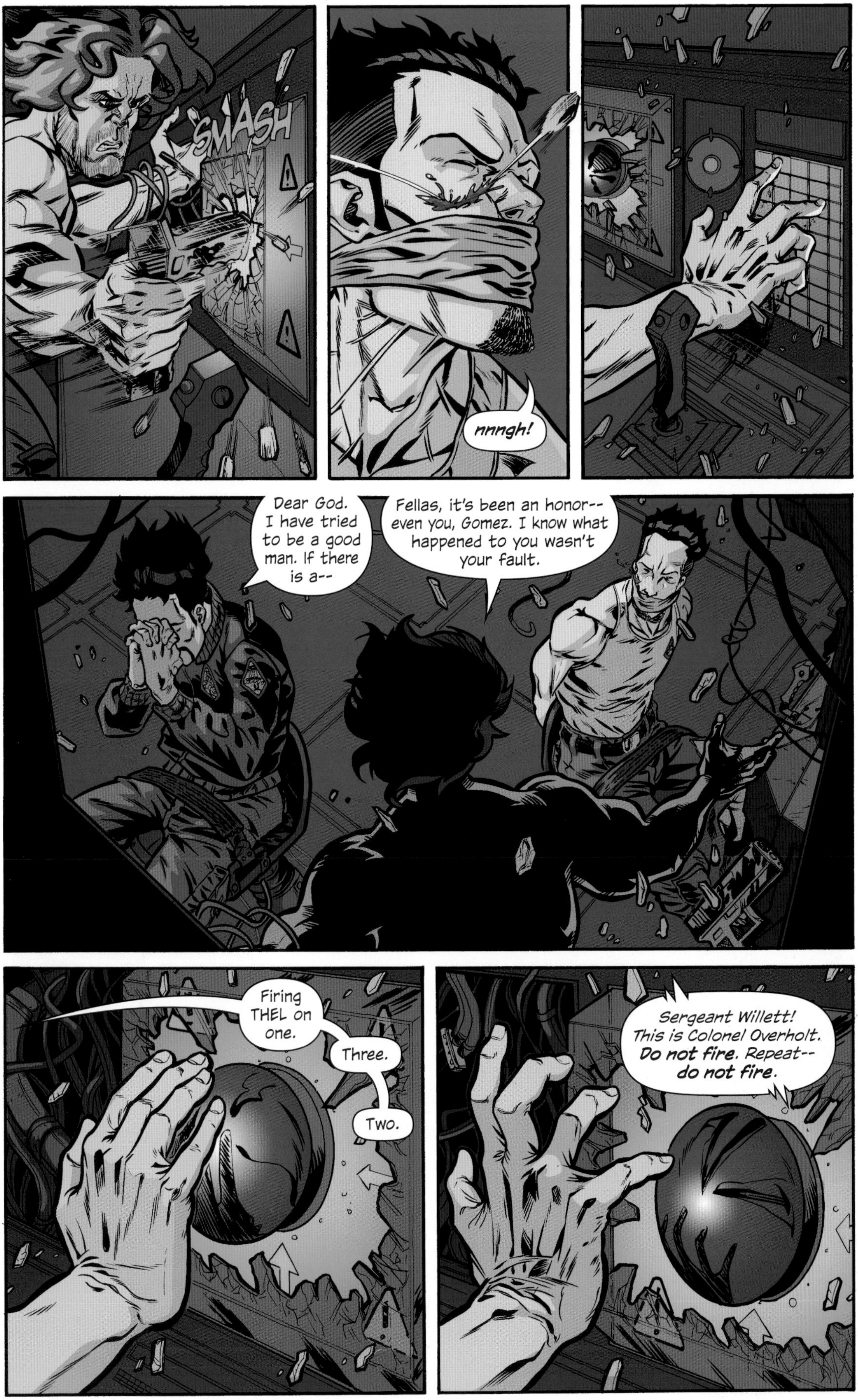
SMASH
nnngh!
Dear God. I have tried to be a good man. If there is a--
Fellas, it's been an honor--even you, Gomez. I know what happened to you wasn't your fault.
Firing THEL on one.
Three.
Two.
Sergeant Willett! This is Colonel Overholt. Do not fire. Repeat--do not fire.

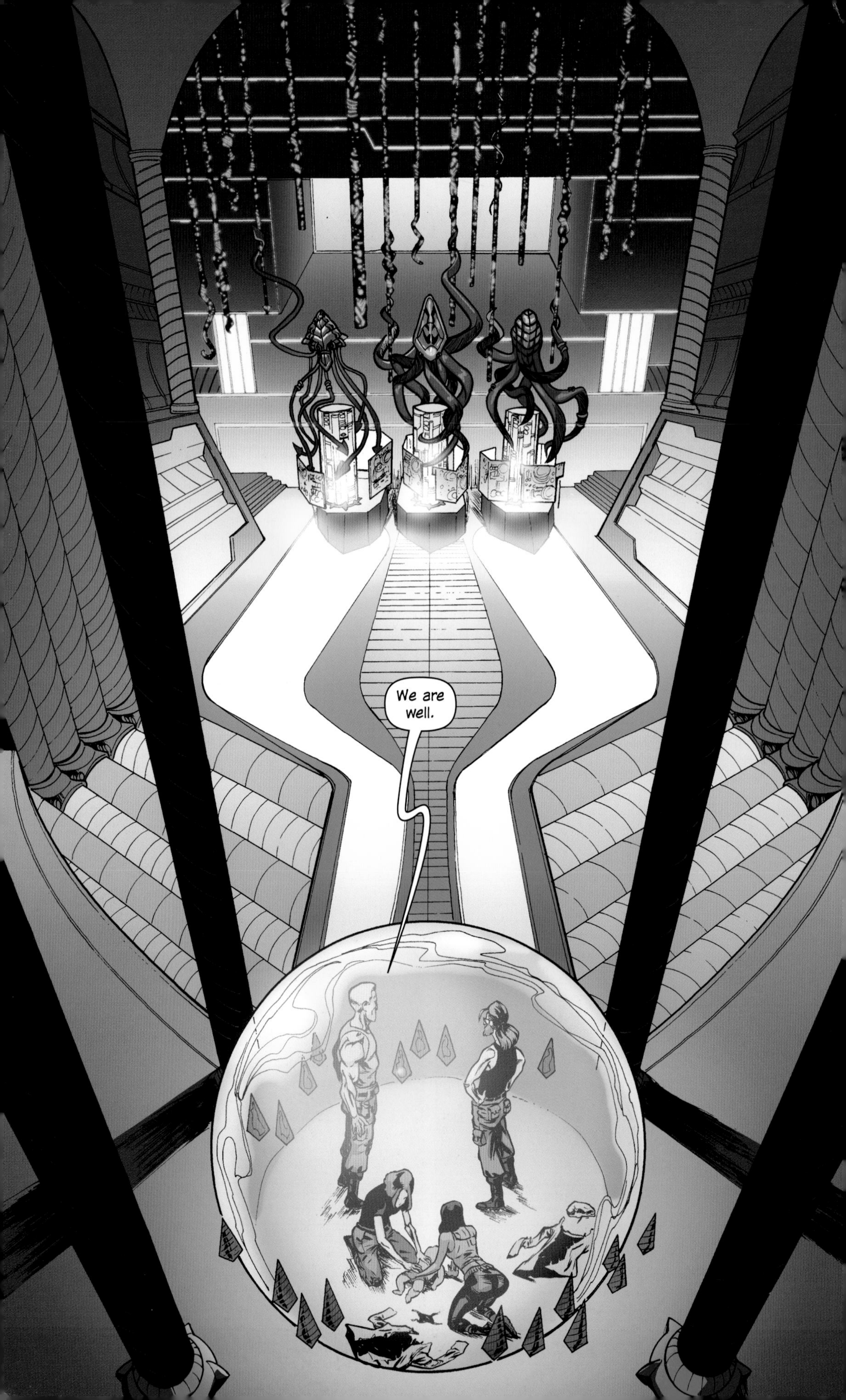
We are well.

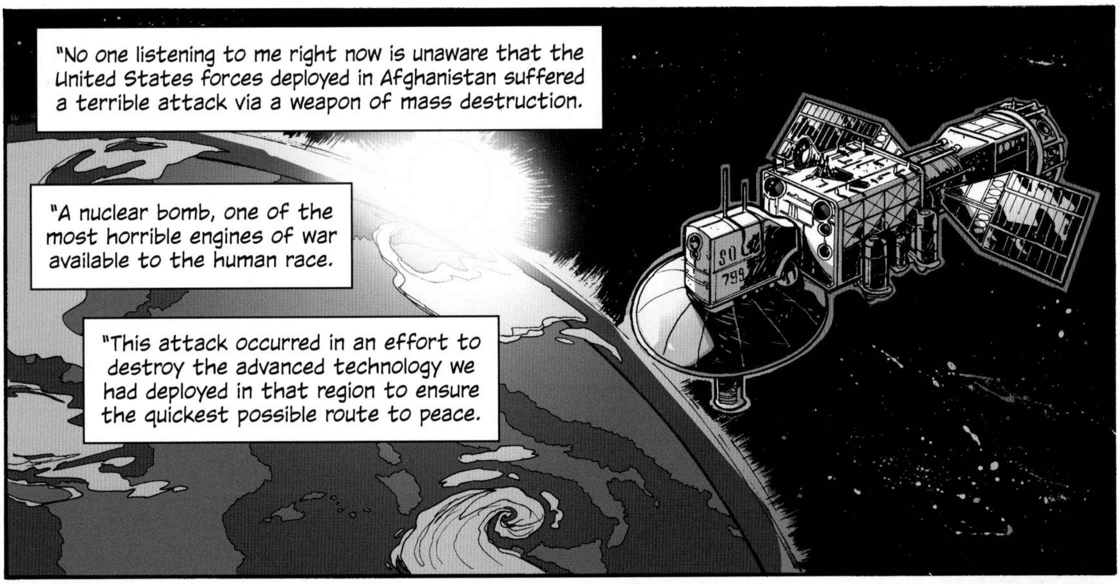
"No one listening to me right now is unaware that the United States forces deployed in Afghanistan suffered a terrible attack via a weapon of mass destruction.
"A nuclear bomb, one of the most horrible engines of war available to the human race.
"This attack occurred in an effort to destroy the advanced technology we had deployed in that region to ensure the quickest possible route to peace.

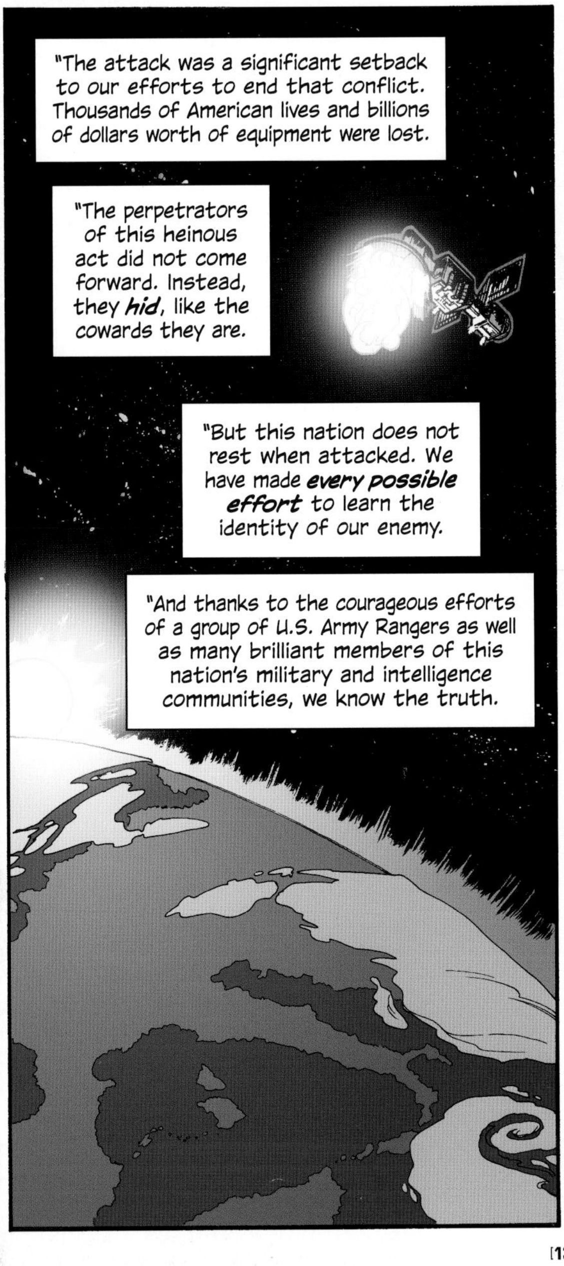
"The attack was a significant setback to our efforts to end that conflict. Thousands of American lives and billions of dollars worth of equipment were lost.
"The perpetrators of this heinous act did not come forward. Instead, they *hid*, like the cowards they are.
"But this nation does not rest when attacked. We have made ***every possible effort*** to learn the identity of our enemy.
"And thanks to the courageous efforts of a group of U.S. Army Rangers as well as many brilliant members of this nation's military and intelligence communities, we know the truth.

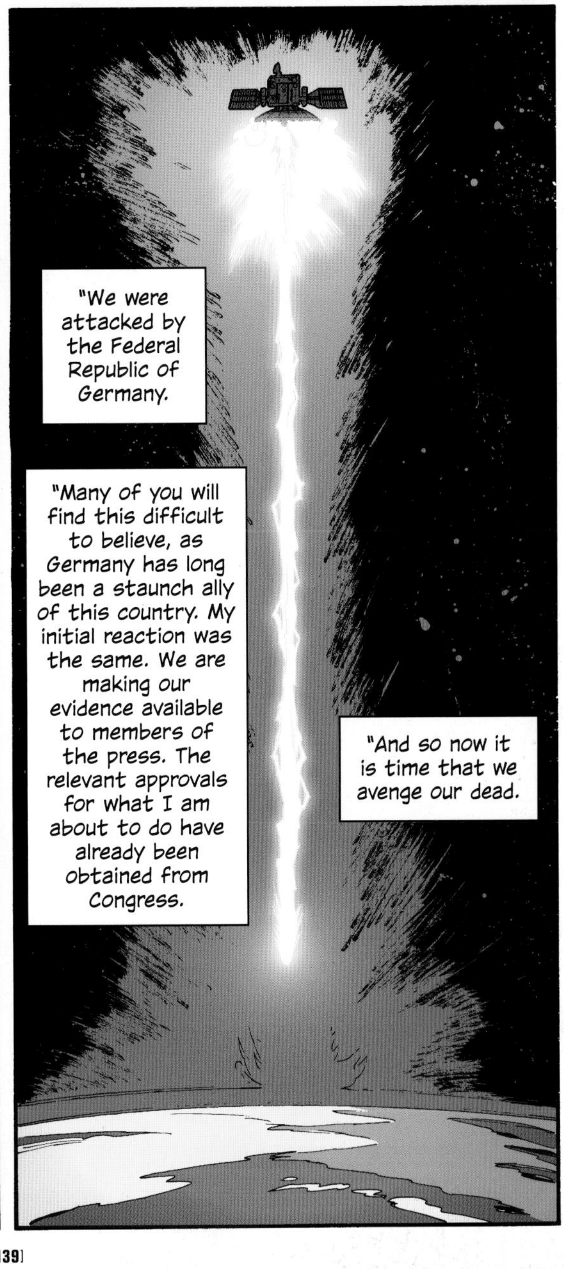
"We were attacked by the Federal Republic of Germany.
"Many of you will find this difficult to believe, as Germany has long been a staunch ally of this country. My initial reaction was the same. We are making our evidence available to members of the press. The relevant approvals for what I am about to do have already been obtained from Congress.
"And so now it is time that we avenge our dead.

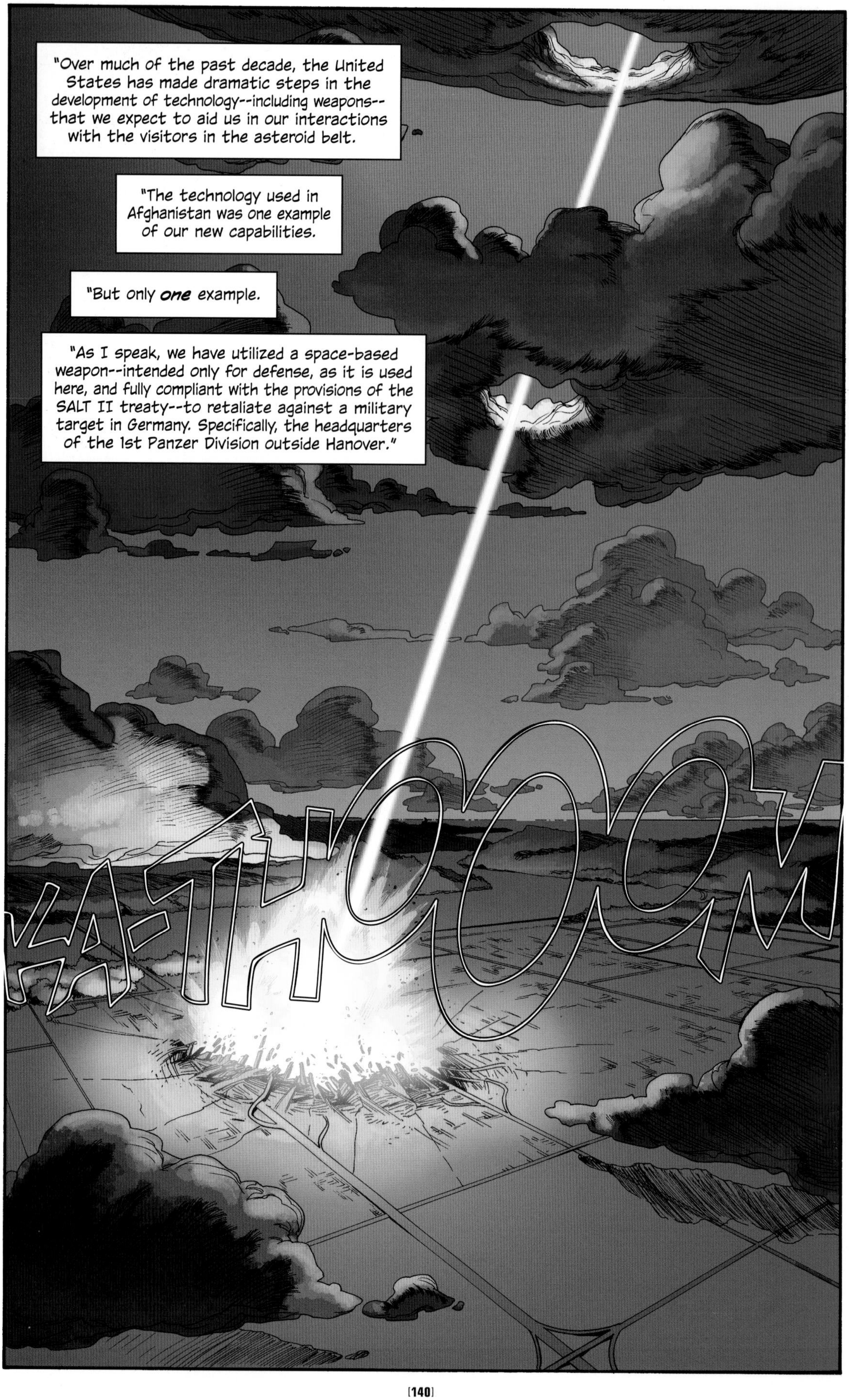
"Over much of the past decade, the United States has made dramatic steps in the development of technology--including weapons--that we expect to aid us in our interactions with the visitors in the asteroid belt.
"The technology used in Afghanistan was one example of our new capabilities.
"But only *one* example.
"As I speak, we have utilized a space-based weapon--intended only for defense, as it is used here, and fully compliant with the provisions of the SALT II treaty--to retaliate against a military target in Germany. Specifically, the headquarters of the 1st Panzer Division outside Hanover."
KA-THOOOM

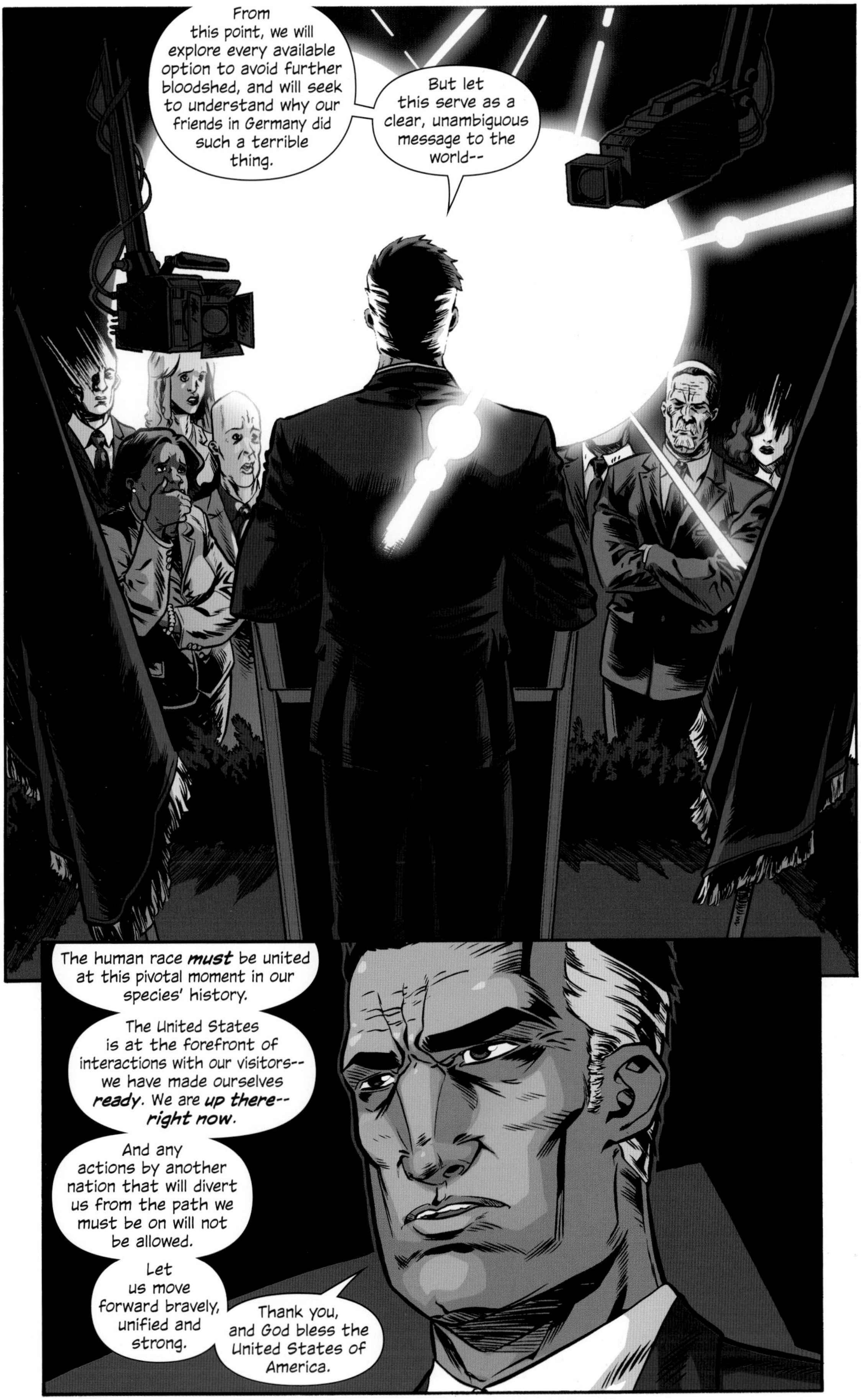
From this point, we will explore every available option to avoid further bloodshed, and will seek to understand why our friends in Germany did such a terrible thing.
But let this serve as a clear, unambiguous message to the world--
The human race *must* be united at this pivotal moment in our species' history.
The United States is at the forefront of interactions with our visitors--we have made ourselves ***ready***. We are ***up there--right now***.
And any actions by another nation that will divert us from the path we must be on will not be allowed.
Let us move forward bravely, unified and strong.
Thank you, and God bless the United States of America.

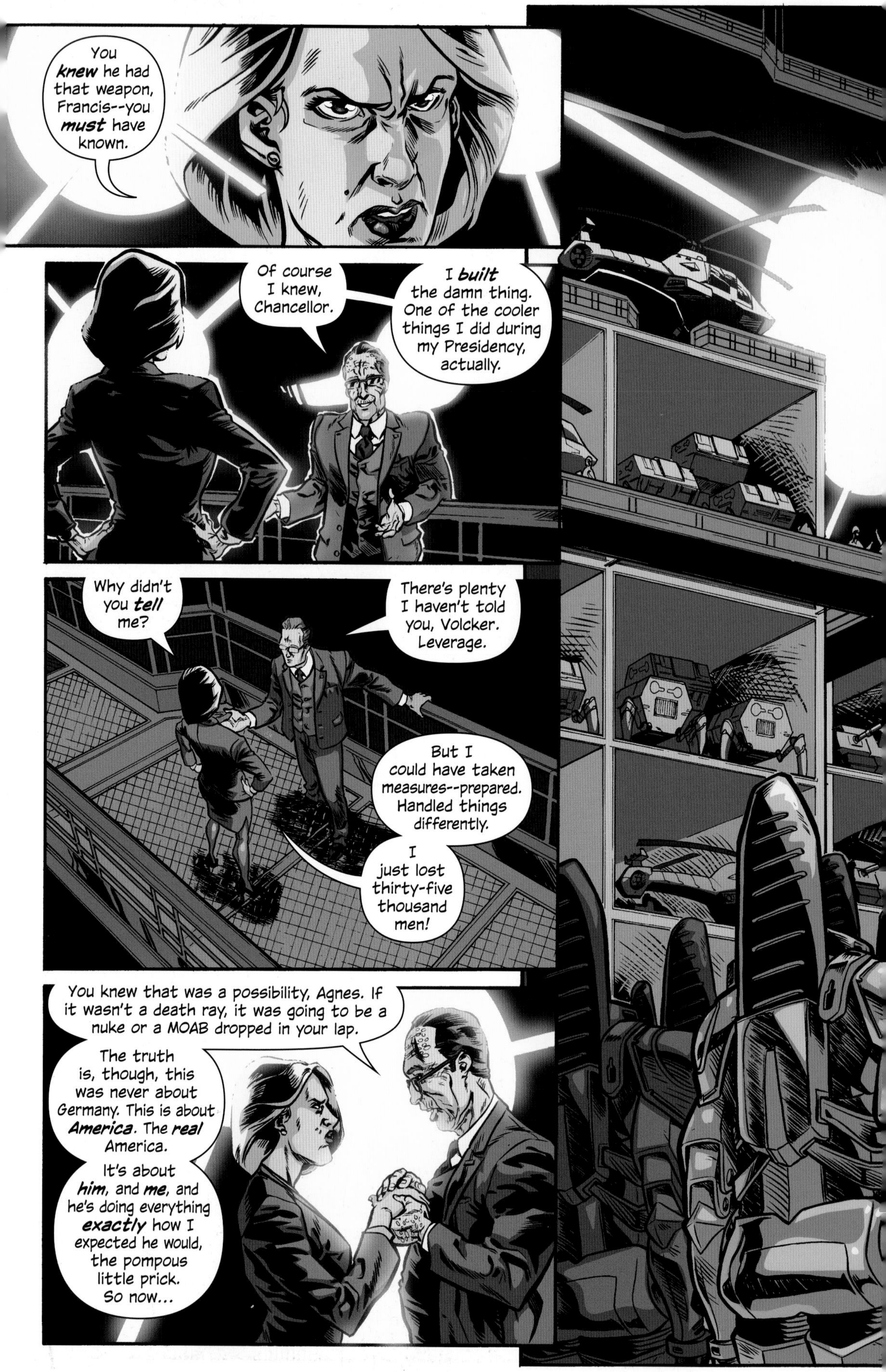
You knew he had that weapon, Francis--you must have known.
Of course I knew, Chancellor.
I built the damn thing. One of the cooler things I did during my Presidency, actually.
Why didn't you tell me?
There's plenty I haven't told you, Volcker. Leverage.
But I could have taken measures--prepared. Handled things differently.
I just lost thirty-five thousand men!
You knew that was a possibility, Agnes. If it wasn't a death ray, it was going to be a nuke or a MOAB dropped in your lap.
The truth is, though, this was never about Germany. This is about America. The real America.
It's about him, and me, and he's doing everything exactly how I expected he would, the pompous little prick. So now...

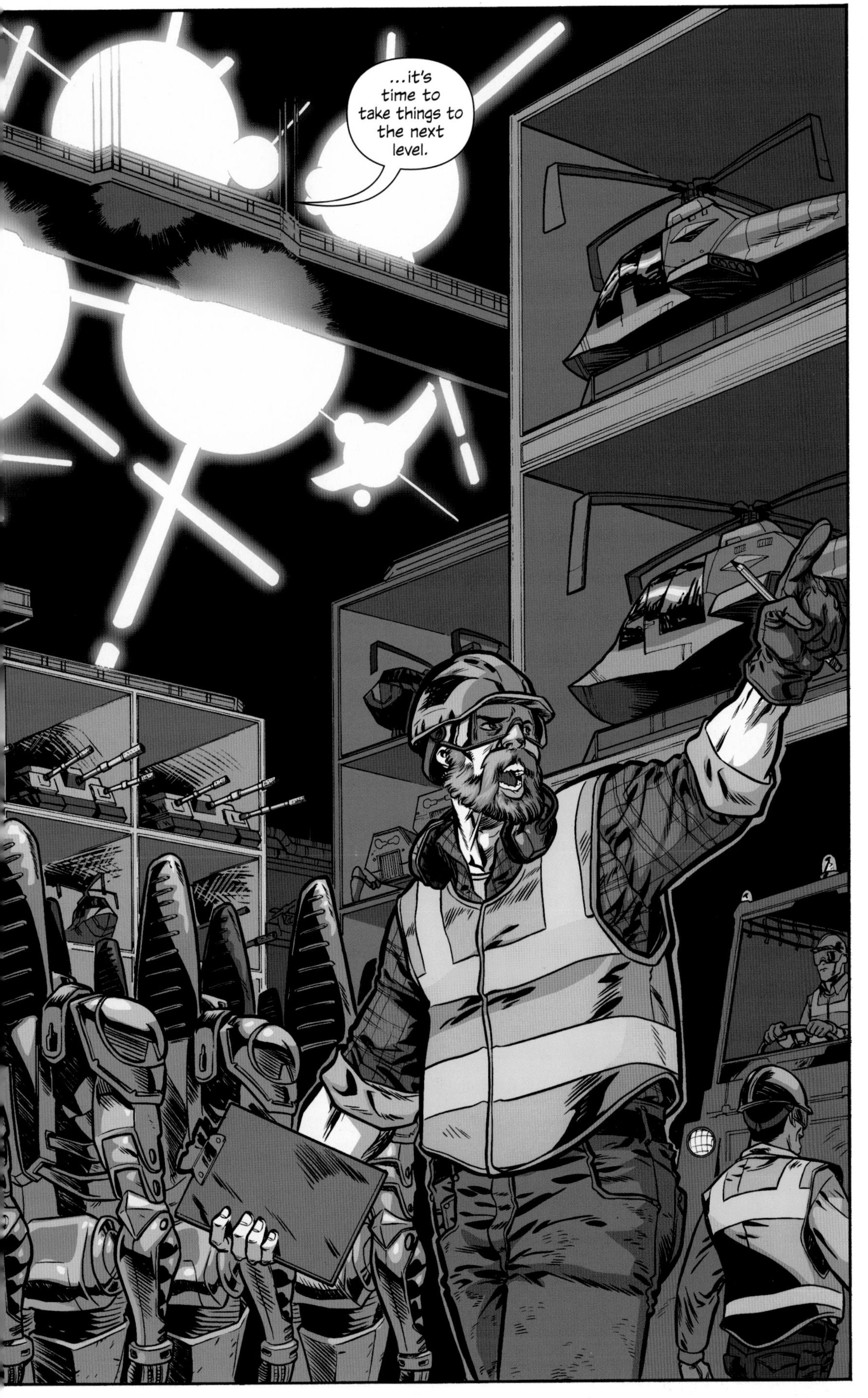
...it's time to take things to the next level.

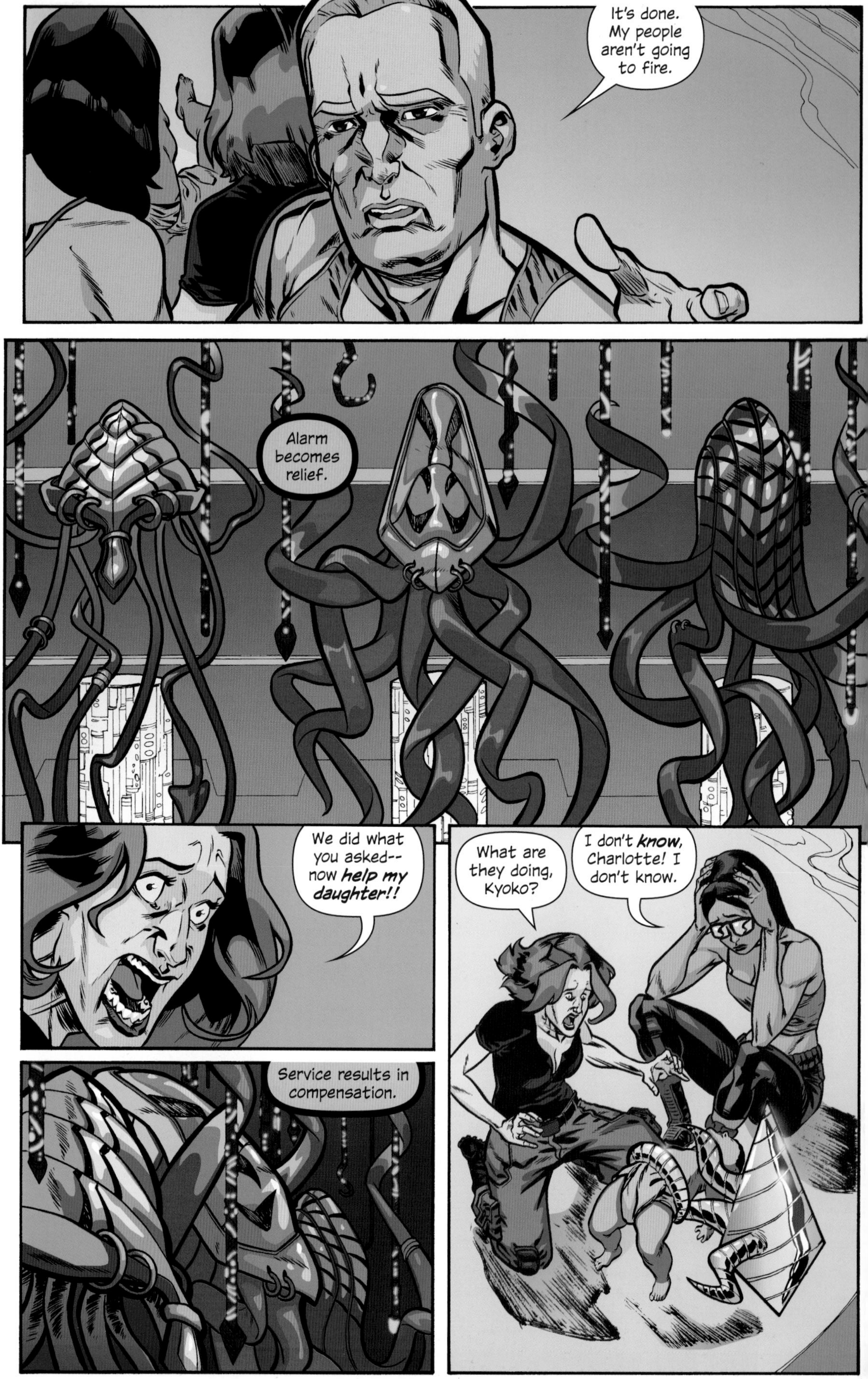
It's done. My people aren't going to fire.
Alarm becomes relief.
We did what you asked-- now **help my daughter!!**
What are they doing, Kyoko?
I don't **know**, Charlotte! I don't know.
Service results in compensation.

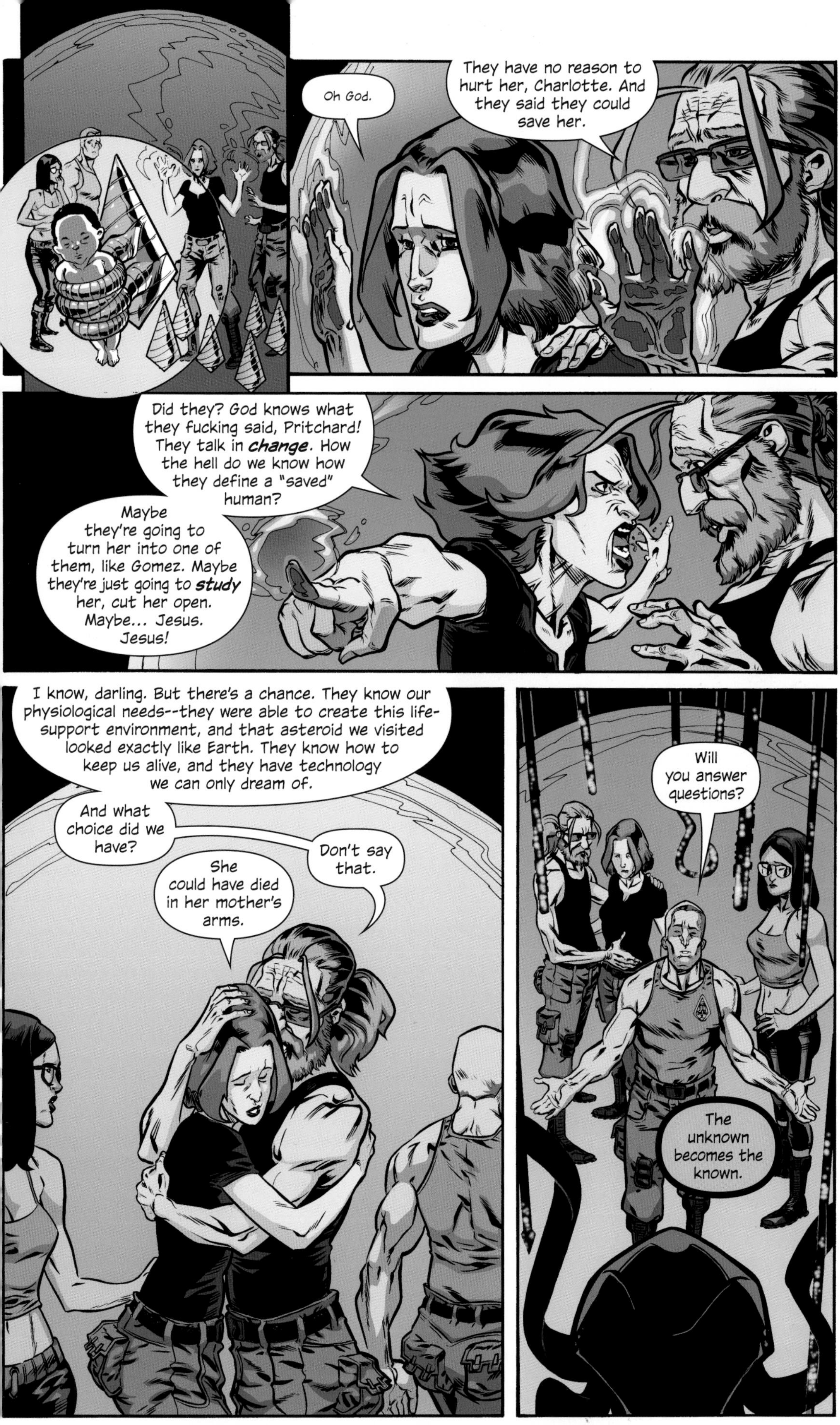
Oh God.
They have no reason to hurt her, Charlotte. And they said they could save her.
Did they? God knows what they fucking said, Pritchard! They talk in *change*. How the hell do we know how they define a "saved" human?
Maybe they're going to turn her into one of them, like Gomez. Maybe they're just going to *study* her, cut her open. Maybe... Jesus. Jesus!
I know, darling. But there's a chance. They know our physiological needs--they were able to create this life-support environment, and that asteroid we visited looked exactly like Earth. They know how to keep us alive, and they have technology we can only dream of.
And what choice did we have?
Don't say that.
She could have died in her mother's arms.
Will you answer questions?
The unknown becomes the known.

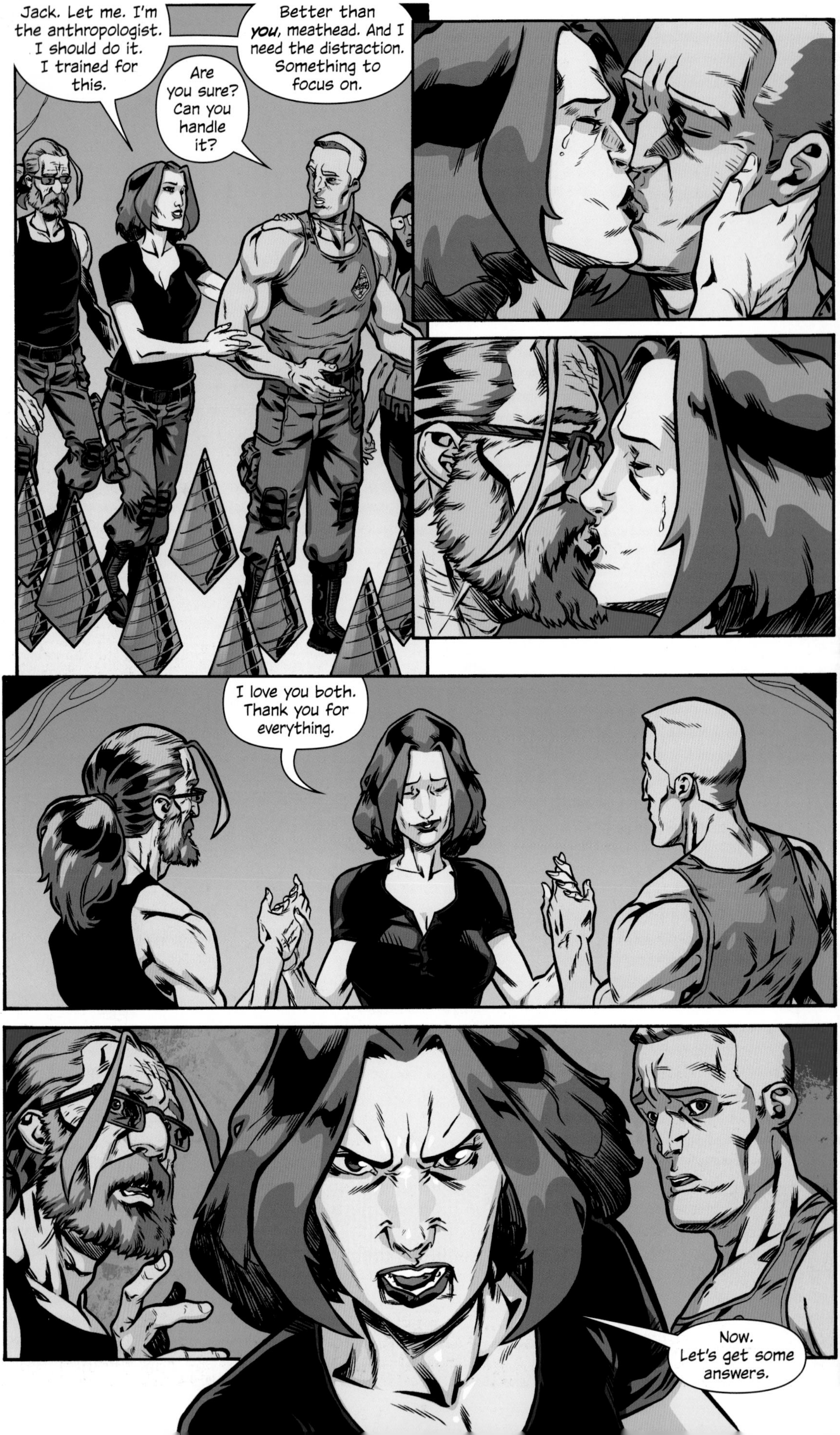
Jack. Let me. I'm the anthropologist. I should do it. I trained for this.
Are you sure? Can you handle it?
Better than *you*, meathead. And I need the distraction. Something to focus on.
I love you both. Thank you for everything.
Now. Let's get some answers.

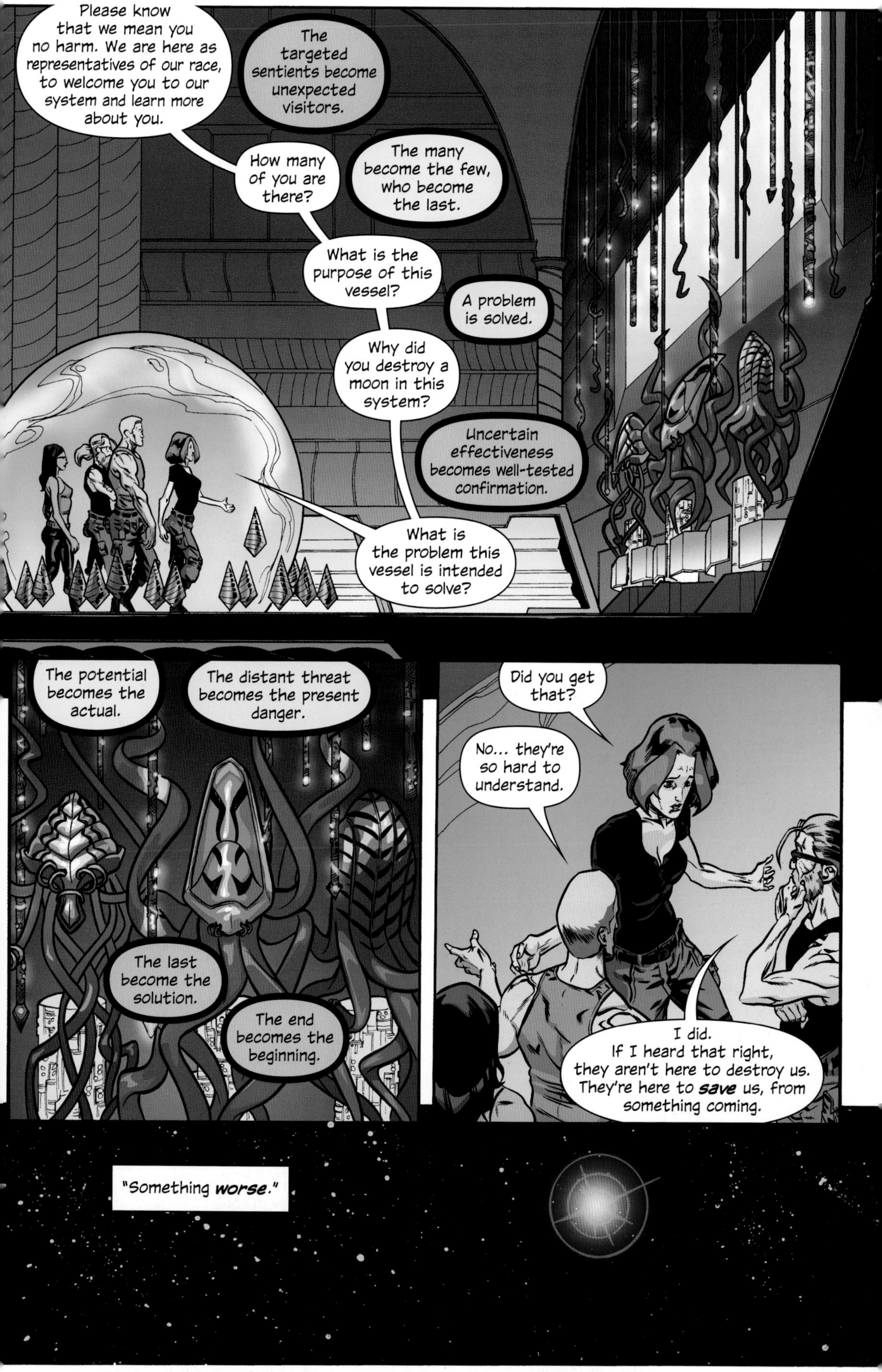
Please know that we mean you no harm. We are here as representatives of our race, to welcome you to our system and learn more about you.
The targeted sentients become unexpected visitors.
How many of you are there?
The many become the few, who become the last.
What is the purpose of this vessel?
A problem is solved.
Why did you destroy a moon in this system?
Uncertain effectiveness becomes well-tested confirmation.
What is the problem this vessel is intended to solve?
The potential becomes the actual.
The distant threat becomes the present danger.
The last become the solution.
The end becomes the beginning.
Did you get that?
No... they're so hard to understand.
I did. If I heard that right, they aren't here to destroy us. They're here to *save* us, from something coming.
"Something *worse*."

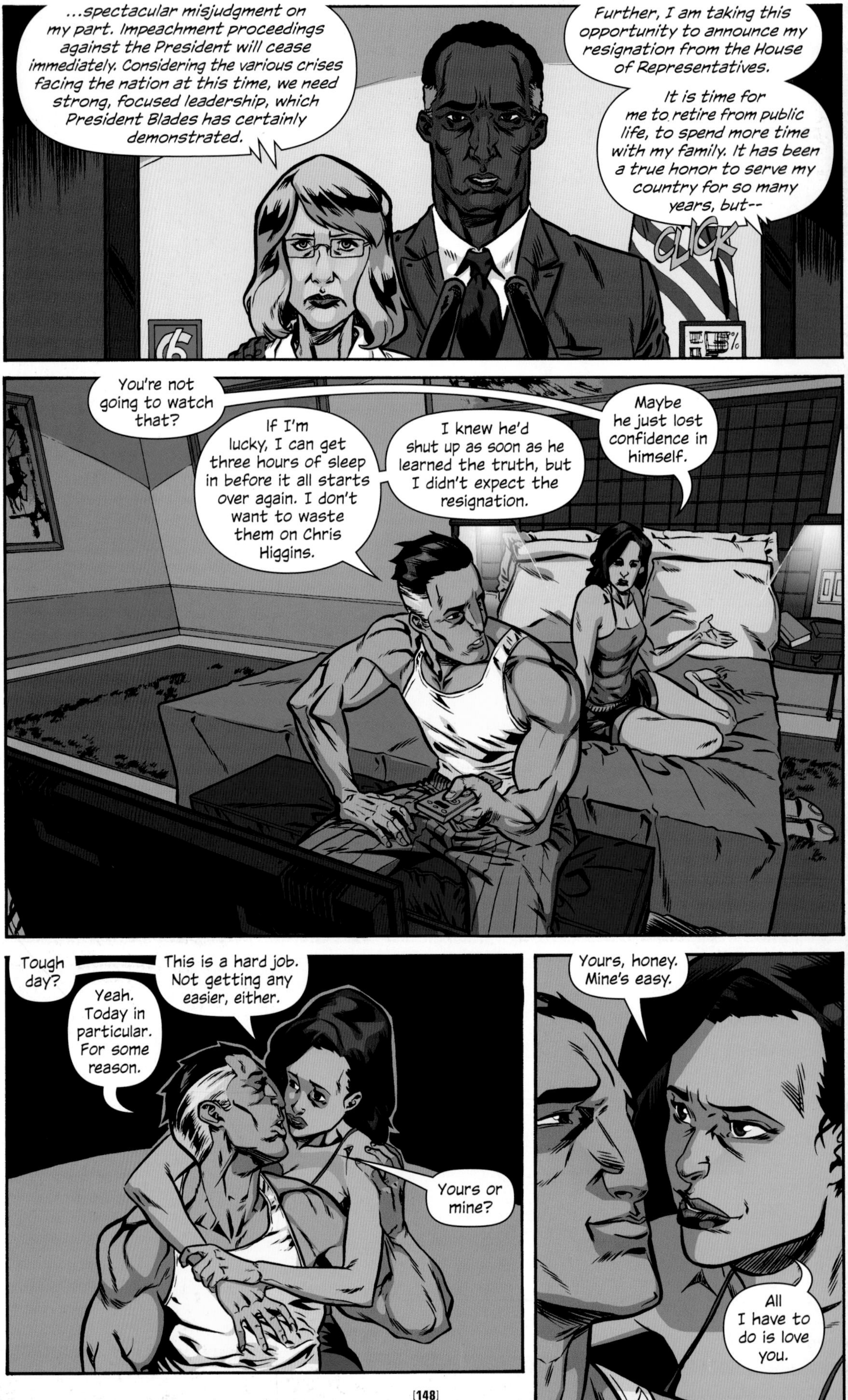

...spectacular misjudgment on my part. Impeachment proceedings against the President will cease immediately. Considering the various crises facing the nation at this time, we need strong, focused leadership, which President Blades has certainly demonstrated.
Further, I am taking this opportunity to announce my resignation from the House of Representatives.
It is time for me to retire from public life, to spend more time with my family. It has been a true honor to serve my country for so many years, but--
CLICK
You're not going to watch that?
If I'm lucky, I can get three hours of sleep in before it all starts over again. I don't want to waste them on Chris Higgins.
I knew he'd shut up as soon as he learned the truth, but I didn't expect the resignation.
Maybe he just lost confidence in himself.
Tough day?
Yeah. Today in particular. For some reason.
This is a hard job. Not getting any easier, either.
Yours or mine?
Yours, honey. Mine's easy.
All I have to do is love you.

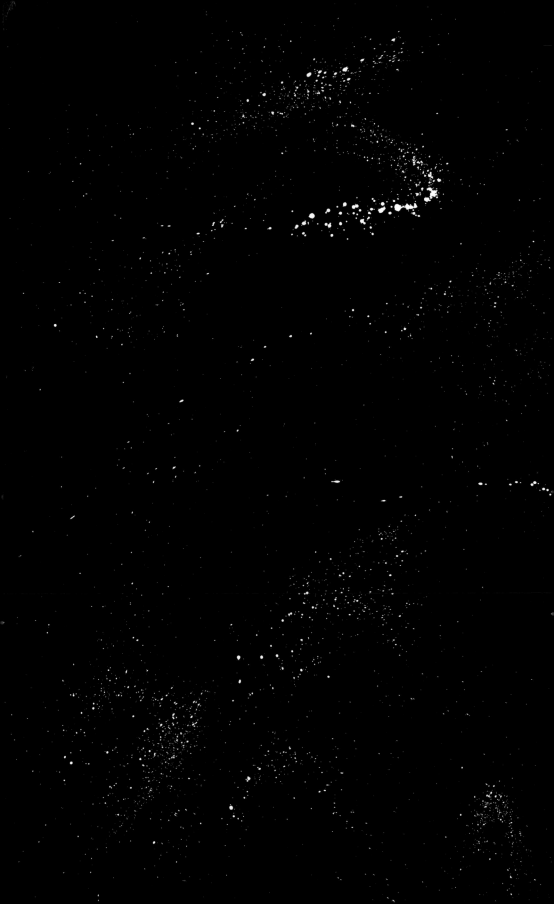

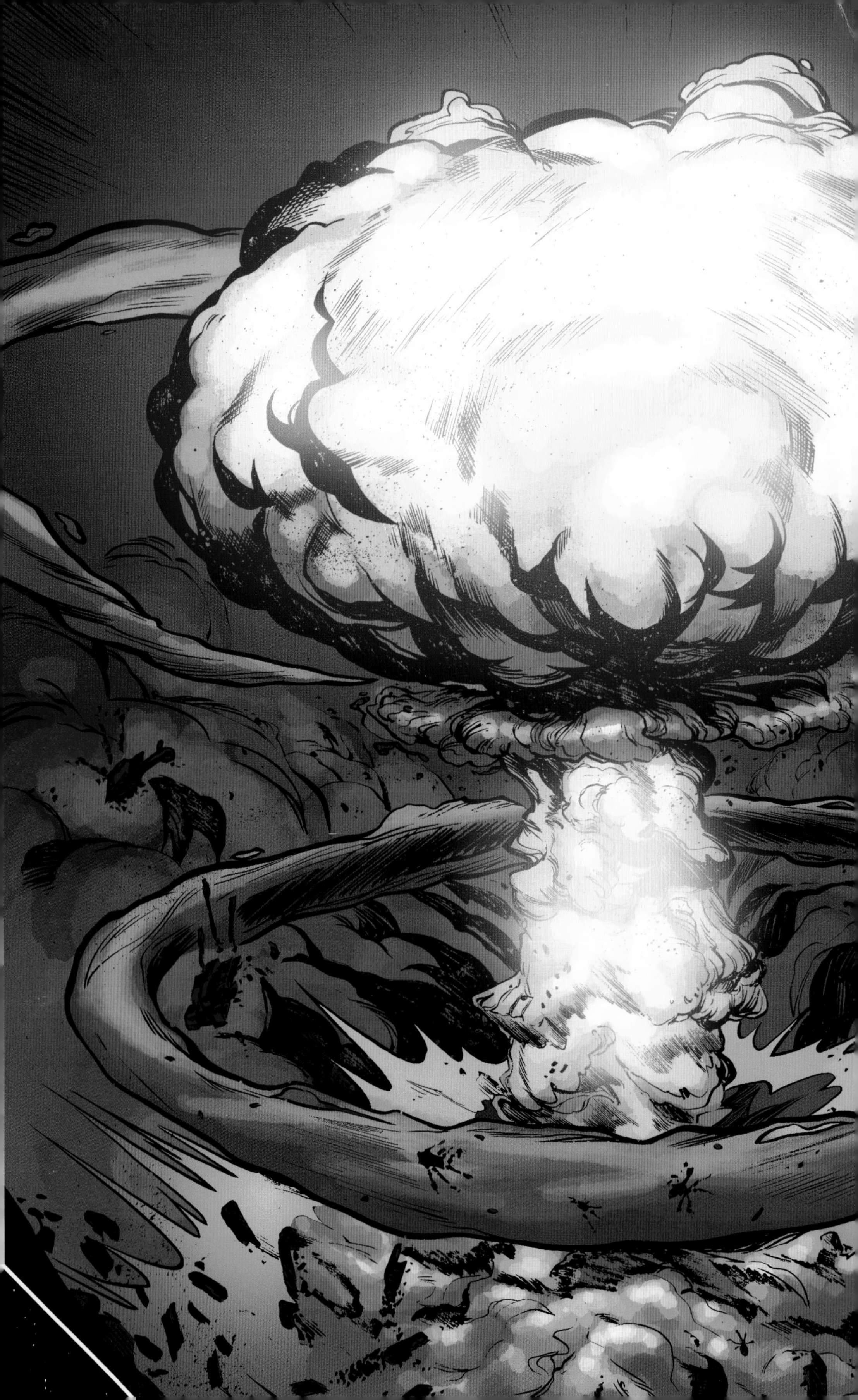

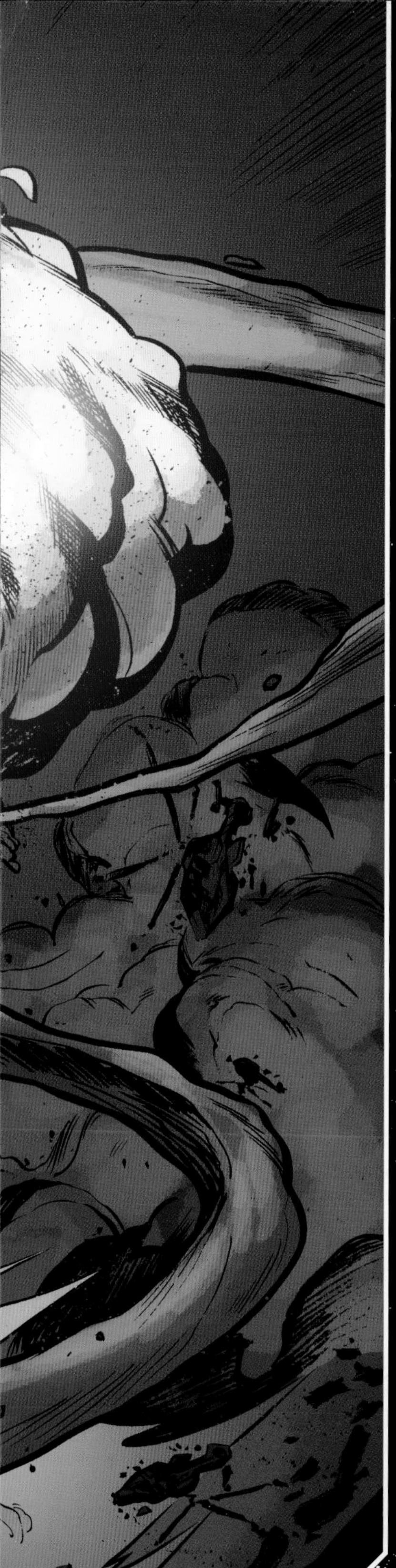

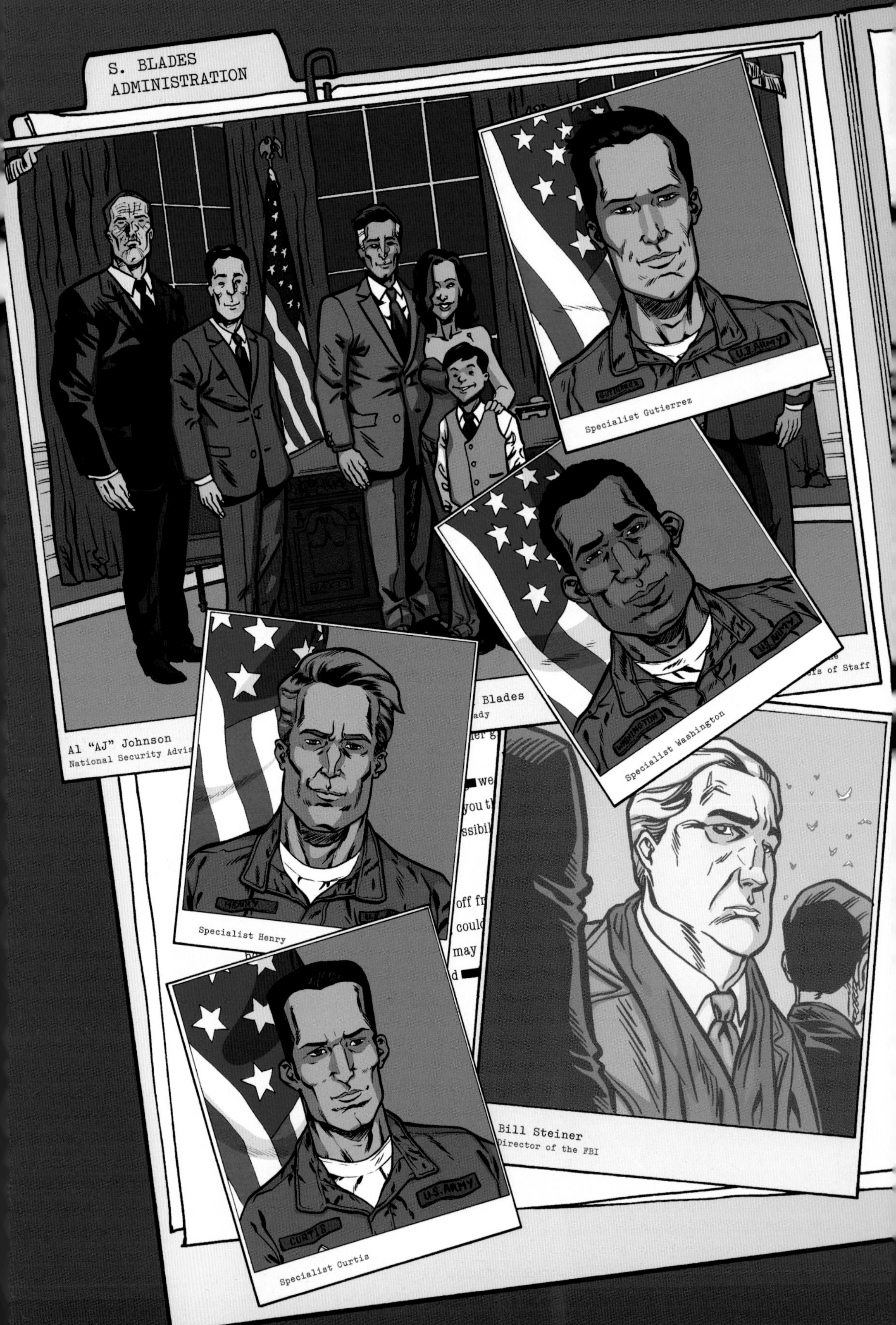

S. BLADES
ADMINISTRATION
Al "AJ" Johnson
Blades
Specialist Gutierrez
U.S.ARMY
Specialist Washington
WASHINGTON
U.S.ARMY
Specialist Henry
HENRY
Specialist Curtis
CURTIS
U.S.ARMY
Bill Steiner
Director of the FBI

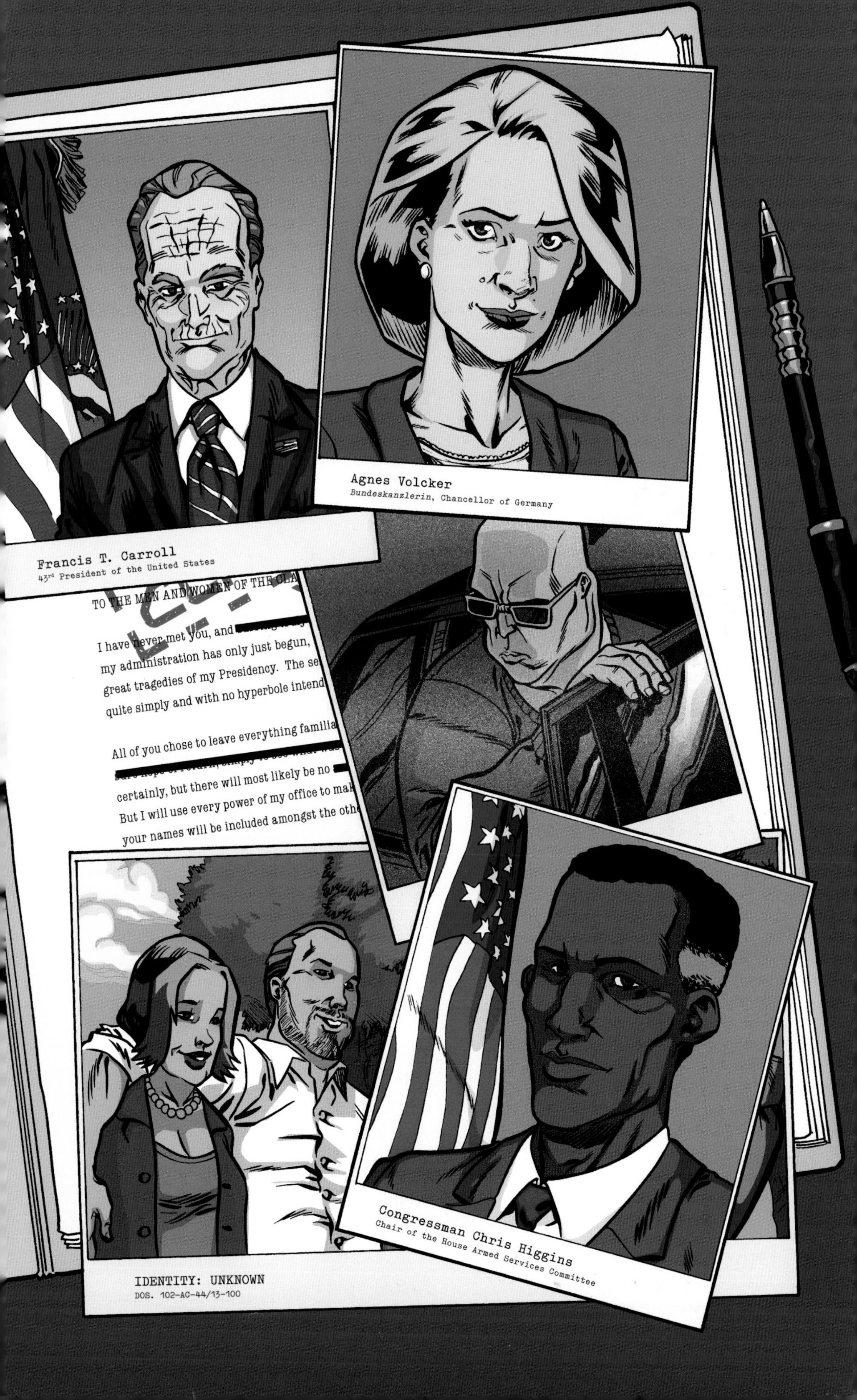
Francis T. Carroll
43rd President of the United States
Agnes Volcker
Bundeskanzlerin, Chancellor of Germany
TO THE MEN AND WOMEN OF THE CLA
I have never met you, and [redacted]
my administration has only just begun,
great tragedies of my Presidency. The se
quite simply and with no hyperbole intend
All of you chose to leave everything familia
[redacted]
certainly, but there will most likely be no [redacted]
But I will use every power of my office to mak
your names will be included amongst the othe
IDENTITY: UNKNOWN
DOS. 102-AC-44/13-100
Congressman Chris Higgins
Chair of the House Armed Services Committee

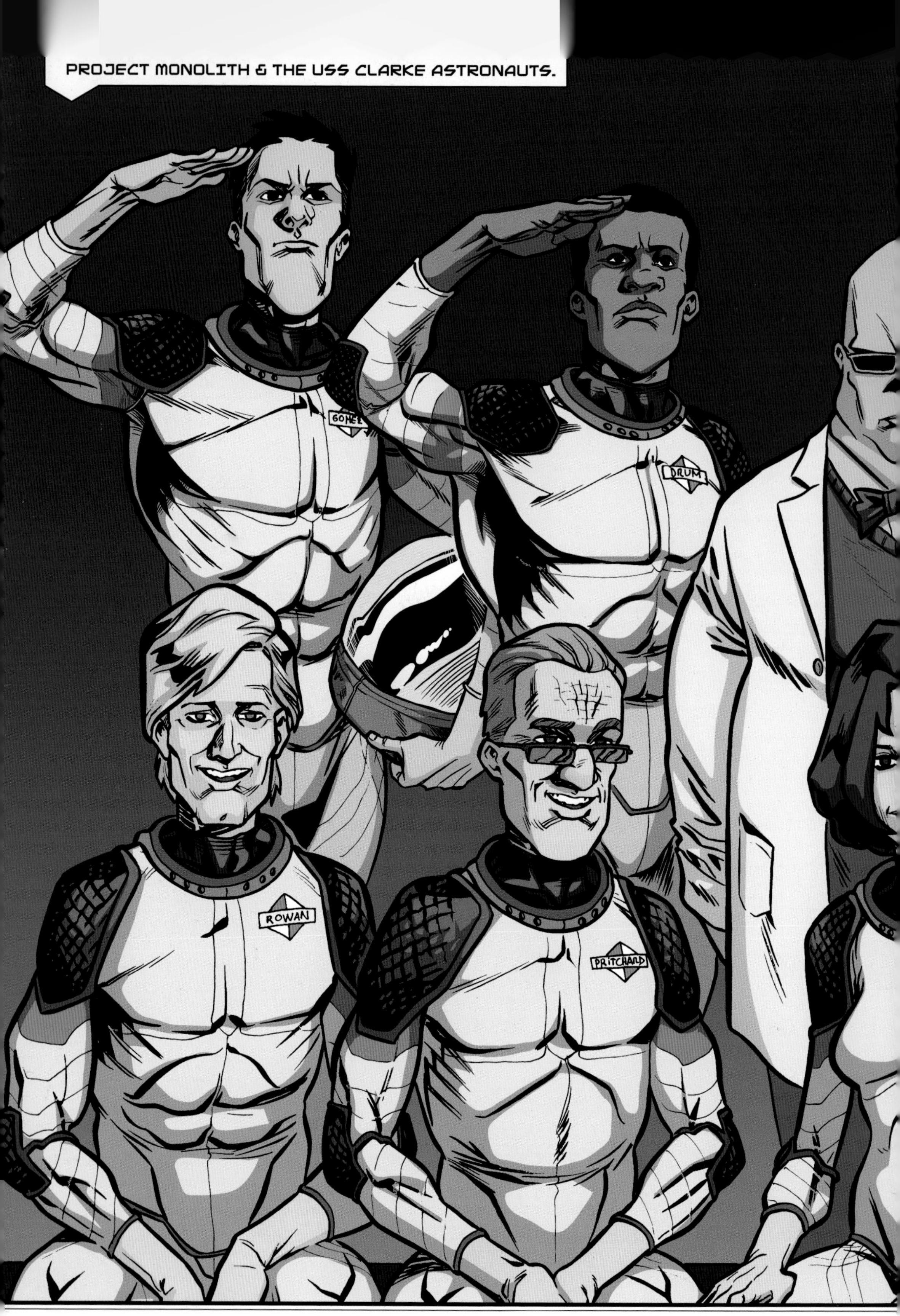
PROJECT MONOLITH & THE USS CLARKE ASTRONAUTS.
GOMEZ
DRUM
ROWAN
PRITCHARD

TOP ROW [FROM LEFT TO RIGHT]:

LIEUTENANT ALBERTO GOMEZ, MAJOR GABRIEL DRUM, DR. PORTEK [HEAD OF PROJECT MONOLITH], **COLONEL JACK OVERHOLT, SERGEANT JOHN WILLET**

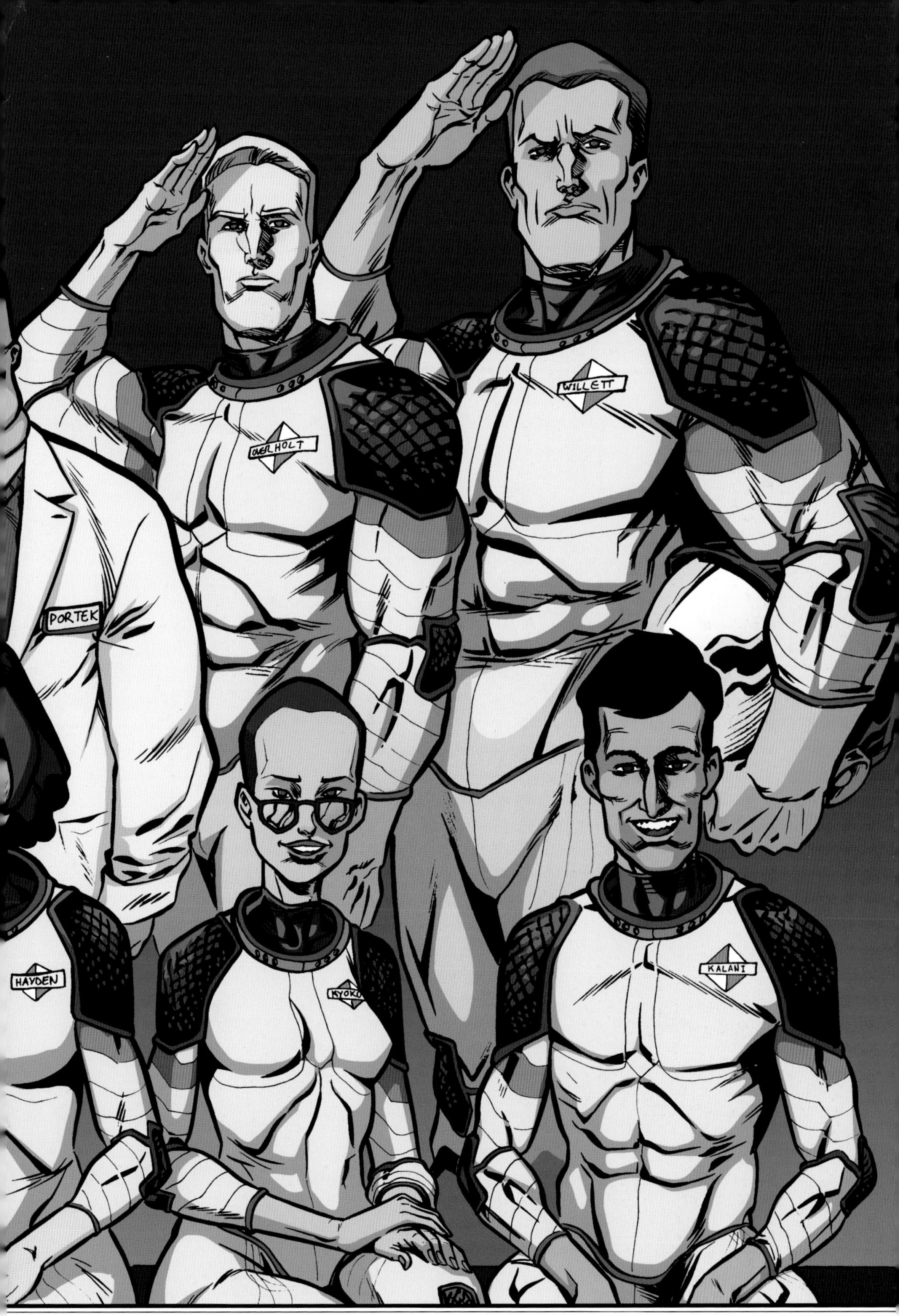

OVERHOLT
WILLETT
PORTEK
HAYDEN
KYOKO
KALANI

BOTTOM ROW [FROM LEFT TO RIGHT]:

CARY ROWAN [GEOLOGIST], **DONALD PRITCHARD** [CHIEF ASTRONOMER], **CHARLOTTE HAYDEN** [SENIOR MISSION COMMANDER], **KYOKO TAKAHASHI** [DOCTOR], **MANESH KALANI** [LINGUIST AND COMPUTER SPECIALIST]